Getting It in Writing

Quests to Become Outstanding and
Effective Writing Teachers

Getting It in Writing

Quests to Become Outstanding and
Effective Writing Teachers

Edited by

Deborah M. Stankevich

Northwest Arkansas Writing Project
University of Arkansas

INFORMATION AGE PUBLISHING, INC.
Charlotte, NC • www.infoagepub.com

KH

Library of Congress Cataloging-in-Publication Data

Getting it in writing : quests to become outstanding and effective writing
teachers / edited by Deborah M. Stankevich.
    p. cm.
  Includes bibliographical references.
  ISBN 978-1-61735-481-6 (pbk.) – ISBN 978-1-61735-482-3 (hardcover) –
ISBN 978-1-61735-483-0 (e-book)
1. English language–Composition and exercises–Study and teaching. 2.
Composition (Language arts)–Study and teaching. 3. Written communication.
4. Rhetoric. I. Stankevich, Deborah M.
  LB1576.G4435 2011
  808'.042071–dc23

                                                            2011016529

4/15/13

Contents

Foreword

Christian Z. Goering
Director, Northwest Arkansas Writing Project

Home from college in the summer of 1997, I worked on the outside maintenance crew of Medicine Lodge High School, the school from which I had graduated a year earlier. Painting, painting, cleaning, organizing, and painting my way through the hot Kansas days wasn't exactly my idea of a good time. Wrapped up in my own nineteen-year-old world, I was oblivious to a magical event happening 325 miles to my southeast in Fayetteville, Arkansas—the first annual Invitational Summer Institute of the Northwest Arkansas Writing Project (NWAWP). Housed and thoroughly supported by the University of Arkansas' College of Education and Health Professions, NWAWP began to change the teaching of writing in Northwest Arkansas that year. For twelve teachers that first summer, what has been termed a "transformation" (Caswell, 2007; Lieberman & Wood, 2003; Whitney, 2008), started.

A few years after working on the outside of a school, I snagged a teaching job on the inside of Washburn Rural High School in Topeka, Kansas and started trying to teach writing in my English classroom. It didn't take me long to realize that writing and teaching writing were two completely different tasks. And it was one of those life-altering—transformational—moments when Dr. Todd Goodson invited me to apply to his first ISI at the

Getting It in Writing, pages vii–xii

Flint Hills Writing Project. It was there, in the sub-zero temperatures of Bluemont Hall, I found a home with the National Writing Project. It was there that just about every practice in my own teaching of writing was challenged. It was there I realized that to become a writing teacher, I needed to first become a writer. I was not alone.

I remember well that group of NWP fellows, writing teachers from around the rural northeast and north central parts of Kansas. Three college teachers, two other high school teachers, three middle school teachers, and three elementary teachers created a tipping point of motivation for me, a "moment of critical mass, the threshold, the boiling point" (Gladwell, 2000, p. 12). Emily Pauly had just completed her second year of teaching middle school English, while Roger Caswell had just completed his 25th year. The range of backgrounds in the classroom helped make the experience for me. The experience made the experience too. Existing as writers and teachers of writing, we grew and developed and learned in ways only possible when a group coexists for an extended period of time together—four full days per week for five weeks. Lieberman (2005) referred to the National Writing Project as a "supportive professional community," and I had found mine.

I returned to my classroom that August with quite honestly a different idea of what it meant to be a teacher, let alone different ideas about how I would teach writing. More than any one tangible activity or approach in the classroom (there were several), I began to identify as a writer in my own professional and personal lives and began sharing my newfound identity with my students. Whether it was that first article that was published or the experience of a rejection letter, I was different because of the National Writing Project, and my students were too. And just as I had been accepted into and flourished in a supportive community, I invited my students into a new one in room 169.

Maybe my experience with the Flint Hills Writing Project—specifically the six free hours of graduate credit—could be viewed as a gateway drug for me. Those first six hours of my Master's degree morphed into the pursuit and completion of a Ph.D. and now find me in my fourth year as Assistant Professor, on the other side of giving out hours. The slippery slope argument holds true for me.

The constant variable in my career since the summer of 2002 is my tie to and passion for the National Writing Project. When I interviewed at the University of Arkansas, I remember confessing to founding director Dr. Sam Totten, "I am a writing project person." I am. I served as Co-Director of Youth Programs at the site in Manhattan while studying under Goodson. I began serving on the NWAWP Steering Committee before even living in Fayetteville and have since continued to seek immersion in the work, people and pride of the site here, serving first as Interim then Associate and now Director of the site. The terrific responsibility and honor is not lost on me.

And while this book isn't about the National Writing Project, any worthy conversation of writing teachers' experiences and development either directly or indirectly tie back to what was started by Jim Gray in a single classroom in 1974 in Berkeley, California. Lieberman (2005) suggests NWP is "arguably the most successful K–12 professional development project ever in the United States" (p. 187). As its stated mission on the project's website (www.nwp.org), "the National Writing Project focuses the knowledge, expertise, and leadership of our nation's educators on sustained efforts to improve writing and learning for all learners." At the core of the belief system are two simple statements: the best teachers of teachers are teachers and the best teachers of writing are writers. While difficult to say quickly, everything that happens involved with the NWP traces back to those two ideas.

While it started as one site in California which quickly spread to other areas of the state and other states through grant money provided by the National Endowment for the Humanities and the Carnegie Corporation, the NWP today is a national network of university-based sites serving all 50 states, the District of Columbia, Puerto Rico, and U.S. Virgin Islands. In 1991, the Department of Education began funding the writing project, the only federal grant solely dedicated to writing instruction. The infrastructure of the national network provides support and programming which allows each individual site to grow and develop over time.

NWP boasts several statistics worth noting as they help place the work in the educational context of American education. In a survey of teachers who participated in National Writing Project inservices or programs over seven years, Inverness Research found that 97% believe it is better professional development than they have experienced prior (John, M. S., 2008). When teachers attend the intensive ISI, 98% ultimately retire from education, most of them from the classroom. Nationally, 46% of teachers leave the profession in their first five years. Teachers are at the center of the work.

At one point, each individual site had to apply for funding through the national network. In 1997, Dr. Samuel Totten, my predecessor, did just that and founded the Northwest Arkansas Writing Project. Since its inception, NWAWP has received federal funding for $410,000 and received or administered, through matching funds from the university, foundations, and public school partners, an amount totaling nearly $750,000 (gross of 1.16 million dollars). For a relatively small grant ($46,000 in 2010, for example), these numbers help to demonstrate the economic effect a writing project site can have in a region. Of course, the numbers, in this case, only tell a portion of the story. Impact is felt in many other ways too.

The work of any site centers around the Invitational Summer Institute, and the ISI at NWAWP could only be described as rigorous and intense, one that separates great teachers from good teachers. While going over the day to day details of such an experience might be interesting, it is those teachers who choose to take on the challenge who have made NWAWP what it is today. These people have existed within the supportive professional community, and their teaching lives have been altered by that experience.

When I think of writing project people, I have to think of people like Scott Sullivan. In 2005, Scott was just about ready to tell public education "goodbye," in not so many words, but he let a colleague talk him into participating in the summer institute. I can speak for others at the site when I say that I am sure glad his colleague succeeded. Scott has been a staunch advocate for NWAWP and the NWP ideals both in his work at the site—presently the Co-Director of Continuity—and through his work as a Teacher Leader in the Bentonville Public Schools.

I think of other people, too. Suki Highers, one of our newly minted 2009 Teacher Consultants, is singlehandedly redefining what it means to be "on fire" about the writing project. Ms. Highers is a high school social studies and sociology teacher in Fayetteville, and she has already attended a national NWP meeting, started working as web editor for our new website, and generally immersed herself in the work here. I cannot count how many times I've encountered her telling her writing project story, one no less transformational than the others.

It was the work of this site and the supportive professional community that lured Deborah Stankevich in the summer of 2005 and her experiences here that have provided the springboard for her to connect with that national network and provide us all with what I believe is an important collection of essays. Before I met her, I encountered her through my role as coordinator of English education in the Master of Arts in Teaching (MAT) program at the University of Arkansas. Specifically and maybe somewhat appropriately, I met Deborah through a writing exercise I have my new MAT students complete each summer. As I attempted to understand my new students, we wrote together to a prompt asking, "What are the reasons you are set to become an English teacher?" Tara Griner volunteered to read first, and as she walked to the author's chair in the front of the room, I noticed an air of confidence about her. She sat and began to read a story about her high school English teacher, a lady by the name of Deborah Stankevich. She was the reason Tara believed she was sitting in front of me and the others. I am thankful for what Ms. Stankevich did to inspire Griner, a bright start now teaching at Washington Junior High School, Bentonville, Arkansas.

The power of that introduction was not lost on me and when, through my work with NWAWP, I encountered that name on a list of TCs, I immediately connected my student, Tara, with her high school English teacher. As this site and this national network continues to change and to enhance the teaching of writing, who better to learn from than the 18 different contributors to *Getting It in Writing*. They help put a face on the history of writing instruction as it is actually learned and practiced. You will read about trial and error, about transformation and supportive professional communities, and chances are, you will identify with all of the writing teachers as they creatively write their stories.

Just as I was invited to attend a site of the National Writing Project, I end this section with an invitation. Please join along and indulge yourself in the stories these teachers have experienced. Whether you are preparing to become a teacher or have been teaching for years and years, you will certainly find kindred spirits in the different authors represented here. With any luck at all, you will both learn from their mistakes and not be bound to repeat them and implement something they have found successful. Whether you are young or old, new or veteran or somewhere in between, I invite you to attend a site of the National Writing Project. Quite simply, it changed my life, and chances are it will change yours as well. In a February 2010 lecture at the University of Arkansas, NCTE President Carol Jago related her story about attending the first ISI at UCLA in 1975. "It changed my life."

References

Caswell, R. (2007). Teacher transformation achieved through participation in the National Writing Project's Invitational Summer Institute. Doctoral dissertation. Retrieved from http://krex.k-state.edu/dspace/bitstream/2097/447/1/RogerCaswell 2007.pdf

Gladwell, M. (2000). *The tipping point: How little things can make a big difference.* Boston: Little Brown.

John, M.S. (2008, April) *Inverness research: The importance of federal support of the NWP.* Paper presented at the Spring Meeting of the National Writing Project, Washington, D.C. <http://www.inverness-research.org/reports/slides-nwp/2008-04-NWP-NationalMtgPresentation-one-paper.pdf.

Lieberman, A. (2005). The National Writing Project: Commitment and competence. In R. Bacchetti & T. Ehrlich (Eds.), *Reconnecting education and foundations: Turning good intentions into educational capital.* San Francisco, CA: Jossey-Bass.

Lieberman, A., & Wood, D. R. (2003). *Inside the National Writing Project: Connecting network learning and classroom teaching.* New York: Teachers College Press.

Whitney, A. (2008, November). Teacher transformation in the National Writing Project. *Research in the Teaching of English, 43*, No. 2.

The Journey to Discovery

Deborah M. Stankevich

In 2006, Dr. Sam Totten, professor at the University of Arkansas and Director of the Northwest Arkansas Writing Project (NWAWP), proposed a book idea to several of us teachers. He asked if we were interested in exploring how teachers became good writing instructors. We all taught writing and were teacher consultants with NWAWP. The idea was fascinating. The four of us, Sam Totten, Anne Lane, Jamie Highfill, and I embarked on a journey that would give teachers an opportunity to tell their stories—how they developed into excellent teachers of writing.

The first year of the project was sending out requests for proposals nationally to journals, publications, and teacher associations looking for those teachers who would like to share their stories. Then came the hard part—looking for a publisher interested in hearing about the struggles and journeys of teachers across the United States who taught writing everyday in their classrooms.

As time progressed, my colleagues were pulled away onto other projects, and I continued to work on this book with Dr. Totten. The work was slow and arduous as we looked for the best selections in all of our teachers' proposals. Interest is always strong in the beginning, but how many of those teachers would continue and complete the chapter once selected? Meanwhile, Dr. Totten's responsibilities sent him overseas to continue his

Getting It in Writing, pages 1–2
Copyright © 2011 by Information Age Publishing

research and to present at a series of speaking engagements. In his absence, I continued to work with my contributors to complete the chapters they were working on. By the time he returned stateside, Dr. Totten was involved in writing his own book while I was working on *Getting It in Writing*. It was at this time, that Dr. Totten asked if I would complete the book without him since I had been working on my own for the last year. I was thrilled to be able to call this book my project. Thank you, Sam, for the confidence in me to see the project through to completion.

I would like to express a special note of thanks to my husband Richard and my sons, Michael, Nicholas, and Jason for their ongoing support as I worked on this book. Thank you for listening to me and reading those passages that needed time to develop. Thank you, Michael, for my Pahu Moe—Hawaiian Dream Box—that reminded me to nana namoe—care for my dreams. Thank you to Information Age Publishing and George Johnson, president, who took a chance on an unknown editor and supported me through this process. Thank you to the Northwest Arkansas Writing Project that gave me the opportunity to participate in the 2005 Summer Institute and join with other dedicated teachers to write over that fateful summer.

And finally, thank you to the teachers who contributed to this book. I know how hard you worked to learn those strategies that created an environment conducive to helping our students become better writers. Thank you for making that journey.

The Sonata Allegro of a Writing Teacher

April Brannon

A typical sonata-allegro form consists of five parts. The introduction sets the stage for the upcoming music. The exposition serves to introduce the theme and all its parts while the development becomes slightly discordant and complicates the piece. During the recapitulation, a conclusion is reached, and the coda ties all the parts together in a restatement of the theme.

Introduction: The Soliloquy of a First Year Teacher

(To be performed in a slightly melodramatic tone by a young, enthusiastic teacher)

My first year teaching I was ready. I purchased sensible shoes in both brown and black, bought the kind of binders that have rings so big they could be worn as a trendy choker necklace, and wrote the most detailed lesson plans ever conceived. I fancied myself a true English scholar, and my goal was to teach my ninth grade students to *analyze, analyze, analyze* the literary classics so they could argue a thesis statement as if their lives depended on it.

When I thought about what my school year would look like, I envisioned neat stacks of analytical essays, carefully typed and perfectly proofread, and I dreamed of spending my evenings in a comfy chair, reading students' words and sipping peppermint tea. Occasionally, I thought, I'd pause to read a well-turned phrase aloud or to contemplate a thought provoking

Getting It in Writing, pages 3–15
Copyright © 2011 by Information Age Publishing
All rights of reproduction in any form reserved.

3

point made by the author. When I felt my eyes grow heavy, I would push through until the early hours of the morning, knowing my hard work would be rewarded in May with astounding test scores and grateful students.

It didn't exactly turn out that way.

That first year was hard. Really hard.

"By taking the time to unpack the prompt, you are building the foundation of a strong essay," I reasoned. "So I am going to give you a prompt on what we've read, and you are going to write an essay." I went on and on about the virtues of careful writing, stopping just one step short from equating following the steps of the writing process to finding a cure for cancer or solving world hunger. As a class, we clustered, bubble charted, and outlined until our fingers hurt; we drafted, revised, and peer edited as if the sequence were part of a religious ceremony and to deviate from it would be blasphemy.

Students tolerated these exercises with a sense of quiet endurance, if not cheerful apathy, and continued to turn in poorly planned and poorly executed essays. In response, I simply assigned more and more writing assignments, and in my perkiest voice, reassured them, "You just need practice." Meanwhile, I slumped in my chair at home and dragged my pen across their pages as I questioned my capabilities. If this was all I could inspire from students, did I really know how to teach? Did I really know how to write?

The days dripped toward the spring semester, and we trudged through the school year following the same routine, mainly because that was what I thought I was supposed to do. When we finally made it to the last act of *Romeo and Juliet,* the part where Romeo finds Juliet pseudo-dead in the vault, students' essays of "careful analysis" had deteriorated to summary at best. In a last ditch effort to invigorate their thinking, I cast myself as Romeo, turned my Diet Coke can into a vial of the apothecary's poison and chugged the poison-filled soda can. But before I drank, I secretly snuck one of those vampire-blood capsules that come out at Halloween into my mouth, so when I spoke Romeo's last words, a crimson flash flood spewed from my teeth with dramatic flair.

In response to the performance, students were supposed to write yet another timed analytical essay. The ones who bothered to do it wrote colorful statements such as, "Romeo's immaturity led to his mouth to being all *Carried* out, which led Juliet to going all Freddy Krueger on herself," while others offered insightful remarks like, "In conclusion, Romeo's death teaches us all to avoid suicide, but if you do have to do commit suicide, don't drink poison that will make you puke out your blood. That's just gross." The only notable evidence of students' reading of *Romeo and Juliet* was a seven dollar and fifty cent dry cleaning bill and a pink stain shaped like Idaho in the carpet of my classroom.

That night, depressed and frustrated, I sat in a haze of self pity, drinking cheap red wine and martyring myself. I saw the hours and hours that I spent grading as an act of generosity not far removed from the type of sacrifice that Mother Theresa made when living with the poor in Calcutta. But unlike Mother Theresa, I didn't know if I would be able to stick it out when I was working so hard and getting so little in return. I was about to start a poetry unit and didn't feel hopeful about its outcome. What if the students weren't excited about the complexity of the narrative voice in Whitman's "Song of Myself" or if they didn't love the way Coleridge's "Kubla Khan" sounded on their tongues? After all, if they weren't excited about Shakespeare, were they going to be excited about anything? *What was wrong with these kids?*

As I sat there, I couldn't bring myself to write one more lesson plan, study question, or essay prompt, so I poured another glass of wine and scouted my bookshelf for something that I liked reading and that had nothing to do with school. I found a copy of the book, *poemcrazy* by Susan Wooldridge Goldsmith. Long before I was a teacher or even thinking about teaching, I bought it at a used book store because I liked the title. *Poemcrazy.* one word. no capitalization. defiant. The first time I read Goldsmith's book, I saw the advice inside its pages as loose, wild, untamed. It was what I wanted writing to be, so I would spend my free afternoons in college tanning and doing the practice exercises on the lawn outside under my dorm room for fun. Long after the sun went down, I'd squeeze words onto my page and play with language.

I decided to ignore the reality of the unplanned impending school day and read *poemcrazy* for inspiration. I didn't get very far into the book before I found myself wanting to pick up a pen and practice my own writing, something I hadn't felt compelled to do since I began teaching. I wrote a couple of journal pages lamenting my sad state and then got bored of my self pity and started to write poems, lines and lines of poems. I wrote about stupid things like my principal's bad breath, my crummy boyfriend, and Cheerios. But I also wrote about the way the light bounced out of the lamp next to me and how it felt to put my feet in wet grass when I got the morning paper. The act of writing made me feel not just better, but alive.

I went to bed that night excited about my own writing. I realized that I never talked about the actual act of writing with any sense of fun when I spoke to my students. Instead, I drilled and pushed them. I pointed out spots of sophisticated writing in the texts we were reading or points that might show up in a test question. But I certainly never gave students a chance to write about crummy boyfriends, how their toes felt in grass, or anything else that was on their minds. It hit me that my belief that analysis was somehow going to save students' souls might be wrong, maybe too much analysis was crushing their souls. Maybe there wasn't anything wrong with *these kids*; maybe the problem was with me.

I don't know how much my students learned my first year of teaching. I learned that writing and reading is not a process that teachers should impose on students. Students should choose their own topics, try new things with language, and do something with words other than analyzing texts. By reducing writing to something akin to a dissolving vampire capsule, students are passive and left to watch an only mildly interesting performance in which they have no role.

Exposition: A Case Study of One Seventh Grade Student

Darien is a seventh grader who is suspected to have autism. His mother refuses to have him evaluated because she does not want him labeled. She believes Darien needs to work on focus and discipline in order to be successful. It is suspected that some form of abuse may be happening at home, but no conclusive evidence has been found.

Darien is small for his age and wears thick glasses. He has frequent inappropriate outbursts in class. Darien has difficulty with social interactions, and his peers recognize that he is different. Generally, classmates do not tease him, but they do ignore him. With no apparent friendships, he spends breaks and lunch periods alone, drawing or reading comic books. He seeks his teachers' approval and is terrified of receiving bad grades.

Darien's language skills are significantly below grade level. He has trouble organizing his thoughts in writing. On expressive forms of writing (poetry, storytelling, narratives), Darien demonstrates strong imaginative capabilities, often drawing or talking about what he is writing, but he has difficulty transferring his thoughts to paper. If he completes an assignment at all, he rarely writes more than a paragraph. His oral skills are also significantly below grade level. He often falls into a pattern of speech that resembles baby talk, he stutters and often refuses to speak altogether, substituting written signs for speech.

Observation 1—Day 5 of a 15 Day Unit on Personal Narratives

Students are getting ready to write their own personal narratives. They are supposed to focus on using specific language and later will incorporate sensory details. As a class, they brainstorm ideas, but Darien is restless in his seat, getting up to sharpen his pencil repeatedly, pulling the edges off his paper, and staring into space. Eventually, he scribbles on a piece of notebook paper and holds up the following sign:

I HAVE TO GO TO THE BATHROOM.

A few students laugh at Darien, and he doesn't recognize that they are making fun of him. I quiet the students. He draws a few more snickers from classmates when he writes more signs:

I AM HUNGRY. I HAVE CHEESE FOR LUNCH.
HOW DO YOU SPELL CONFUESING?
SAM DOTS HER I's WITH 0's.

To keep Darien on track, I help him list topics with details for his paper. When students share their topics, Darien writes his into sign form and shows the class:

MY DAD TOOK ME TO SEE BATMAN.

Observation 2—Day 8 of a 15 Day Unit on Personal Narratives

Students work in small group workshops to revise their papers, and the students in Darien's group are tolerant of him, but not welcoming. Darien reads other students' work, but he failed to complete a paper for the workshop. Because students are uncharacteristically energetic and unfocused today (probably because of the pep assembly they just attended), I am not able to monitor Darien closely. I do notice that he writes short, superficial comments such as "GOOD" and "LONG" on torn pieces of paper and hands them to his classmates. When it is his turn, he gets out of his seat, walks to chalk board and writes a sign on the board:

I MISS MY DAD.

He then sits down, visibly upset. Students start to laugh, but they quickly stop when they recognize he is not joking. I try to calm Darien, but he is too agitated to talk or write. He reads silently for the last ten minutes of class.

Observation 3—Day 9 of a 15 Day Unit on Personal Narratives

Today students add sensory details to their personal narratives. In pairs, they read one another's papers and then ask their partner questions about what he or she saw, smelled, and so on. Darien is smiling and seems to have forgotten how upset he was yesterday. He is fully verbal and asks his partner, Samantha, all kinds of questions about her draft. He occasionally stops the conversation to make a signs that say

> THAT PART IS FUNNY.
> I LIKE THE OCEAN TOO.

Since Darien completed one sentence of the assignment, when it is Samantha's turn to ask questions, she asks him about what happened in the movie, not his narrative. He explains the plot of the movie to her in great depth, making noises to illustrate the sound of the Batmobile, wings flying through the sky, and so on. I prompt Sam to ask him questions about his experience and take notes for him. By the end of the period, she has transcribed almost a page of notes. I praise the pair for all their hard work and hold up the page of writing to show the class what good work they did. Darien is clearly pleased and rushes to complete a sign that says

> THE SMELL OF BUTTERIE POPCORN MAKES ME THINK OF BATMAN.

Another student in the class off-handedly remarks, "I always think of *Shrek* when I have Dr. Pepper because I drank a mega-size Dr. Pepper when I saw that movie." This comment pleases Darien, and he walks around the room showing each student his sign.

Observation 4—Lunch Time Tutoring Session

Because Darien has not written any cohesive type of narrative, I request that he stay in at lunch and work with me. He is pleased by this requirement and brings a sign to the tutoring session that says

> LUNCH IS MAGNIFISENT.

For fifteen minutes, Darien tells me the "plot" of his narrative while I take notes. He describes sensory details with extreme accuracy, pausing to draw the pattern on the movie theater carpet and describing the movie seats as "the color of batman's wings." Occasionally, he slips into telling me the plot of *Batman*, but I steer him back to his narrative. I number the ideas on Darien's paper so that he can write them into a cohesive paragraph.

Observation 5—Day 10 of a 15 Day Unit on Personal Narratives

Students re-write their drafts to include the sensory details they brainstormed during the previous class. Darien is completely silent and on-task. He writes the entire period and covers his work with his hand, so I can't see it when I come by to check on him. It appears that he has about one third of a page of writing by the end of the period (more than he has ever completed without prompting). He doesn't write any signs.

Observation 6—Day 15 of a 15 Day Unit

Personal narratives are due today, and Darien draws a picture of a sad face on a sign and holds it up, indicating that he did not complete his homework.

Students sit in a circle and read their narratives one by one. Darien sits up straight, listening. After each presentation, he holds up a sign that says

CLAP PLEASE.

When it is his turn, he takes the notes I helped him with to the front of the room and clears his voice. He holds up a now wrinkled and stepped-on sign:

MY DAD TOOK ME TO SEE BATMAN.

"That's the title," he clarifies. He then holds up another used sign

THE SMELL OF BUTTERIE POPCORN MAKES ME THINK OF BATMAN.

and starts to tell his story, using his notes to guide him. At points, his voice slips into inaudible baby talk, his stutter covers his words, and the focus of what he is saying gets off track.

The gist of his story is that his father took him to see Batman the same day he left home. It isn't a happy story about getting a reward; it is a painful story about being left behind. At the end, Darien re-displays the previous sign

THE SMELL OF BUTTERIE POPCORN MAKES ME THINK OF BATMAN.

and says, "I miss my dad." Another student in the class holds up Darien's CLAP PLEASE sign, and everyone applauds Darien's performance. He smiles the rest of the period.

Reflections and Conclusions of a Researcher/Teacher/ Human Being

Darien's performance on this assignment was well below grade level. He wasn't able to sequence events into a cohesive narrative or to create more than a few sentences of writing. He did come up with some ideas, but he needed prompting and help transcribing them. It is difficult to evaluate his knowledge of grammar and usage because he completed so little of the assignment. He misapplied spelling rules for making long vowel sounds, spelling words such as "make" as "maike." His oral skills were also below grade level. Rather than speaking, he often reverted to signs to "say" his points, and when he did use oral language, parts of his presentation were inaudible. By all academic standards, Darien's performance on this assignment was a failure.

I have taken university classes and have participated in professional development workshops, and I've learned all about the rhetorical triangle and the importance of having students write for real audiences. My experience tells me that student writing *does* improve when they have a real audience, but I think there is more to it than that. In English professor G. Lynn Nelson's article, "Warriors With Words: Toward a Post-Columbine Writing Curriculum," he argues that telling our personal stories is a deep human need that is as old as the caveman and says, ". . . when we are allowed to write our stories and when someone actually listens to us, powerful language emerges. Voice emerges. Sense of self grows. Maybe that is all we need (could it be so simple?)" (p. 45). The smile on Darien's face tells me he got something valuable out of this assignment. It may not have been a good grade or even much skill development, but there was something there. And I think Nelson is on to something when he talks about listening, *actually* listening. As teachers, we need to create a space where we not only allow students to write their stories, but also where we set up an atmosphere that allows both our students and ourselves, "To listen. Not: To Grade. Not: To Psychoanalyze. Not: To Solve. Just: To Listen" (p. 45). I am not so naive to think that Darien's classmates instantly became best friends with him when they heard his narrative, but I do think for a few minutes on a Wednesday afternoon, he had an audience who saw him as more than the "weird kid" to tolerate. He got to genuinely communicate how he felt and thought, and his peers really listened to him, which is a pretty remarkable thing since Darien's own mother blames his abnormal behavior on his lack of discipline.

Perhaps Darien is really onto something with his signs. In a world that doesn't always listen when it should, he posts his message where it can't be missed. When I think about Darien and what I learned from this case study, I am compelled to make my own sign:

THE SMELL OF BUTTERIE POPCORN MAKES ME THINK OF DARIEN AND WHAT HE TAUGHT ME.

Development: A One Act Play About Writing in the Age of Testing

Be aware that you will be required to write a response to a standardized test question after you have finished reading this play.

Written by: A Teacher who will remain nameless for fear of losing her job

Directed by: Policy makers who endorse high stakes testing but who have never been in a classroom

Acted by: Thousands of students and teachers everyday

Setting: A ninth grade reading classroom where class periods are exactly one hour long. Students must pass an end-of-the year standardized test or their school will be penalized, and their teacher must follow a prescribed curriculum. Once a week, students are given a computerized multiple choice test to monitor their progress. They complete monthly benchmark writing tests. The classroom walls are completely bare, except for black and white posters with lines and lines of state standards written in tiny print. Students are seated in straight rows and stare forward with vacant, lifeless stares. A giant clock ticks loudly at the front of the room.

Teacher: Who remembers what a thesis statement is?

Class: (*In unison and mechanically*) An opinion.

Teacher: Do you know where your thesis statement goes?

Class: (*In unison*) It is the last sentence of the first paragraph.

Teacher: Write an essay in which you state whether Odysseus was or was not a hero. Make sure to support your position with specific examples.

Brian: What if you think Odysseus is complicated? What if he had moments of heroism and moments of weakness? What if your answer can't be boiled down to just agreeing or disagreeing whether Odysseus was a hero?

Miss B: That's an interesting point. Can you talk more about it?

Jennie: (*Interrupting*) Right. Odysseus was brave when he fought the monsters, but he was also selfish. He stayed with Calypso while his wife was home waiting for him. He was prideful when he blinded the Cyclops, and everyone suffered.

Students are starting to wake up and leave their dazed expressions behind.

Joe: But does a hero have to be perfect? Aren't all humans flawed? To be a hero, you don't have to be sub-human.

Miss B's eyes light up as more and more students begin to join the conversation.

Sara: Heroes have to . . . *Her voice is drowned out by the increasing volume of the clock ticking off precious seconds to the standardized test.*

Teacher: (*Nervously*) Oh, we have to get back on track. You have to be able to identify ten literary devices by the end of the week. Write a thesis statement about Odysseus's heroism and worry about actually thinking about the text later.

Joe: What's the point of writing an essay that doesn't really say much anyway?

Students' eyes glaze over, and once again they look like drones slumped in their chairs.

TEST QUESTION

Write an essay discussing reading and writing in a language arts classroom. Make sure to have a thesis statement and evidence to support your points.

Thoughtful reading and writing are not common practices in American language arts classes. The absence is easily explained; English classes have been transformed into a process of creating measurable and quantifiable data and have taken on an almost grocery store checklist type format. Teachers are forced to go through the list: Students write a how-to manual. Check. Develop a thesis statement. Check. Never mind the artistry of a simile in the literature, there isn't time for that. Never mind the possibility of ambiguity in a work of literature. You cannot test ambiguity. The beauty of language: Students should learn to notice on their own time. Or not. There isn't time in class. In the current educational climate, writing is a performative exercise; its success is measured by the students' output on a five-paragraph-essay written in the pages of a test booklet.

For the teacher who wants to promote a reverence for language, who wants to examine language as an art form, and who wants to help students ask questions and wonder about real issues through reading and writing, well, she better not let anyone know about it. She must secretly sew her agenda into the seam of a standards-based lesson plan, careful not to deviate from its format. In doing this, she unavoidably creates a corset that often constricts her students' thinking and smothers their intellect.

This answer received a failing score but was published as an editorial in a local newspaper. Despite a multitude of studies that support the authors' claims, lawmakers continue to ignore her message.

Recapitulation: A True and Good Short Story about Lily

Lily was a kid in my sixth grade class. She seemed very typical. Short, standard school uniform, always trying to write in that glitter ink that makes teachers crazy. In class, I insisted on silent reading. She needed a book. I recommended Sharon Creech's *Walk Two Moons*. She read it and liked it so much that she read all of Creech's books. She even got the other girls in class to read the Creech books.

Good job Sharon Creech. End of story. Almost.

I gave a writing assignment. I taught the kids, Lily included, the formula for the five paragraph essay. I called it a test-taking genre, and everyone followed the format on the standardized test. Our class did fine. End of story. Almost.

We did a lot more than the test-taking genre in our class. We wrote poems, personal narratives, and short stories. We imitated Sandra Cisneros and Li Bo. We created movie reviews, collaborative reports, definition essays, evaluations, and visual reports. And Lily, twelve years old and a little boy-crazy, wrote an entire novel, *one hundred and twelve pages of novel* to be exact and emailed it in chapters to me. She wrote because she loves Creech's style (her word choice, not mine). She wrote because she wanted to make something original. She wrote without being forced.

Here is where I like to believe I enter in a very small way. No five paragraph essay I assigned ever compelled anyone to write on her free time. No writing practice test ever inspired a kid to write a poem, tell a story, or do anything beyond what was required. I believe that when I let kids write with their own voices, they felt language and its power. I believe they wanted to be better writers. End of story. Almost.

Beyond exploring language, my students became better readers. I watched kids notice literary devices and elements of story in books we were reading without my prompting them. I listened to them make insightful comments and make meaning from text by themselves. In short, they read closely and with a scrutinizing, sophisticated, and perhaps most important-ly, motivated eye. Then they transferred their skills from careful readings into thoughtful writing.

Over email, Lily used to ask me questions about the material she was writing. She would say things like, "Do you think that a character like Bryan would really do something like that? Is it believable?" and "I need to say this so that it sounds pretty. What do you think of this phrase? Is it too much?" I think I don't know what more an English teacher could want. End of story.

Epilogue: I used to lose papers, my jokes weren't always funny, not all my students did their homework every day, and sometimes I got toothpaste on my shirt before work. In reality, I was an okay sixth grade teacher, and Lily was an extraordinary student. However, I do believe something extraor-dinary happened in my classroom. We became better readers and writers because we experienced the power of language and what it can do. Our improvement certainly wasn't because of working towards good standard-ized test results.

Coda: Diary of a Teacher

I began my teaching career with the intent to teach a "serious and rigorous" English class, and I saw writing at the center of this plan. I wanted the work my students did in class to leave an indelible mark on their psyches and to affect their growth as both humans and as intellectuals. I believed—and still believe—that reading and writing both develops and uncovers some-thing deep inside of me, something like truth, in the wisest sense of the word. I believe this because as I go about my everyday life, lines from novels and poems shuffle through my head whispering their lines and shaping my thoughts. When I write a newspaper editorial about the genocide in Sudan, I am reminded of Dante's *Inferno*, which warns, "The hottest places in hell are reserved for those who remain neutral in a moral crisis," or when I work on my own poetry, I remember H.D.'s dictum in *Trilogy* to "be indigestible" as I strive to maintain the integrity of my own creative vision. As a teacher, I want to share this passion and belief in the power of the written word with my students.

I am no longer interested in teaching "serious and rigorous" English, although I do believe that is exactly what I do. I am now interested in learning through reading, through writing, and with students. I am still captivated by the written word, but my understanding of writing is conducted through my experiences working with my students. Last night before I went to bed, I was re-reading *Mrs. Dalloway*, a book in which Clarissa, an ordinary woman on an ordinary day living an ordinary life, reflects back on all her experiences—both good and bad—and thinks, "Ah, this is life!" as she realizes that the unpredictability and messiness of life are what make it extraordinary. As a student, teacher, writer, and reader, I can't but help feel the same way.

A typical sonata-allegro consists of five parts; a typical Shakespearean play consists of five acts; a typical standardized test consists of seven sections; a typical student's notebook consists of six subjects; a typical understanding of literacy takes more than five parts, five acts, seven sections, or six subjects.

References

Nelson, G. L. (2000). Warriors with words: Toward a post-Columbine curriculum. *English Journal, 89.5*, 42–46.

Goldsmith, S. W. (1996). *poemcrazy*. New York: Three Rivers Press.

Teaching the Art of Writing
A Journey to Learn How

M. P. Cavanaugh, Ph.D.

I am a professor of English, and my specialty is English Education. One of my teaching responsibilities is to prepare undergraduate students to incorporate writing in their future teaching. I believe two elements must be in place for that to happen successfully: 1) they have to be taught many methods of teaching writing; and 2) they have to see purpose and some enjoyment in their own writing. I took a long journey to develop those beliefs; I am glad I did, and I think my students have benefited.

How I Learned to Teach Writing

I followed the traditional path of undergraduate education where I majored in English at Western Michigan University and became certified to teach in the state of Michigan. Unlike many of today's students, I graduated in four years, and I did get a job immediately in Bay City. I began my career teaching at T.L. Handy High School with five sections of a variety of English: 9th grade "regular" English and 10th grade "general" English. In every section, I had my students write, and I duly marked each paper with my red pen. I saw myself as a teacher, certainly not as a writer. I demanded that my

Getting It in Writing, pages 17–30
Copyright © 2011 by Information Age Publishing
All rights of reproduction in any form reserved.

students read "good" literature like *Great Expectations* and *Romeo and Juliet* and write essays that reflected their understanding of the literature and any research I asked them to do. I have some memories, but much of that early period of teaching is a blur—perhaps fortunately.

Except Roger. I took my 9th graders to the library for orientation, and I instructed them in proper behavior. They must sit quietly and listen politely to the librarian even though I knew the librarian's orientation was hardly spellbinding to adults, let alone 9th graders. Most of the students complied with my disciplinary demands even though I seemed to care more about their behavior than their learning. A few didn't, and after the presentation I went over to Roger, put my face very close to his, and practically hissed, "You are NOT behaving according to my standards."

Roger hissed back, "I'd have to be dead to meet your standards." My point is that I think I was teaching out of a conservative mode that prized behavior and rote learning. But there must have been a spark deep within me because I did get along well with my students. At the end of one of my early years, many of the newer teachers received "pink slips," which were notices of a lack of employment for the following school year. It was a safe-guard for the district in case they did not have the funds to pay salaries. News of these "pink slips" went out quickly, and one of my 10th graders came to me and reported, "I talked with my father, and we can use you on the farm in the fall." What could I say? I had never even been on a farm, but what a thoughtful gesture.

I was re-assigned to a different high school at one point in my career, and I was given reading improvement classes to teach. These were classes for 10th graders who had failed Freshman English. I knew absolutely nothing about teaching reading (which I now know is a sad state for an English/Language Arts teacher to be in), but I knew enough about teaching to know that workbooks that required students to practice the alphabet ____ c ____ by placing the letter that comes before and the letter that comes afterward on the blank lines is not the right way to go about it. I decided to work on a Master's degree in Reading—at Michigan State University, and that was eye opening and enriching. It got so my colleagues would walk the other way when they saw me approaching in order to avoid hearing yet another wonderful way to teach and why we should all be teaching reading and writing. They were logical ideas, but they hadn't occurred to me until I heard them in graduate classes:

- Treat developmental readers and writers like the good people they are—not like second class citizens.
- Encourage all kinds of reading and writing as much as possible.

- Use interesting, motivating books and stories rather than dull textbooks.

I established the practice of reading aloud to my 10th grade developmental reading students in a class that met after lunch. One day as I was reading a King Arthur tale, I heard one boy remark to another, "Look how into it (the story) she is." I suspect it was my passion rather than the story itself that hooked them.

Another suggestion I took was having students read short sections of the stories aloud while I stood or sat close by the reader and softly whispered pronunciations of difficult words. Allowing poor readers to "master" the art of oral reading was also a motivational factor. My students and I were becoming used to this practice, but one day the trance was broken. The assistant principal, generally known as The Disciplinarian, came to my class to observe. He sat down in an empty chair and watched. I took a book from the shelf, turned to the page we were on and gave it to him. I had in mind simply to let him know what we were doing and where we were. The students had something else in mind. When the reading rotation came to him, they "politely" waited for him to read a paragraph or two aloud. When he stumbled over the pronunciation of a word, they were quietly triumphant, and I could literally see it in their faces and their postures.

I moved from the Master's in Reading to my continuing connection with the National Writing Project. I co-led the Saginaw Bay Writing Project Summer Institute in the summer 2008. I strongly believe that we "learn by doing," and I certainly did a great deal of writing as a high school English teacher, but I don't think I really knew what writing was and what I was capable of until I went through the Red Cedar Writing Project at Michigan State University. I had begun a graduate program and had studied the previous summer in England under the direction of Stephen Tchudi, who is widely known for his work in English/Language Arts. So, the next summer I became a participant in the Summer Institute which was also under his direction. I learned so much—not only about the teaching of writing but about myself as a writer, which became a strong influence on my teaching of writing. I learned the art of close reading and close revision and revision and revision and re-vision. As all teachers who have spent a summer in a Writing Project Institute know, the total immersion into the land of composing—thinking it, breathing it, sharing it, comparing it—learning wonderful teaching of writing concepts from the Summer Institute leaders and consultants and from each other, changes each participant. Writing Projects start their participants down a road from which there is no turning back. And who would want to? The joy of knowing how to write and how to teach writing is compelling.

In addition to the summer class, we had to commit to a reunion in January where we would share stories of success having incorporated some of what we learned in the Summer Institute in our classes. It was a joy to see again those teachers with whom I had shared so many hours and ideas. But my report was not one of success. Again, I had to learn the hard way. We learned about the power of students keeping journals, and I could certainly see the merit in that practice. What we hadn't learned or what I hadn't learned was the importance of timing and planning. I taught high school English; I had five classes, and I had over 125 students. I explained and demonstrated the art of journal writing, and for each journal entry I gave them three to four topics with a "Create Your Own" topic option as Steve Tchudi had suggested. But I collected 125 journals one Friday afternoon. I spent the entire weekend writing responses to their entries. Not every single one, but still by Sunday evening I could barely hold a pen in my hand. So when the participants of the Summer Institute met to share their successes, I shared what I considered my failure. It wasn't a complete failure, of course, but I did have to learn how to stagger due dates because my students really liked keeping journals, and they really liked my responding to them. One Monday in May of that year, instead of three different suggestions for their journal entry, I wrote a quote on the board: *It was the best of times; it was the worst of times.* We were about to begin Dickens, and I thought reflecting on those words and possibly connecting them to their lives would be a good start, but the looks on their faces told me a discussion was necessary, and not about literature. My students had their prom that weekend, and several prom/party attendees had had situations with the local police. They thought somehow I had found out their deep and dark secrets. I hadn't, but in time, I learned the entire and not so dreadful story—the power of journal writing.

The summer in England and the Summer Institute led to my doctoral studies—another long and ambitious road. For most of my coursework, I continued to teach in the high school, so I could practice what I was learning. At the end of my course work, I moved down to campus to join the academic community and got the thrill of my lifetime: the opportunity to teach college students.

My dissertation was a history of holistic literacy. It also changed my attitude, my teaching, my views on much of education. I looked at a span of 100 years from just prior to the Civil War to the 1950s. I studied five phenomenal educators: Colonel Francis Wayland Parker, John Dewey, Rudolf Steiner, Hughes Mearns and Laura Zirbes, and I learned that in too many cases we are reinventing the wheel. For example, today we are concerned about the reading abilities of young children. In 1949 Laura Zirbes wrote about the serious curriculum issue of the day: recurrent failures in beginning reading. Seventy-five years earlier, Charles Adams discovered that while the students of Quincy, Massachusetts, could read the words of the examination pages for which they had prepared, they seemed to have no real understanding of what they read. Some of the successful contemporary literacy strategies were developed and taught in the 1850s. I was astounded, but this information continued to convince me of the importance of these holistic and process approaches. (My dissertation has been published by Greenwood Publishing Company and is called *A History of Holistic Literacy*.)

Initial Successes in My Teaching

College-prep seniors: At T. L. Handy High School, I was eventually given the opportunity to teach four sections of college-bound seniors. What a joy! The students were all planning to attend college, and they really wanted to be prepared. I did have a mentor—the man who had developed the course—but one day after school, I looked over the empty desks and wondered, "What do the colleges want? What are the expectations?" Not long after that wondering moment, I learned about a small day-long conference to be held at Delta Community College for area high school students. They had a poetry contest (teachers could submit poems their students had written), and a play was to be performed. They also had several workshops on short story writing, poetry analysis, and persuasive writing. We took a school bus to the campus, and I told my students they could attend whatever they wanted to, and we would meet in the auditorium for the Poetry Prize Presentations and the return trip to our school. One of the workshops was on College Writing Expectations. I really wanted to attend that one, and I went early. Good thing. There wasn't an empty seat in the large room. It was filled with students—high school students—and when the panel of instructors and college students began to talk, we could have heard the pin if it were dropped. So many high school students cared about college expectations, and they wanted to hear it from the college, not from their high school teachers. (One of my students did win a poetry prize, and what a thrill when they read his poem aloud.) That conference propelled me toward my passion today of developing a "true" link between the high school and the college.

I loved teaching those students. I taught world literature, research, persuasion, note-taking, test-taking including essay writing. I made their research project one of great importance because I wanted them to respect it and the process. I made it clear, absolutely clear, that all papers must be submitted on the due date. One student was so anxious she called me at home during a dinner party I was giving because she had a citation question that simply would not wait. Another student whose father was a central office administrator told of having to go to his father's office at midnight to finish typing his paper. I would teach all those kinds of writing genre again: world literature, research, persuasion, but I would do so in different ways as I have learned along my journey, and as I will explain. For example, I would use the multi-genre approach in the research process, voice exercises prior to having students write persuasive essays, and use pre-reading, guided reading, and post reading writing strategies to guide their reading of world literature.

Content Area Reading courses: At two universities, I had the opportunity to teach Content Area Reading. What an impact that can make on teachers! In Content Area Reading, we divide reading strategies into Pre, Guided, and Post. In university courses, teachers of many subject areas (or undergraduate students preparing to become teachers) take a course like this. As in Writing across the Curriculum, we believe in Reading across the Curriculum. "Every teacher a teacher of reading." As in writing, reading is far too complex an undertaking to be relegated to the English/Language Arts class. I taught a variety of these pre, guided, and post reading strategies and had my students develop them in their disciplines to be used in their classrooms. This was widely successful and teachers who "buy into" the idea were so pleased. For example, have students write answers to background and prediction questions and discuss their answers prior to reading; have students keep a character map as they are reading; and have students draw a graphic organizer of what they have read and translate the graphic organizer into a summary.

Graduate course in the teaching of writing: I had the opportunity to teach graduate courses in the teaching of writing, and this is a delight because those students really want to learn more to enhance their teaching. The kinds of teachers who elect to partake in the Summer Institutes of the NWP, the kinds of teachers who will read this book, and the kinds of teachers I had the privilege to teach are the ones who are eager to learn new—for example, copy changing in poetry, fiction, and non-fiction—and tried and true strategies and techniques, such as the 5-paragraph essay and the research process, to improve their writing and their teaching of writing. I love teaching practicing teachers or when my undergraduates "go out to field," which means they are in a classroom for several periods to teach. I encourage them to try the ideas they have learned and bring back to our classroom the news of their successes or if they experience problems; perhaps as a whole class we can brainstorm suggestions for alterations and revisions. Students have returned to report that they have tried using the RAFTT strategy or the Multi-Genre Research Project, and they show what "their students" have created.

Teaching the Art of Writing: This is a course for both elementary and secondary majors, and we attempt to cover the writing process and the teaching of writing: have students pay attention to their own writing and then see how they might teach writing. We begin with excerpts from Sandra Cisneros' *House on Mango Street* (1985) and Tobias Wolff's *The Boy's Life* (1969) in which the authors describe their feelings toward their names and give the reader some insight into their lives and some of why they feel as they do. Our students are then asked to do a "copy change" and write about their own names, their feelings about them, and some insight into their lives.

We teach the teaching of narration, poetry, writing across the curriculum: description, exposition, persuasion. We have lessons on evaluation, revision, specific, and general grammar issues. They write a variety of papers from the opening "My Name" piece, a Life Map (Kirby, Kirby & Liner, 2004), a Writing Self-Profile, a description, a voice exercise, several poems, and a digital story. They develop a grammar mini-lesson, a research project on some aspect of the teaching of writing, and a teaching demonstration. Research topics include autobiography, description, grammar, graphic organizers, journals, letter writing, narration, persuasion, poetry, writing across the curriculum, and the writing process. Readers who have been through the Summer Institute of a Writing Project site will recognize the similarity to it. All of the writing pieces and all of the writing that comes out of each teaching demonstration goes into their Writing Folders. In addition, a hand-out that explains each student's research project and one that can be used in the teaching demonstration are placed in the Writing Folder. This, then, becomes a collection of thirty to thirty-five writing lessons with a sample of each written by each student. Former students report that this Writing Folder is an enormous help to them in their teaching. One student told me that during her initial meeting with her host teacher, the teacher remarked that she hoped that the SVSU student would be coming to her classroom armed with many writing ideas. Rather than being intimidated, which is how many undergraduates react to comments from their brand new host teacher, my student smiled, "Oh, yes, I will."

The Frustrations I Had and/or Continue to Face: A Confession

Frustration and Barrier # 1: As I high school English teacher I did not know what colleges expected students to be able to do.

How I Overcame Barrier #1: I earned a doctorate and taught at the college level. Now one of my major interests is connecting high schools with colleges so we can communicate and help each other. Recently, a high school English teacher told me when she receives a very poorly written paper from a student, she does not know what to do or how to help that student. This is why I have studied so much and so long; I want to help her.

Frustration and Barrier #2: One semester, a Content Area Reading student told me his host teacher said not to listen to anything I taught. I assumed it was a case of the teacher feeling as though college methods courses don't teach anything useful. Unfortunately, this is sometimes the case.

How I Overcame Barrier #2: I vowed to continuously conduct research on the best teaching strategies and techniques and to become the most practical teacher and in-service provider so that students and teachers with whom I work would not have that feeling that they are not learning anything useful.

Frustration and Barrier #3: My students don't seem to understand. I work so hard at teaching; I want my students to work hard at learning. I worry when I believe I have converted them to a new way of thinking, and I see they have not.

How I Am Overcoming Barrier#3: Sometimes an individual conference is necessary, and sometimes many individual conferences are necessary. Advertisers know that people need to hear the message seven times, and yet teachers want to say it just once. I have a situation now in my Methods of Teaching English class. I have just finished reading a set of lesson plans. Several of my students who were in my Teaching the Art of Writing course where I stressed giving motivating and creative writing assignment have placed nothing but the five paragraph essay in their lessons. I will ask them why, of course, but I suspect the answer lies somewhere in William James' notion of habit. These students probably had nothing but essays to write in high school and in most of their college classes. One class with me is not enough to change this cycle.

Types of Writing They Produced

Traditional Compositions: Of course, as a teacher of writing, I must teach my students how to write a variety of essays such as description, comparison/contrast, persuasion, and response. I like to give a definition, an explanation, a graphic organizer designed to follow the type of essay, and an example prior to having students write. I urge them to pre-write by brainstorming and filling in the graphic organizer prior to drafting.

Research/Multi-Genre/Multi-Genre Project: Tom Romano, a former high school English teacher, developed an amazing way to have students present their research. While he was in Stratford, and in between plays, he went to a book store and happened upon a biography of *Billy the Kid* by Michael Ondatgee (author of *The English Patient*). It was written in multi-genre format, and he was instantly inspired. He returned to his high school English class and had his students change the format of their traditional research papers. Instead, they wrote a poem, a short story, or a one-act play. It has since been opened up to almost any kind of genre from birth certificates to recipes to interviews to top ten lists.

In the English Department, we have a course that follows our initial Freshman Composition, which is a research-based course. When I taught it, I taught the traditional research methodology with topic selection, searching for information, topic narrowing/broadening, searching for information, categorizing information, outlining/graphic organizing, drafting, revising/editing, and final draft. I always have students present their research. I allow just two to three minutes for these presentations. I must admit, for the most part, these presentations were somewhat stiff. Then, I had the students take their research and develop a Multi-Genre Project. When we gathered for their presentations, the atmosphere in the classroom was literally charged with energy. They presented like scholars, and even though I had set a time limit for each presentation, they each really wanted to give more of the very interesting information they had already discovered. The Multi-Genre Project did not require that they locate any additional information. But as they manipulated or transformed the information into genres, they were thrilled with their projects. One student had researched sleep disorders, and she submitted her new multi-genre project in a pillow. The pillow replaced the traditional cover or 3-ring folder. Another had studied Freud, and she submitted her project in a suitcase because she had framed pictures, framed diplomas, a photo album, and more. Another studied Watergate, and she created a Watergate Yearbook. One young man finally changed topics altogether. He had selected the topic: gender bias in films. He knew nothing about this, yet I could not convince him to select a new topic. The result was dismal, and when we switched to Multi-Genre, he switched to sea turtles and created an amazing project. The creative manner of presenting information motivates students to write about and think more about their research. They are eager to present information in creative genres rather than traditional paragraphs.

My Name: On the first day of *Teaching the Art of Writing* class I have my students write a "My Name" piece. In the course packet I have an excerpt from

Sandra Cisneros *House on Mango Street* where she is talking about her name, where it comes from, how it sounds, and an excerpt from Tobias Wolff's *This Boy's Life* where he is talking about changing his name for several personal and serious reasons. Following these readings, I have my students write their names across the middle of the top line—first, middle, and last. They then write what comes to mind. Of course, we do this in a computer lab, and I will have shown them samples—one which has a can of Campbell's Tomato Soup in the background because the student author's last name was Campbell.

Voice: In this exercise I give a list of possibilities from Kirby, Kirby, and Liner (2004) such as Fast Talking, Mad Talking, Sad Talking, Talking Back to Self, How do I Love Thee? and Multifaceted Self-Portraits. I talk them through each of these with suggestions, and I let them at it. I say if you are really angry about something today, Mad Talking is just for you. If you have ever been home alone, you are absolutely certain you are alone, and no one could possibly get in, but still you hear that creak, you begin Talking Back to Self: "Don't be ridiculous, no one is here—uh oh, I just heard that creak again." I've had students do "How do I love Thee" as a collage. Multifaceted Self-Portraits is my favorite. Students select several people close to them: parent, sibling, friend, teacher, and enemy. They describe themselves as each of these people would describe them using their voice. One of my students chose the Multifaceted Self-Portrait voice, and she used her mother and her twin sister. She wrote in "their voices" how she thought they would describe her. After class, she called them, told them the assignment, and asked them what they would say in a description of her. They were closely aligned with what she wrote, and she was just delighted. In fact, she came running to my office to tell me. I was delighted, too. They could describe themselves as their mother would describe them using first person and their mother's voice and point of view. This teaches students to more carefully consider point of view in this Voice exercise, but also to consider point of view in all writing.

Life Map: This is also from Kirby, Kirby, and Liner (2004). I begin by asking students to list answers to my prompts: Where were you born? What is your first memory? Where did you attend kindergarten? First grade? Did your family move? Third grade? Middle School? What sports or clubs or hobbies did you have? I prompt them into high school, and then I tell them to bring themselves to now. From this Life List, they move to creating a Life Map, literally a map of pictures, clip art, graphics, or drawings that portray some of these events. They draw it like a map with one event moving toward the next. This exercise contains a list of facts and images and graphics that represent those facts. Students enjoy thinking back over their lives and sharing those memories in their writing groups. This can be used to help students prepare to write a memoir. The Life List helps sort out the facts of their lives and the Life Map conjures many powerful memories. These "pictures" of their lives could assist in creating word pictures in their memoir.

Digital Stories: I attended a Professional Development Conference at Saginaw Valley State University in the Winter Term of 2006 sponsored by our Saginaw Bay Writing Project. The session I attended was on digital stories. I was so impressed I spent the next morning creating my own. So, when it came time to teach narrative writing in my class, I developed a pre-writing chart with the elements of the short story, and I shared my new digital story. I told my students that if I could create one, they certainly could do so, and they believed me. Their creations are so fun and motivating because of the pictures, designs, and formatting. I also do some oral warming up to short story writing. I explain and discuss the elements of narration: setting, protagonist, antagonist, conflict, resolution, and theme; and I have lists of story starters in the course packet. I ask for four volunteers, and we sit in a circle in the center of the room. I let them select one story starter, and I explain that we are going to make up a story from the starter they chose. We will each take a turn talking aloud and creating as we go; we must consider the elements of narration, so someone has to declare a setting, and someone else has to determine our conflict and so on. It is usually a lot of fun because the students who volunteer are the precocious ones who can jump right into almost anything. Following our demonstration, all students get into their Writing Groups and follow suit. It gets pretty noisy, and I hear a great deal of laughter. Some of the story starters are "I don't believe in magic pencils but…" "The fog set in at midday…" "The day the teacher overslept, we…" and "Suddenly, the lantern sputtered and went out…" It is a non-threatening way to practice understanding the elements of fiction, and it is a fun way to have students begin to think about the story they will write.

Found Poem and one Formula Poem: I garner from both Kirby, Kirby, and Liner (2004) and Tompkins (2007) a series of Formula Poems: Name, Auto-Bio, Bio, Diamante, French Triolet, Concrete, Cincain, and others. I teach Found Poetry from both sources. After defining, explaining, and showing examples, I give each of my students a magazine. The assignment is to create one of the Formula Poems and find/re-work a Found Poem. For the Found Poem they must take the page right out of the magazine and attach it to the poem they create. Again, we spend time in a computer lab, and I urge them to make their poems look like poems: page centered. By this time in the semester, my students have become enthusiastic about color and font and appropriate illustrations. So, while they still struggle as writers creating a poem, they are assisted by the formula for a Bio Poem:

> First name
>
> Four traits that describe character
>
> Relative of
>
> Who loves (list three things or people)
>
> Who feels (three things)
>
> Who needs (three items)
>
> Who gives (three items)
>
> Who would like to see (three items)
>
> Resident of
>
> Last name

Students in a high school English class studying *The Great Gatsby* could write a paragraph describing Jay Gatsby or they could write a Bio Poem:

> Jay
>
> Confidant, jealous, ambitious, inventive
>
> The former James Gatz
>
> Who loves Daisy, money, power
>
> Who feels depressed, anxious, unwanted
>
> Who needs life, love, and happiness
>
> Who fears Tom, his identity, and his past
>
> Who gives parties, his soul, and his life
>
> Who would like to see Daisy, her divorce, and their merger
>
> Resident of West Egg
>
> Gatsby

They add color; they care about font selection; they add pictures that represent meanings and images in the poem; and they are proud of what they have written.

RAFTT: Role, Audience, Format, and Topic. Instead of the traditional approach in which the student assumes the role of him/herself, the audience is the teacher, the format is the five paragraph essay, and the topic is determined by the teacher. Now, the student assumes a new role—perhaps that of a newspaper reporter; an appropriate audience might be readers of the 1870s; a unique format: an obituary; and the topic possibly the death of General Custer. One of my students created the role: a wheat thin; the audience: other wheat thins; the format: a travel brochure; the topic: the digestive system. I created the second T on RAFTT, and that is tone. Thus, what tone would the reporter adopt in the obituary? What tone would the wheat thin adopt in the travel brochure? Another student created the role: a plant; the audience, the sun; the format, a top ten list; the topic, the plants needs; and the tone: lovesick and infatuated. These RAFTTs can even be used as assessment in the sense that if the role is a plant, the audience is the sun, the format is a thank you note, the topic is the sun's role in plant growth, and the tone is grateful, we know if the students understand how the sun effects plant growth by what information they include in their thank you note. The students are more motivated to create the thank you note than they might be to write a report or take a test.

Lessons Learned through My Career

I have learned so much about teaching and learning throughout my career both as a teacher and as a learner. I encourage my students to be creative with not only what they write but also how they represent their work. I have learned that students must not only understand but also be competent in writing the basics. If we don't continue to demand this, we are not really teaching our students. In fact, we do them a disservice. So, I have to encourage, motivate, gently correct, and listen.

Successes

I am very happy with my teaching, and as I look back I see that I have been lucky because I have been willing to learn and change. When I began teaching high school English, I, like many other new teachers, had high standards for my students. Remember Roger? The 9th grader who did not behave well during the library orientation? Time passed, and Roger became a senior. He was on the football team and had sustained an injury. The seniors had their own hallway with lockers and benches. One day toward the end of the school year, I happened to see Roger sitting alone on one of the benches. His football injury had required that his jaw be wired, and he had a neck brace holding his neck steady and stiff and his mouth closed. I sat down next to him and said nothing for a few minutes. Then I murmured, "Now you are meeting my standards." Laughter shone in his eyes and delightful laugh-tears slowly rolled down his cheeks. Our eyes met, and we knew that somehow both of us were right, and we had learned that from each other.

References

Cisneros, S. (1985). *House on Mango Street.* New York: Vintage Books.

Kirby, D., Kirby, D., and Liner, T. (2004*). Inside out: Strategies for teaching writing.* Portsmouth, NH: Heinemann.

Tompkins, G. (2007). *Teaching writing: Balancing process and product.* Upper Saddle River, NJ: Pearson Education, Inc.

Wolff, T. (1969). *This boy's life.* New York: Grove Press.

My Journey

Teaching All Students the Joy of Being Writers

Cheryl Cormier

"**H**ave you ever thought of becoming an English teacher?" questioned Ms. Binks, my junior year English teacher.

"No," I replied, still a high school student.

Today, I actually am a sixth grade writing teacher. My students and I are so fortunate because I have taken a circuitous route. This chapter is my journey through so many changes in education and in me. The journey also became personal as writing became a part of my entire life.

It began in the 1970s when I was a student and then a young educator who knew only to follow a textbook. My interest in language led me to the field of speech-language pathology rather than English. Through the years, my experiences with inclusion led me to believe *all* students can learn the art of writing when given the proper tools and guidance. This became my passion—to teach students that they all are writers. The students needed to gain confidence and become invested in the joy of writing. My job as an educator was to facilitate this process.

I have come full circle since those early years. I am currently a full-time sixth grade writing teacher in a small town in New England where the

Getting It in Writing, pages 31–54

middle school model is housed in the town's lone elementary school of about 650 students. Every sixth grade student attends my writing class for four class periods a week. It is twenty-one years since I received a phone call to be a six-week substitute speech-language pathologist. I believe I am truly where I belong—teaching each student the joy of being a writer.

Early Writing Roots

In the 1970s, I became an elementary education/communication disorders major at Boston College. In my education classes, I was given a college textbook for language arts and learned about entertaining activities to promote speaking, listening, reading, and writing. We created "centers" to address prescribed language arts skills such as parts of speech, contractions and many others. I have no recollection of direct methods of teaching writing, except in the area of conventions and forms of writing, like the "friendly letter." I remember the term "Creative Writing," but I do not remember any training on how to teach "creative writing." I tried to give an imaginative prompt to entice them to write creatively, "You have been stranded on a desert island. Name 5 objects you would bring and describe your experience." I do not remember teaching about leads and narrative structure.

After my graduation from Boston College, I spent a few of my early years in education tutoring small groups of children in a federally subsidized program. This led to a middle school position where I taught two grammar classes to eighth grade students, as well as literature classes to seventh grade students. In those grammar classes we took out our *Warriner's Grammar and Composition Book* to drill and kill each day. "Do exercises one through eight on page 82." Then we corrected them. I assigned a chapter test on the prescribed skill and so it went for an entire year. I'm lucky any of us survived and it only lasted for one year.

In Massachusetts, Proposition 2½ was passed, and this led to many teacher cuts and changes of assignments. I became a primary grade speech and language classroom teacher to about six students with language learning disabilities. These are generally students who have difficulties with the expression and comprehension of language that affect academic skills. This position allowed me to work with the development of language and the foundation of literacy. I felt my first waves of passion about the connection between language development and literacy.

We started our day with morning news generated from the students seated around an easel that they then read back. They told about their world. They were invested in these stories and could see the direct relationship between the spoken word and written word as I scribed their stories on the chart tablet. I was able to guide them to higher forms of language and literacy skills. "What's another word we can use in this sentence? What more can we say?" We worked on sound symbol relationships as they hunted for letters and sounds. My enthusiasm for the teaching about the written word started right here. I saw how my enthusiasm became contagious as we used our "magic eye" to find end marks of sentences. With a smile on our faces, we all shouted, "*stop*!" when we found one.

As happy as I was in that position, I made the decision to stay home for a while to raise my own children. It wasn't until five years later that a phone call looking for a substitute speech pathologist would bring me back to the schools. Since that time, my circuitous journey through teaching writing has been ongoing in this one small school district in Massachusetts. I continued to work part-time after my substitute position was completed. I also received my master's degree in speech-language pathology. After graduation, I worked in a full-time speech-language position for the next sixteen years.

Speech-Language Pathologist as Teacher

I returned to my love of blending my speech-language pathology background with my education background. My services were classroom-based, not exercises in isolated skills. I looked for ways to include classroom skills into my speech-language therapy. My caseload mainly consisted of students with language-learning disabilities and articulation disorders. The therapy was still conducted in any small area we could find outside of the classroom. What speech and language skills did my students need to survive in their daily life as a student? Did the vocabulary words contain my students' target sounds? Could I use the vocabulary of the classroom to develop my students' language skills? The answer was a resounding, "Yes!"

I watched and listened to the teachers' concerns. "My students just don't listen" was a common statement in the primary grade teachers' room. During my graduate level research, I explored the collaboration approach to therapy where therapist and teacher combined their efforts in the classroom. My knowledge of language as the foundation of literacy could be very beneficial working together with a classroom teacher as we blended our knowledge to enhance literacy skills.

I chose a teacher who I knew would be comfortable working with me and I with her. We respected each other and were friendly as fellow colleagues. I offered Mrs. K weekly "Listening Lessons" to her second graders, who included many of "my students." Each week, I went into the classroom and gave whole class lessons on how to be a good listener: eyes watching, ears listening, mouth quiet and hands and feet still. We practiced following direction activities including concept words used during regular classroom instruction. They sometimes followed directions by coloring the items I referred to, "Color the bear in front of the line brown." They learned strategies (Classroom Listening Look) to listen for those "special direction words." The students looked forward to a special teacher coming to the classroom. The teacher looked forward to the new understanding she gained about her students as she truly observed them. As for me, I received wonderful feedback that this was truly meaningful work, not only for "my students," but also for the regular education students and for their teacher. The teacher could use these lessons to refer to during classroom lessons. Get one positive teacher and others followed.

First and second grade teachers wanted their students to have this special attention that might guide them to better listening skills. I also had another motive. The teachers stayed in the classroom so I could role model teaching techniques for my learning disabled students, such as giving them extra wait time and giving them increased cueing so that they may be successful in answering questions. With experience, I could see how my role could be expanded, as the teachers and I were more comfortable with our roles.

What does this have to do with writing? I was breaking my way into the real world of my students to improve their language skills. Language skills are the basis of literacy skills, including writing. I was making headway in my circuitous journey as I broke into the classroom and established rapport and respect among the teachers. As my journey moved on, this became very important in my work as a teacher of writing.

I saw with my very own eyes how important early language skills are the foundation of literacy skills. Expressive language consists of semantics (word knowledge), syntax and morphology (sentence construction and grammar), and phonology (sound system). Having these skills intact are crucial to the process of reading and then to writing. Phonology affects decoding and encoding (spelling). Vocabulary enrichment, including developing background knowledge, is so important in all areas of academic and social development. Students must also have a good command of syntactic structure (sentence constructions) when they speak but also so that they can anticipate words that make sense when reading and writing sentences.

Therefore, my listening lessons in grades one and two continued to develop vocabulary skills, as well as listening skills. It wasn't too long before we worked on expressive language as well, and I expanded my role into the pre-school and kindergarten. The teachers told me of the difficulties my speech and language students were having in the classroom.

My role changed from grade to grade, teacher to teacher. As a culminating activity for the integrated special needs pre-school program, the classroom was transferred into a three-ring circus. The good kind! Mary, the lead teacher, and I were the ringmasters with high boots and top hats, but no whip. The students showed their amazing feats, such as our "strong men" lifted their weights up high, higher and highest and the "balance beam artists" walked to the right and then to the left. Their parents cheered in the stands. So many foundations for language learning and literacy development were enthusiastically practiced and learned.

I believed the blending of my knowledge of language and disabilities within each teacher's classroom curriculum provided seamless language and literacy instruction. It was at this time that my assignment changed to grades three through six and to writing instruction.

My journey took a turn toward where I was ultimately meant to be. In the upper grades, the expectations rose for the students to comprehend and use more complex semantic and syntactic structures. It was time to listen to the teachers as I had at the primary grades. "My students' writing skills are atrocious." I saw my opening. I volunteered my knowledge of expressive language and its relevance with writing skills to the classroom setting.

I began to see at the intermediate and upper level of elementary school that the language-learning disabled (LLD) students were having trouble with written language. They couldn't initiate writing because they had no idea how to start or worse yet, they could not hold their experiences in their memory long enough to write about them. Organization of thoughts, memory difficulties, and word retrieval difficulties are common with this disability and greatly affect writing skills. Their disabilities now caught up with them as they tried to transfer thoughts into the written word.

Ramona, age ten, was my home-school student who came in for stuttering therapy, but it became more of a concern to her mother that Ramona was not writing her thoughts out. Ramona was a bright child and her vocabulary and creativity in her oral expression were well beyond her years. Yet, when required to write something on paper, she would stiffen and refuse. I knew I had to meet Ramona at her comfort level. She frequently brought in a stuffed animal or doll. I asked her to tell me about the doll, thus evaluating her fluency in conversation that day. Then came the time I suggested it would be wonderful to write about the doll. Of course, the pout came on her face immediately. I responded that I would like to write about the doll if she could tell me about her. With gentle encouragement and knowing Ramona well, I convinced her to help me write some sentences. It wasn't that she couldn't spell. Her fine motor skills were slower than her verbal skills. We took turns writing about the doll. She had put up a brick wall to writing, but bit-by-bit it was torn down by praise, patient guidance, and her sense of accomplishment. The pout was replaced with a sense of pride as her mother and I praised her truly creative writing. As each week went on, she was willing to write on her own and then in longer pieces as I guided her when needed.

After writing about her doll, Ramona's pieces were about herself, and then she started to show off her creativity with fantasy. She then wrote her first full-length story. Seeing the mother's tears in her eyes was the moment when I became committed to teaching students how to express themselves in writing. Ramona became passionate at home about writing, writing longer and longer stories, essays, and finally a letter to the President of the United States about the lack of prayer in our public schools. Unfortunately for me, they moved away that summer, but I would never forget that stubborn, bright child and the excitement on her face and her mother's face when her fantasy story was written on paper.

The refusal of a student to write even one word on paper is disturbing. The source could be a disability, academic or even emotional. Too often this refusal appears to be a behavioral issue, when in reality, it may be a cry for help. The student needs to trust us and develop a relationship with us through our authentic praise and encouragement.

During third grade writing time, Anthony sat off by himself and stared at his paper. He had been given a prompt, but the pencil remained on the table. "Get started, Anthony," the teacher called from her desk. I sat beside him and made some personal connections with him that led to a discussion of the prompt, "Describe a time when you were lucky." There are many occasions when the backgrounds of some of our students are far from ideal. "Lucky" was not something that he seemed to relate to.

"I've never been lucky," sulked Anthony.

"That's lousy. Sometimes I don't feel lucky either," I replied.

Anthony peered up, quizzically.

"I need to think really hard about this. There must have been a time when I felt lucky," I answered. I then started to rattle off small lucky events hoping that Anthony would relate to something.

"I found a dollar bill on the ground this summer," Anthony jumped up in surprise. Further discussion ensued as he related his story.

"Let's write it down," I suggested. "How about we work together with the first line? Remember Mrs. B said we should include part of the prompt in the first sentence." He dictated his first sentence as I scribed. Again, I met him at his comfort level but still had him practice thinking of ideas and related them to me in a meaningful sequential order. That day he wanted me to be his scribe for the entire piece. I did it because he needed to see his ideas could be put on paper and see a successful result. As I came into writing time each week, there was decreased writing by me. Later on, when he was ready to write a story independently, we started using a web graphic organizer. It was a slow process. The main goal was for him to gain skills to develop his self-confidence and work toward independent writing. His teacher became more aware of his needs. A graphic organizer, such as a web, let him get his thoughts out, given some prompting. I often have students number the logical order of events on the web. Some students prefer a series of events graphic organizer that is more linear; some would rather just list or make the organizer on their own. Some, not usually the special education child, have the ability to organize in their heads. I have learned to give choices in regard to the graphic organizer, but planning remains very important.

The LLD child has great difficulty with organization of thought, as well as retrieval of information. The main purpose is for the student to see that pre-writing (planning) for them is important. When an educator experiences success with one of these students, the feeling is euphoric for both the student and teacher. It is a self-confidence booster for the student and teacher.

I was more determined than ever to get into the classroom. The more experience I gained from the different grade levels I serviced, the more passionate I became. The teacher side of me was bursting to come out and teach with the language background knowledge of a speech-language pathologist. Teachers became increasingly receptive to me entering their classroom. Many teachers were confused about how to teach the content of writing. In the third grade, I started whole classroom modeling of narrative structure (about four to five sessions long) for the students and their teacher. I first read aloud *Sylvester and the Magic Pebble* (a technique now called "using a mentor text"). Then, as a class, we filled in large story map to organize our thoughts to recall the story. These days there are a multitude of story maps, but in the early 1990s, this was a new concept. I first saw this concept used with language learning disabled students in Springfield, Massachusetts. The chart had different colored shapes labeled with the necessary parts of a story. This allowed the students to identify and record narrative story elements of a story they read or wanted to write. As we recalled the story, we first filled in the main character shape and then the setting shape. Next, we wrote in the "kick-off" football shape of the story, the event that lead up to the problem. After that, the class determined the problem in the story. Then, we discussed all the ways the characters tried to solve the problem and we bulleted them in our large rectangle. The winning resolution was put into its own shape and the conclusion was the last shape to be filled. All of these shapes were connected in a vertical fashion to show the sequential relationship.

The next time I came in, we discussed writing a class story making sure we had all the story elements. We used a blank story map chart to organize our thoughts. I guided them as they collaborated on a group story plan. The story was then ready to be written. Each student in turn dictated a sentence for the story, guided by the story map. I used a "think aloud" method to get them to stretch their vocabularies and details. The students were very pleased with themselves with the end result. They loved reading their own class story.

During another lesson with the classroom teacher, the students independently filled out a printed story map for their own narrative. A wealth of details grew by using this story map method. It is a time consuming introduction, but I believe if this is done in the early grades, the students gain a better understanding of story structure in reading and in writing.

Teachers again were buying into my knowledge of writing. They learned from me as much as I learned so much from the teachers. I "borrowed" many of their methods, such as writing workshop structure and creative ways of teaching different aspects of writing, into my own future teaching endeavors just as they borrowed from me. I was no longer an isolated speech-language pathologist. My joy continued as I blended into the teaching community. This was not as common as it is today when this began in the late 1980s and into the 1990s.

Another successful venture was the "hamburger method." Today, this is a commonly known method to organize a paragraph, but at the time I hadn't heard of it. For the time I presented these lessons around the school, I was known as the "hamburger lady." I used this in grades three through five as a whole class introductory lesson on paragraph structure. I made a very dramatic analogy between hamburgers and paragraphs with student participation and colorful drawings. High school students have been heard to say that the "hamburger method" was one way they learned to write.

I made the process of learning into a theatrical production. I told the students they were receiving hamburgers that day, although there were many sighs when I said we had to live in the world of pretend. When the pretend "delivery man" came, they were to pantomime the reaction to my description of the hamburger that they received. Third graders can be very dramatic, especially when this "over the top "teacher was describing the pantomime. They were horrified as ketchup and mustard were running down their shirts when they found out their hamburgers were without buns. They ate with disgust when the deliveryman gave us hamburgers without meat. After the deliveryman forgot to bring the students their "hamburger specials" that included all the condiments each student loved, the word "bland" was only one word of many to describe the tastelessness in their mouths. When the deliveryman brought the correct order, the delicious hamburger brought many descriptive words of delight.

After the pantomime, we discussed what each part's role was in the sandwich. It was an exciting adventure, but then came the moment of truth. A paragraph could have a similar structure. The students easily comprehended the comparison and were excited to talk about paragraph structure and its need for cohesiveness. A paragraph needed a topic sentence and a concluding sentence to keep the paragraph together. The paragraph needed the meat of information, and was very bland without the details and special sauce of vivid vocabulary. This was a visual and dramatic event that was hard to forget. Many teachers hung homemade hamburger posters in their classrooms. Now you can commercially buy them. Students and teachers were learning methods on the "how" to write a paragraph.

The students experienced joy while learning about paragraphs and the teachers experienced joy when students began to use this information in their writing. I experienced joy that I was increasing learning throughout the school and there was visual evidence to prove it. Hamburger graphic organizers were made to allow primary children to write their paragraph.

The joy of writing was increasing across the school. My LLD students were now learning the same language for writing with their fellow classmates. They all were learning methods that they could remember and be helpful to them. For many, writing became less and less of a chore. Confidence was building and enthusiasm was contagious.

In response to the Education Reform Act of 1993 in the state of Massachusetts, the Massachusetts Comprehensive Assessment System (MCAS) was created. This standardized statewide assessment program brought frenzy to administration, teachers, parents and students. For teachers, the race was on to figure out how to blend best teaching practices and ensure the students were prepared for these tests. In those early years it took time to figure out what the state wanted and for the state to figure out what was appropriate. It often led to frustration, but persistence prevailed as the state hammered out standards for each academic area and the schools began to "get it."

For language arts, two special educators and I created a teacher's resource book on how to create open response prompts and how to help students respond to these prompts. We divided each section into different expository structures (description, sequential, cause and effect, problem and solution, and persuasion) and gave teachers ideas on how to word each prompt, a graphic organizer to match that type of prompt, a student list of words they could use in writing each type of paragraph, and examples of a simple prompt and response. It was a way for teachers again to have something concrete on the "how" to teach writing.

Most important of all, the students needed to see what "proficient" and "advanced" writing looked like, as opposed to "needs improvement." I was lucky enough to be on a panel to score long compositions for one summer and learned first hand what was needed for each category according to Massachusetts standards. Getting these examples from the online MCAS site, the students would huddle in groups and defend why they thought certain pieces of writing deserved a certain score. Then they held up their poster board number as if they were judges in a skating competition, only now the contest was writing. It was my attempt to put some enthusiasm into this type of writing. The students did enjoy the challenge and the interaction.

During this time there was a change in administration in our school. All of a sudden, LINKS: Strategies Across the Curriculum (Porcaro, 1997) became the new program to help with the teaching of writing and, more importantly, help our students prepare for the language arts section of the MCAS. I was crestfallen. This decision was made over the summer before I even met this new principal. I felt that my identity in the school and my joy in teaching writing were in jeopardy.

Kathy Porcaro came in with her polished power point presentations and taught two workshops. We were all given magnificent professional binders with inserts to go along with the presentation. The writing portion was on strategies for the teachers to create various prompts that could be used in the context of their teaching. It also guided teachers on how to help children plan for writing through specific graphic organizers associated with the type of writing they were to write. This was not a new concept for our teachers. Porcaro presented many ideas that were similar to ours, but hers were in an expanded form, professionally researched, and professionally presented in her workshops and her binders (Porcaro, 1997).

I feared I had lost a role that I loved within the school. I spoke to the new principal about my previous role in the school. He explained his vision for the school with the LINKS program and improving MCAS scores. I explained my informal melded role as a speech-language pathologist and writing teacher. I spoke to the principal about my passion for the teaching of writing and my opinion of its success within the classes that I taught.

It was not too long after that when he called me into a meeting and explained that there needed to be a trained teacher leader within the school system to continue the LINKS training program. He must have researched what I told him because he asked if I was interested. It was just as Helen Keller said, "When one door closes, another one opens," and an even better door at that. I received further training in being a leader in writing. I went to teacher leader workshops. I now gave the polished power point presentations to not only my school, but to the school district. Some were wonderful experiences, such as voluntary after school workshops for new staff and paraprofessionals. Others were dreadful. I learned my lesson as an elementary special educator not to try to present a mandatory in-service to a large group of seasoned high school veterans from my own school district. As soon as my presentation started, the principal was nowhere to be found. The resistance was not only palpable; it was vocal. Basically, the message was we know what we are doing and we are not changing our ways. They seasoned me a few years that afternoon.

I went back to my safe elementary school and continued my work, now under a specific title of "LINKS Writing Trainer." At first, I was given a few hours per week to work in that role, but as my special education role became more filled I went back to my "catch as catch can" availability. I continued to grow each year in experience and confidence with teaching writing and guiding other teachers. For a few years, the LINKS program was a frequently chosen writing tool. In time, I found that we had to be careful not to over generalize this method. We needed to be cautious not to use it as an exclusive canned approach. Students' written voices could become lost when the guidance in writing became too narrow. For example, many students were concluding their paragraphs with the transition phrase, "All in all." It became a habit that was hard to break. It validated my belief in a balanced, eclectic approach to teaching writing.

Teacher as Writer

Another influence on teaching the joy of being a writer to every student is my own interest in writing. I love the English language. I love words. My love for reading was a natural foundation for my love for writing. Two major influences provided me with the ability to become a "writer." First, at the same time I was beginning my journey as a teacher mentor in classrooms, I was dealing with depression and a subsequent divorce. I played the role of teacher by day, and then dealt with my personal demons at night. With depression, my journey went inward, yet there were so many feelings and thoughts that needed to come out. Journal writing became the answer for me. I bought books on this type of writing and became fascinated with the techniques they introduced. I loved "stream of consciousness" writing where thoughts come out on paper that you didn't even know were there.

My journal became my safe haven and my friend. I looked forward to my time with my journal. The night of my divorce, I began attending a four-week workshop on journal writing at a local college. This became a blessing to me. When the workshop was over, a few of us started our own journal writing group, meeting each month sharing our writing. This group lasted for the next two years. As I grew as an independent woman, I grew in my writing. My life became more positive and it also helped in the teaching of writing.

The methods we practiced in our group and read about in journal writing books could be used in the classroom as well. Stream of consciousness writing was one way of loosening students' thoughts on paper. In this process, we kept the pencil on the journal page, didn't let the pencil leave the page and wrote the thoughts that flew through our minds, even if at first we wrote, "I don't know what to write." I also cut a multitude of words and phrases for the students to randomly choose from to create a poem, similar to magnetic words. On its cover, *Journal to the Self* (Adams, 1990) proclaims that a journal "opens the door to self-understanding—by writing, reading and creating a journal of your life." I added this aspect of introspective writing to the writing workshop at the upper grades. Examples of such writing include writing dialogue between themselves and a real or imagined person or writing an "unsent letter." Especially for pre-adolescents and adolescents, this introspective writing was important and appealing.

In journal writing, I also found out what it was like to have a blank page in front of me and string word upon word together as my students must do. For me, the more I let my mind go and my pencil stayed on the page, words flowed from my fingers. The outcome was often a surprise to me, whether it was the content or form. When writing became a daily practice, I grew in my ability and I gained more self-confidence. Isn't that what we believe when we have students write daily in the writing workshop method?

Teacher as Writer and Student

Participating in the Boston Writing Project (BWP) 2001 sealed the deal as "teacher as writer" for me. It also gave me confidence in imparting my knowledge and joy of writing to my students. I received a fellowship in the summer of 2001 to participate with other teachers of all different grades in the Boston area to share our knowledge and share our writing with one another. Despite the five weeks of a long commute, with homework given every night, this remains a highlight of my professional career. I was surrounded with passionate "teacher writers." I was "at home," despite our different backgrounds and cultures. They shared the same passion for writing.

I learned what it felt to be a student writer. Each morning as we entered our room, we were encouraged to "free write" until the class officially started. It was lovely to actually carve out a consistent time of day when I could just let words flow upon the paper as I was accustomed to doing. In particular, I loved the time to experiment with stream of consciousness writing. It was also the time where we could express particular frustrations or joys. An especially frequent topic was the excruciating commute to the class. We were then given a short time to share.

In later years, I found this technique especially helpful as a transition technique in my sixth grade classes. It became soothing to switch gears, whether it was from a previous class or from lunch. It was time to focus on writing and experiment with ideas. The free choice not only helped the students in their interest in writing, but that awful downtime between classes was quickly filled with more writing. For the reluctant student, a daily prompt is there or they can look at resources such as their writing territories or topics from their writing reference folder. This is a warm up activity that sometimes leads to a full-length writing piece. Tracy's humorous start about a cookie monster's plan to catch a cookie that included "come swim in my pool of chocolate milk" is just one example of these creative quick starts. We do a quick share as we did at the BWP.

After that free writing activity at the Boston Writing Project, we were assigned for a day to read aloud a favorite piece of text to share with the others. Because of our passions for writing, this was an especially relaxing, enjoyable experience. After the short reading, we wrote for five minutes in our journal. I now felt like my students when they filled out their response journal. Was it easier to have free choice here or would I rather have a prompt? For me, I loved the freedom to make any kind of connection I wanted and to write in any form I wanted. For students, I believe some benefit from free choice, while others need a prompt. We need to meet the students at their comfort level and then stretch them to higher levels.

At the BWP, we were asked to share from our response journals. This gave me insight into the courage it took to raise my hand and share something as personal as my writing to a group. It put a new perspective on how and what I said to my students about any piece of writing. I immediately liked the idea of students sharing favorite pieces of another author's writing. The students needed to read from the eyes of a writer. Why is this a great passage? What technique did the writer use to make writing so vivid? What can we learn from this so we can do the same in our writing?

Bringing this activity to a higher level in my sixth grade classroom, I had groups of students modernize Robert Frost's *Walking in the Woods on a Snowy Evening.* This Frost activity was a class favorite. It had a life of its own. It was supposed to be a short-lived activity in December as Frost's New England weather descended upon us. Not only did it teach my students about writing, it taught me many important lessons about teaching at the middle school level.

I allowed the students to choose their own groups resulting in friendship groups for what I thought would be a two-day lesson. I found the students to be *more* focused. They weren't wandering around the room looking for their friends. They were working with them. They seemed to bond together and wanted to make their piece the best. This was supposed to give them a taste of a New England nature poet, but suddenly they wanted to finish it to full publication. This required deep analysis of the poem before translating it into everyday English. One group successfully portrayed *Walking in the Woods* in a rap style. It may sound insulting, but in actuality, the creativity was undeniable and the joy of writing within this group and others was authentic.

While the students and I were talking about the importance of imagery, we suddenly had the art teacher involved. After they typed up their group poem, they had choices of mediums in order to portray their poetry in art. Our classroom turned into an amphitheater with a podium and a microphone for poem recitation and the snapping of the student audience's fingers for applause. The poems later were displayed in our sixth grade hallways.

I felt the passion of writing during so many of those December days as they discussed what Frost meant and how they could make it their own. There was an excited buzz in the room as heads huddled in groups, animated faces discussed word choice and students discovered reasons for rhythm, stanzas and rhyme, learning much more than I could have taught them in a mini-lesson. The joy of writing could be sensed as soon as you walked in the room, no matter what group was working, no matter what academic level or background. The students loved being creative with their friends and having such choices over what and how they were going to make their presentations during the final piece, both visually and in recitation. They had an audience and a purpose for their writing. As their teacher, I felt I had come home to where I was meant to be all along. I also knew I never could have come to this place without following that long journey of learning best practices in writing, as well as finding how to meet the needs of each child.

During the Boston Writing Project, we also experienced peer revision. We participated in peer revision groups every afternoon, another eye-opening experience. I was in a group of six adults who either timidly or confidently began to share writing. For some, like me, it was my first experience sharing my writing with anyone, other than family and friends. To others, they already had experiences such as these. No matter what our backgrounds, we were all eager to listen and share thoughts about writing techniques. Six people, six different writing styles, but all wanted to learn how to become better writers, even when it meant our piece of writing was given the close eye of peer revision. I learned from each and every one of them. I learned how to cut my poetry to the bone to make it more effective.

Having a copy of each other's writing pieces helped in this process. I still have them today. Some are wry and clever; some are warm and wistful of memories long ago. Some are short stories; some are poems. Many of mine are memoirs, some magical and some painful. All pieces are ones I am proud of even today. They represent a time in my life when for five weeks I put writing first and received my first feedback from impartial people who had the same passion for writing as I had.

I learned poetry was my strength as the imagery of my days on Mayflower Beach with my two growing daughters flowed across the page. Yet in some personal narrative writing, I could not seem to reach my response group about the horrors I felt waking up alone in a hospital after complications from surgery. I was privy to some outstanding writing of others as well. Elaine had such a knack for writing with an edge, as she wrote pieces about procrastination or how natural disasters seemed to follow her in travel. Her parody piece about procrastination read like a women's magazine article as if procrastination were some personality disorder. It even included a multiple-choice quiz and "constant procrastinator" quotient. I was in awe of this ability, and as much as I loved the genre I couldn't see me becoming a master of it.

I understood how it felt to be a student again. With writing you share a piece of yourself. Writing is personal no matter what the genre. Words are from a place deep within you. It takes courage to offer yourself up for scrutiny. I also learned to accept compliments and respectful suggestions and then go back and learn the true art of revision. As a student, I had a first hand feel of what it was like to be in a peer revision group. As a teacher, this was helpful for me to set up the peer revision groups in my classroom and the positive guidelines needed. Positive comments needed to be a priority in any discussion.

Back in my own classroom, I now have a peer revision table that has peer revision rules and checklists about giving and receiving important feedback. Students care about what their peers think. If the students know other peers will be commenting on their writing, I have already stepped up the quality of their work.

I came away from the BWP much more confident as a writer and, more importantly, as a teacher of writing. I was still a speech-language pathologist/writing trainer at that time when I participated as a BWP fellow. The Boston Writing Project was the last experience that led me to the crucial step in my journey, going back to being a classroom teacher.

Writer as Teacher

I was chosen for the fourth grade teaching position in 2002. I tried to put into practice all the knowledge that I had gained in that long journey of mine. I had a self-contained classroom of 24 students. Now there was also reading, math, science and social studies and the looming dread of MCAS. I was challenged to put the workshop method to work, a daunting task. I found the logistics the most difficult task. How did I fit it all in? How did I let my students go into workshop when my mini-lesson always seemed to need much more time? The long composition of the MCAS happened in the spring of fourth grade. It took me awhile to find a balance between the necessary elements of the workshop method of writing and the importance of my students having practice with "high stakes" assessment writing. My workshop structure was balanced between genre writing and six-trait writing throughout the year and I treated assessment writing as another genre to teach.

A tragedy struck during my third year, the year that I thought things were coming together for me as a classroom teacher. It was Thanksgiving weekend. I planned to return to start an Andrew Clemens author study that I had worked on all summer. I had been looking forward to seeing my plans in action. That was never to be.

My precious 21-year-old daughter was in a fatal car accident on her way back to her senior year in college. My life as I knew it stopped. It would be months until I went back to work part-time. Passion left my life, including my passion for teaching. This was another time where I used writing as an outlet, but to be honest this time the words did not come easily. Yet there were times I needed to release pain. The blank page could listen to my pain and not talk back to me in platitudes. This time I let the pain go through my fingers as they clicked mindlessly onto the computer keys.

A Month

December 27, 2005

Today is a month.
Reality cuts like a jagged blade
Turning round and round
Into the very core of the self.

Please come right back through that door.
It was just a big mistake,
But I can't live that lie anymore.
It's been too long since I've heard your voice
And hugged you close.
People are easing back to their lifetimes.
No lifetime exists for me.

I can't seem to pick one up yet.
I'm in a Twilight Zone
A Purgatory on Earth
Waiting for a new life
A life without Jill
I cannot grasp that kind of life.

The next year and a half was a professional and personal nightmare. I believe I remained a competent teacher, but I was not the "same," for whatever that meant. It seemed to mean different things to different people depending on their vision of me through their own eyes. One person thought I was courageous, while another thought I was emotionally unstable. I thought I was a grief-stricken mother who was just trying to put one step in front of the other to make some meaning on this new journey. The mounting misperceptions of me were adding to the hell I was living in. People were afraid to talk directly to me so they made up their own conclusions. Many times they were the wrong conclusions. I was to find this out months later when damage to my career had already been done. I was afraid I was being pushed out of my job; instead a miracle happened.

This next step on my journey brought back my sense of self and the passion of teaching writing again. I was given a sixth grade classroom position teaching writing. Every aspect of my journey, both good and bad, led me here: learning the foundations of literacy and language, learning about the needs of special education students, experiencing co-teaching and inclusion, knowing the personal journey of being a writer and having the experience of being a writing/language mentor at a variety of grade levels. I became a writing teacher to four fully inclusive classes. All of the aspects of my career merged together as I entered this position.

Especially important to me was the team-based middle-school inclusion model. Special educators and teachers worked together with the same positive philosophical approach—all students can learn by including all students using a differentiated and flexible grouping approach, with a positive discipline philosophy. No student had to stay in the same group all year. We worked to meet students at his or her level. All teachers worked as a team. Each student was the concern of each one of us. We planned and taught with this in mind. My passion returned; the administration was thrilled. My team members accepted me for who I was.

I found that choice at the sixth grade level was a major motivator. Throughout the year, they added to their writing territories (ideas for writing) in their own writers' notebooks. I learned that mini-lessons really ought to be mini. Students needed to write, not listen. They needed a highly focused lesson on a writing strategy or concept and then they went to the business of writing. Here was where they found the passion for writing. Students are much better with the action of learning rather than passive learning. I needed to remember that individual conferencing could have more impact than a whole group lesson. The Robert Frost activity made that clear. Students authentically learned what they needed during conferencing. They were invested in their own pieces of writing.

When I did have whole group mini-lessons, I often used texts as models. The students still loved stories read aloud to them. I usually gave them the text version or an overhead of it so they could read along. They learned different writing techniques from seeing it used in actual published writing pieces.

No better illustration of this was our Dr. Seuss project. As a member of our school's literacy committee, I was part of a discussion on how to celebrate Read Across America Day, Dr. Seuss' birthday. Still in the honeymoon stage of my sixth grade writing position, I offered that the sixth grade groups create their own Seussian books based on a Seuss favorite. The students could read them aloud to the primary grades on this special day as part of a community service project and have an authentic purpose for writing.

I was determined that my students would not only enjoy this project, they would also grow as writers. We analyzed Dr. Seuss books for style, theme and purpose. The students learned that Dr. Seuss was not just a humorous rhyming author. In fact, many of his books had deeper meaning, such as *The Lorax* and *The Butter Battle Book*. He was a social activist.

I allowed the students to work in friendship groups after I saw the success of the Frost project. Again, they delved into this project with palpable excitement. My students were immersed in the analysis of an author's rhyming pattern, style and theme. The buzz was back. This time there was a true publication deadline: Read Across America Day. They had to work cooperatively to write an original book based on a true Dr. Seuss book and have Seussian illustrations included. The students soon learned that they had to give each other certain tasks in order to reach the final deadline. Compromise was a necessity. Every one of my 98 students met the deadline. This resulted in books such as, *The Ghoul who Stole Halloween* and *The Chap with a Map*. This project was a rousing success at all levels. The primary students loved the big kids visiting them and sat in awe as they listened to these special books based on books they were familiar with. If the primary students were lucky, some sixth grade groups stayed and helped them with their own attempts at writing and drawing. The teachers enjoyed seeing former students making an impact on their current students. Administration loved the community involvement and I loved the joy of writing being spread around the school. What about those big kids? I had them complete a reflection paper about their experience. Here are some excerpts:

- "Even if you didn't like another's idea, it might turn out better than you thought."
- "I have good ideas and I didn't know I was such a good artist when I try."
- "I think Dr. Seuss is an amazing author and illustrator... He was a wise man because his stories sometimes have meanings."
- "I learned that when my group is counting on me it is a big responsibility."
- "I learned that rhyming is hard when you have to stay on track and get a point across."
- "I learned that writing in a group is harder than writing alone, but the result can be better."
- And the one that tugged at my teacher's heartstrings was from my usually non-compliant writer: "It's hard to draw and think of ideas. And it's also fun when you're learning and drawing."

It's fun learning! Someone who rarely tried to write in class felt the joy of being a writer. Tom's comfort level was drawing. Ted's motivation improved when he was at his comfort level, pairing writing and drawing, as well as working as a team with his peers.

I learned that group writing could be one excellent teaching method that satisfied these pre-teens' social needs and motivated writing. The task needed to be clearly defined. The students had to be invested in it. Having an authentic purpose made students more goal-driven and successful.

Given their social needs, many students love animated discussions with each other in small or large groups. I still have goose bumps about the day my class was involved in a heavily animated discussion over commas and semi-colons. A sentence was on the board that could be punctuated in several ways, but the meaning would change according to the punctuation. I believe this discussion happened because I did not directly answer whether the student's answer was correct or not.

Our sixth grade team uses a technique we learned at a workshop where the philosophy is that the teacher should not be the leader of the right or wrong answers. Let the students learn to question and apply higher level thinking skills, instead of passively sitting back and waiting for the teacher to deem what is correct and what is not. I needed to let the students work out the answers.

During this punctuation mini-lesson, students wrote in the correct punctuation and the remaining students had the choice of saying "I support…" or "I respectfully challenge." or "In addition to what _____ said…" A discussion on commas and semi-colons began. I wouldn't have believed what ensued unless I had been there. Their discussion went beyond what had originally been taught. A heated discussion about comma and semi-colon use filled the classroom. Students eventually went to grammar resource books until they decided on their own when it was appropriate to use a comma or semi-colon, backed up with evidence. They owned that piece of information much better than if I had just corrected it on the board.

Growing as a Writing Teacher

My mentors have been many: Nancie Atwell, Fountas and Pinnell, Ralph Fletcher, Lucy Calkins, Vicki Spandel, John Collins, and Barry Lane. My first experience with Nancie Atwell was during my Boston Writing Project experience. Atwell's second edition of *In the Middle: New Understandings about Writing, Reading and Learning* (Atwell, 1998). This was the book I chose to review for the BWP. I actually missed my subway stop for UMASS Boston because I was so absorbed in the book. Atwell has a way of writing to an educator as if she were having a chat with you in your classroom. Her ideas are practical and soundly based. You can use many of her ideas the day after you read about them. They can easily be modified to an elementary classroom, not just to a middle school. Atwell's insights into adolescence are also helpful in planning a writing program. I recently had the opportunity to hear her speak and she brought the nuances of the writers' workshop to life for me. I now see next year's students receiving my truly mini mini-lessons and benefiting from the freedom of writing from their heart. I've decided that next year I will try my own idea of a "Writers' Binder" (a 1 ½ inch loose-leaf binder) to be divided into the following sections: writing territories, writer's notebook, writer's reference pages, personal spelling list, word study pages. I had included all these things in separate folders this year. I believe this new organization makes more sense and is more fluid. The students will still have a writer's folder for completed work. Writers' Reference Pages are many resources and checklists the students receive about writing, such as editing checklists and synonyms for ordinary words. I use Rebecca Sitton's method of spelling as outlined in Nancie Atwell's book, *Lessons that Change Writers* (Atwell, 2002, pp.216–219). I have learned that the world of writing is a continual growth process, for the student and the teacher.

I consider Fountas and Pinnell's seminal work, *Guiding Reading and Writers Grades 3–6* (2001) and Lucy Calkins' *The Art of Teaching Writing* (1986) as encyclopedias of research-based ideas for forming readers' and writers' workshops. My original framework for setting up my programs began with these sources. I found that setting up these workshops was not a one-year process. There was no cookie cutter format. A teacher must find out what works for his/her own personal style, setting, and, more importantly, the students who are in front of you.

Remember, my ultimate goal is that *all students learn the joy of being writers*. I do not believe that there is one foolproof teacher's manual for writing, nor should there be. Fountas and Pinnell and Calkins have excellent techniques and practices, but nothing is one size fits all. The number of ideas on developing writing workshops and methods is daunting, and I have found that there is no one easy way if you want a productive and successful workshop program that will reach each and every learner.

Process writing is usually at the crux of most elementary writing programs. Students start with choosing a topic, do some pre-writing organization, create a first draft, edit and make revisions, write a final draft and publish. This is an organized and logical way to accomplish finished writing pieces. I believe in process writing, but I also find it to be a time-consuming task. Some of my students ended up getting caught in the process, and the quality and quantity of writing experiences became compromised. By the end of the process, some students were bored with a piece of writing that at first they were very excited about. Therefore, the end result became mechanical. I became frustrated with how slow the process of one writing piece became for the students. Although I believe in the importance for process writing, I don't strictly use every part of it for each writing piece. The joy seemed to leave the room when the students lost interest in a piece. When the entire process was limited to pieces that they were invested in, the students were motivated to see the end result.

John Collins (Chadwell, 1999) was the first author that gave me permission not to have to evaluate every aspect of writing in every piece of writing and not all pieces have to go to final publication. What a welcome relief. Collins and Chadwell (Chadwell, 1999, pp. 59–71) outlined five types of Writing Experiences:

Type 1: Brainstorming and activating prior knowledge;
Type 2: Quick Writes to show the writer has knowledge about a subject;
Type 3: More formal writing using Focus Correction Areas (FCA's), correction is focused on a few specific aspects of a writing piece rather than the entire piece;
Type 4: Same as Type 3 but peer revision is included;
Type 5: Full Publication.

If Focus Correction Areas were a relief, then rubrics were a lifesaver for writing assessment. With FCA's and rubrics, I give specific feedback on specific elements of writing. Receiving a single letter grade on a paper is meaningless. On a rubric, the student understands where his writing performance is on specific areas of that piece of writing and sees what he needs to do to reach the next level of writing. The students also may self-assess using this document.

I was overjoyed when I found Six Trait Writing (Rice, 2004; Spandel, 2005). It is another way to focus my instruction and assessment. I was pretty clear about the framework of a writers' workshop from reading many excellent authors, talking with other teachers, and implementing it, but I was still in a quagmire of all the possible aspects of writing instruction. From a special education background, I knew many students do not learn through the osmosis of practice. What about them? Six-Trait Writing gave me a focus on a framework for instruction. This program focuses on six characteristics of developing good writing based on: ideas, organization, word choice, voice, sentence fluency, and conventions (Culham, 2003). This also seemed to fit in perfectly with the Language Arts Massachusetts State Standards and Frameworks (2001). My focus has been on what's best for the students in front of me. Write, write, write. Give opportunities to choose pieces to edit and revise. Give the students guidance to publish a few writing pieces each term. Expose the students to different genres of writing. Utilize the writers' notebook almost daily to practice various writing techniques. Practice the six traits of writing to add to their quality of writing.

We may conference, use rubric assessment through self-editing and teacher assessment, or peer revise many pieces, but they do not all go to that last step of final publication. I try to find authentic reasons for the final publication, such as the Read Across America celebration. Another reason may be the piece is a model piece of writing or is evidence of student progress. At least two pieces a trimester should go through all steps of process writing. This year, certain genres have gone to final publication: a memoir, a narrative, poetry, the Dr. Seuss project, descriptive writing and an essay.

I practiced the wizardry of teaching writing, mixing and merging practices that best meet my students' needs, constantly changing, adding and deleting as my wizardry powers improve. This year going back to middle school writing, I decided to use some frameworks: Nancie Atwell's *Lessons that Change Writers* (2002) and *Creating Writers through 6-Trait Writing Assessment and Instruction* (4th ed., Spandel, 2005) and then use other resources as needed. I wanted to concoct the right mixture of choice and guidance so that the students improve their writing, but I especially wanted to meet my goal to let *all* students gain confidence and joy that they *all* were writers. If I can give them this foundation, they will want to improve their craft. It was my responsibility to find the right tools for each student, including students with disabilities, to believe in themselves as writers.

It has been a wonderful, as well as an arduous journey. For me, writing is now not a subject to be taught. It is an experience to be shared with other student writers. When I watch the faces of my students excitedly write and wave their arms to share their pieces, I feel like proverbial "Rocky" at the top of those Philadelphia steps. It started way back in the 1970s at the middle school level. I have had personal and professional triumphs and tragedy. I have come full-circle to teaching writing again in a middle school model. The end looks nothing like the beginning. The lessons I've learned are maybe more than the lessons I have taught. It has been a wonderful opportunity to improve 100% from those first years of teaching. I am now teaching writers instead of writing. I am trying to keep writing authentic. I model texts to portray excellence in writing. I challenge my students to choose writing opportunities and create pieces that they care about. My goal is for my passion for writing to become infectious. Writing is about the writer, not about marks upon the pages. During my many stops on my journey of teaching writers, I have watched my students grow in their confidence in writing and thus grow in their passion and in their abilities as writers. They have experienced the joy of being a writer.

References

Adams, K. (1990). *Journal to the self: Twenty-two paths to personal growth*. New York: Warner Books

Atwell, N. (1998). *In the middle: New understandings about writing, reading, and learning* (2nd ed.). Portsmouth, NH: Heinemann.

Atwell, N. (2002). *Lessons that change writers*. Portsmouth, NH: Firsthand.

Calkins, L.M. (1986). *The art of teaching writing*. Portsmouth, NH: Heinemann.

Culham, R. (2003). *6 + 1 traits of writing: The complete guide grades 3 and up*. New York: Scholastic Professional Books.

Chadwell, G. (1999). *Developing an effective writing program for the elementary grades*. West Newbury, MA: Collins Education Associates.

Fountas, I.C. & Pinell, G.S. (2001). *Guiding readers and writers grades 3–6*. Portsmouth, NH: Heinemann.

Porcaro, K. (1997). *LINKS: Strategies across the curriculum*. Woburn, MA: Educational Performance Systems.

Rice, L. (2004). *Resource book: 6 trait writing*. Petersborough, NH: Staff Development for Educators.

Spandel, V. (2005). *Creating Writers through 6-Trait Writing Assessment and Instruction* 4th ed.). Boston: Pearson Education, Inc.

The Journey to Become a Writer
Then a Teacher of Writers

Helen Eaton

I am a writer. I have always been a writer. I have always known that I was a writer. Although no one ever told me it was so, I know—I am a writer. I have searched my memories, and I cannot remember a single teacher—at the elementary, secondary, undergraduate, or graduate level—that encouraged me as a writer, an artist of words. On one hand, that makes me sad. What would I have become if I had known that it was not odd for me to feel pleasure and receive comfort from writing? How could a student go through that many years without having even one teacher who valued writing for the sake of writing? On the other hand, years of skill-and-drill exercises made me great at grammar, usage, and mechanics—I even enjoy that part of the writing process. It also gives me hope that a young writer can blossom and grow under less-than-perfect circumstances.

Perhaps it is because writing has always been important to me that I have vivid memories of specific writing activities and assignments from each part of my schooling. Surely my memories are skewed—how can an adult recapture a child's perspective with complete accuracy? Although a touch of sarcasm may creep in occasionally, my hope is to recall and retell them with a sense of humor and fondness. I can look back now and see how

Getting It in Writing, pages 55–71

55

each one—even those that were negative—has influenced me positively as a teacher of writing today.

There are a few events that I remember in great detail from my first year at Louise Durham Elementary School in Mena, Arkansas. I remember that some guys went to the moon, so all the first grade classes had to sit in one hot room and watch the gray fuzzy pictures and hear the crackly sounds of their voices. We thought surely that was the most boring thing ever. I remember that the school began serving breakfasts, that my best friend and I got a spanking for swinging double, and that Snoopy had a new friend named Woodstock. I remember that my reading book had a little blonde girl that always wore a dress. She and her brother had a dog named Tip and a cat named Velvet. I remember that being in the bluebird group meant that the teacher didn't help you sound out hard words—like Velvet. And, I remember that I was the shortest one of the 31 six-year olds in my first grade class.

I also remember writing in first grade. Like all the others, I had the required Big Chief tablet in my little plaid satchel. It was red with a fierce looking Indian chief. He stared out of his frame wearing feathers and war paint. Everyone knew that when the tablet was used up, he would be cut out and saved to be collected and traded. Inside were pages and pages of news-print type paper with red lines for the letters to sit on and blue lines for the letters to reach. Sitting on the red lines and reaching the blue lines was very important. In fact, it was imperative. If they didn't, they'd have to be written over. That wasn't the hardest part. Sharp pencils would poke holes in the thin paper, but letters written with dull pencils smeared across the pages. "Always make letters from top to bottom," the teacher said again and again. If you tried to make sure your letter sat on the red line correctly and tried to draw a letter from the bottom to the top, then the paper would wrinkle at best or tear at worst. Even erasing was risky. If you pushed too hard or erased away rather than toward yourself, a rip was sure to follow. The final step was tearing the finished page out of the tablet. There was a trick to that too. You had to tear it up and away—farther than little arms could reach. If you dared pull down, your hard work would be torn in half from the top. Learning to write letters must have been very stressful because there were so many ways to mess up. Getting it right the first time was expected. For some reason, however, I loved filling pages with letters, adding to my Big Chief card collection, and then beginning a new tablet.

That same year, my teacher, Mrs. Kelly, whom I loved and adored, read a novel to us—the first big, fat book I'd ever heard. It was called *Little House in the Big Woods*. Read aloud time was the one time of every day that I know I sat very still and listened intently. I loved that little girl character named

Laura. She reminded me of someone—me! I loved the fact that her story went on and on. There was a new adventure every day, and it all happened in the same book. The best part was that Laura Ingalls had been a real person, and the stories were true.

By second grade, writing on Big Chief tablets was replaced with writing on ditto sheets. The ink was purple and could be easily deciphered—if there hadn't been a fold or wrinkle in the master as they were being made. I especially loved it when the teacher left one student in charge of taking names of talkers while she went to make these ditto sheets. When she returned with the hot-off-the-press dittos, we would hold them as long as possible to our noses as we passed them down the rows. The aroma of the still-drying ditto fluid was divine—although probably toxic. After a study of some interesting topic, there would always be a "writing" assignment. My teacher would review what we'd learned, pass out the sweet-smelling purple ditto sheets, and tell us to copy the sentences or paragraph from the board onto them using our best penmanship. Once we'd finished, we were allowed to color the picture that was either above or below the "writing." All letters, words, and sentences had to be copied exactly, but creativity was encouraged in the coloring of the illustration—as long as people and objects were the color they were supposed to be. We knew our grade would be based on the perfection of our "writing," but there was always the threat that coloring outside the lines could endanger a good grade. One particular assignment stands out in my memory. We'd learned about aurora borealis, the northern lights. I can still picture the ditto sheet. I could hardly wait to finish copying the required story so that I could color that amazing patterned sky using every crayon I had in my box. Certainly, I put every capital and period in its proper place so that I could get to the highlight of writing class—coloring. I doubt that I knew then that the embellishments of publishing were what made me smile. I just wanted to color it pretty so it would look good if it got to hang on the wall.

Third grade brought a new "writing" focus—slanted letters hooked together with lots of curlicues and flourishes—cursive! It was back to special tablets with special lines that letters had to sit correctly on and others that letters had to reach. While I don't recall any type of creative writing, third grade was when I first attempted personal writing on my own. It started with the opportunity to order books through a weekly student news magazine, *Weekly Reader.* Through these orders, I discovered that Laura Ingalls Wilder had written other books about her life. I saved my allowance money and ordered a new *Little House* book each month. I loved that the story of her life seemed to never end. Her entire life was chronicled through the stories in this set of books. If I wanted to follow in her footsteps, I knew I must begin to record my life so that I could make a book out of it when I was old. That Christmas I asked for my first diary. It was blue with a floral cover, and I loved it. The first entry read, "January 1, 1973 – I watched the orange bole parade and traist in my coloring Book. And I got mad at you know who." That was the genesis of my love for and dedication to journaling.

I suppose there was more writing done at school during my fourth and fifth grade years. I do know that I wrote dozens—even hundreds—of "I will not talk in class" sentences. As the content of subjects became deeper, that gave yet another opportunity for writing—copying definitions of vocabulary words. And I did get a solid foundation in grammar, parts of speech, and mechanics during these upper elementary years. Copying sentences from the English book and circling nouns, underlining predicates, drawing arrows from direct objects, or correcting punctuation consumed the biggest part of the daily English classes. (How I managed to separate writing as a punishment or as busywork from writing as a form of creativity is still a mystery to me.) I was sporadic with my diary entries during these years, but no matter how many days I missed, I always returned to write again.

Little House on the Prairie became a television series when I was in fifth grade. I was heartsick that I didn't get to play the part of Laura. If only the people in Hollywood had known about me, I was sure they would have chosen me. Every Monday evening at 7:00, I would watch my hero's life on the television then recommit to keeping my diary. Now I had the dream that not only would I write my life story for a book, it might be on television as well!

Home writing was very different from school writing. I will never forget my first research report. It was assigned during sixth grade. I was actually excited about learning all I could about a topic of my choice. I chose "Animals." My teacher said that was too impossibly broad, so I narrowed it to "Fish." Apparently that was also too broad. I learned the backwards lesson that the narrower the topic, the more specific information could be found. Eventually I wound up choosing "White Amurs." The library—which was a long room in the basement of our school that doubled as a cafeteria—didn't have any books on white amurs, but we found some information in the encyclopedia. My dad had a brochure on them since he'd purchased a few to eat the grass out of the bottom of our lake. And, we even took a trip to the Lonoke Fish Hatchery so that I could interview an expert on the topic. Finally, it was time to begin. I wrote and wrote. The most important part of the report (in my mind) was that it must be three pages long. That did not include the title page. I wrote and wrote to state and restate my information in various ways in order for it to be just the right length. Once complete, it was time for revision. That meant recopying and recopying and recopying and recopying. It had to be written in blue ballpoint pen and must be error free. (If only I'd been born a decade later there would have been the invention of correction tape, erasable pens, or even eventually liquid paper.) One incorrectly formed letter, forgotten capital, or misspelling and the paper was wadded and tossed into the trash. (Yes, this was before the idea of recycling had occurred to anyone.)

Of course, there was the requirement of an outline. Once my paper was finished, I was able to quickly do that bit of prewriting—since I then knew what the paper was about and in what order the facts came.

I was so proud of that body of writing. It felt real somehow. Seeing it in its finished—blue ink, title page, outline, 3-paged—form made me feel that my status had been raised from "plain old kid" to "expert on white amurs."

There was plenty of other writing that year—the new skill of sentence diagramming, more grammar, more definitions, more practice with mechanics, and lots more "I will not talk in class" sentences. That was the balance of the writing curriculum as I recall it in the bicentennial year. It makes me sigh today.

We buried a time capsule that year that contained some of our writing. I wonder whether it was the research papers or the diagrammed sentences that were chosen to go in that box. (I should leave a note to have my grandchildren check on that in 2076.)

By the time I was in junior high school, daily diary writing had become a priority—maybe even an obsession. I never went to bed without recording the events of the day. Switching classes, friend issues, boys . . . my diary became the place to keep track of the ever changing saga of teenage life. A young girl never knows when she might need to remember exactly who said what and when, or who had admitted a crush on whom, or when someone had had a crush on someone else. Interestingly enough, I also thought it was important to note when tests were given, what scores I made, and how much I studied. I've tried to analyze why this thread of writing managed to stay alive without outside encouragement, but the answer is elusive. It may have been a habit, the desire to be the star in my own book, the fixation of recording life, therapy, or simply the passion to be who I was—a writer.

My first impression of my junior high English teacher was that she was so cool—at least in a teacher sort of way. She wore bell-bottomed pantsuits, high heels, and had a Farrah haircut! As if that wasn't enough, she thought journaling was a good idea.

She gave us a small amount of time each class period to free write in a spiral notebook. She encouraged us to write about what was going on in our lives and how we felt about it. Adding the emotional side of journaling was new to me, but the time allotted to this activity felt perfectly natural to me—another diary.

My teacher had said, "If you ever write about something personal, you may fold that page in half so that it will remain private." This is where my trust in this journaling activity came to an end. One day that teacher had caught me alone in the hall. She smiled and told me that she noticed that I'd begun "filling out." I was mortified! I don't know if she was complimenting my new teenaged figure, hinting that I should wear a bra, or simply making awkward conversation. Well, I did indeed write about my emotions that day! I wrote, "My English teacher told me that I was getting fat!" I filled that page with emotion and, according to her procedures for personal entries, folded it in half. The next day she made a point to find me before school started. Now it was her turn to be mortified that she'd hurt my feelings when she was apparently only trying to compliment me . . . Hmmm—the only way she could have known that was if she'd opened folded page and peeked at my private journal entry! That was the end of my ability to express myself freely in that journal. From that point on, I was back to events only.

Something good did come from that horrific junior high journaling experience. It changed how I wrote in my diary at home. During my high school years, I found that expressing emotion on paper was a good way to let it go. These days we'd call that therapy. My nightly page of diary writing became a time to express my emotions, organize my thoughts, and sort out teenaged life. (I have my students begin every morning of school with a paragraph in their journals. Maybe a few of them will continue the routine, and it will help them through their teenaged years.) Although I was past the age of reading my beloved *Little House* books, deep down I still held on to the idea of writing my life's stories when I was old. So, I didn't forget the aspect of recording simple events of the day in my diary so that I'd have them straight when that time came. I thought surely my friends would want to do the same thing, so diaries were my usual Christmas and birthday presents to them—although I doubt many of them continued writing in them more than a few weeks.

There were plenty of other skills that were honed in junior high English classes—grammar, usage, mechanics, parts of speech, vocabulary definitions, and book reports which were straight summaries. I'm ashamed to say that I remember a specific time that I actually copied the summary off the book jacket and made an A. If I could remember the title of that book, I'd go back now and read it just to make up for that dishonesty and lack of effort.

I enjoyed English classes in high school. The skills (grammar, mechanics, sentence diagramming, and parts of speech) never changed, so I became very good at them. While I may have become bored with the repetitiveness of the skills, I also actually grew to love those aspects of writing. I challenged myself to do these assignments with perfection and even hope to find some error that the teacher hadn't known was on the page. Maybe this is why I have an affinity for editing to this day. Perhaps it is also why my greatest pet peeve is incorrect grammar or spelling on signs, newspapers, or other published materials. (Pick up you're school supply's, while your their!!!—Ugh!)

I remember doing only one research project in high school. It was for my junior year world history class; however, because there were apparently only a small number of famous political people in history to choose from, the kids in band had to choose famous composers. These were graded by the band director.

I chose to research the life of Richard Wagner. I looked him up in the encyclopedia and in a couple of non-fiction books and then got busy rewording sentences and paragraphs. I don't believe I'd heard the word plagiarism, but I did know that I couldn't copy word for word in something so important as a research paper. I'd honestly hate to see that paper now. I'm guessing that I paraphrased pretty closely on most of the paper, but I got an A for it—there were no grammatical or mechanical errors. (If those papers turned up today, decades later, what kind of content would be there? I wonder if my memory is faulty, or if the biggest part of the grade came from error counting.) I also learned a few facts that I remember to this day: Richard Wagner was born in Germany. The correct pronunciation of Wagner is "Vogner." And, if you squint when you look at his pictures, he looks a little bit like John Wayne.

When I was a senior, I took a class called English V. I suppose that would equate to the AP English classes of today. We were expected to have a strong knowledge of grammar, usage, mechanics, and all the rest. That didn't mean we didn't continue to practice those skills; it simply meant we were expected to be good at them. Because we had mastered those, we actually got to use them in creative writing during the second semester. I remember a project in which we were assigned to write a story. I chose the desert as my story's setting. I wrote and wrote, describing every aspect of that setting. The next step was to put all those editing skills into place and rewrite it. I worked hard and was very pleased with my piece. I was shocked to have it handed back the next day with an F at the top. The teacher said it wasn't a story, it was an essay—a description without a plot. So, that's how I learned the difference. I reworked the assignment by adding a couple of characters and putting them through some events with a little action. I did receive an A this time, but I cared little for the piece. A positive thing that I took away from that experience was the idea of putting words on the page in such a way that they would, in turn, put pictures in a reader's mind.

The last and most important piece of writing I did in high school was for my graduation salutatory speech. (This is the one piece of school writing that I still have a copy of.) It was an opportunity that called for me to write something from the heart and then to share those words with hundreds of people. I was very, very nervous. As my speech and drama teacher helped me with how to say my words, she also helped me with the flow of the words and the choice of vocabulary—the writing domain we call style today. I made it through the delivery of that speech, and I was pleased. The words that had come from my heart and head then traveled through my hand onto the page became real as they were heard by an audience. I was both pleased with what I had written and with the fact that I had shared out loud with my friends, my family, and with many strangers something that I had written. I had a captive audience for those few short minutes—the final words brought a feeling of triumph and of deep satisfaction.

I began my college career by taking Composition I at our local college branch of Henderson State University the summer after my senior year in high school. I remember feeling so timid. I was 18, and everyone else was so old—probably 30.

After some review of grammar, usage, and mechanics (again), we received our first writing assignment. We were to write an essay entitled "Pride." I thoroughly enjoyed writing about helping children build pride in their work, the importance of letting someone know you're proud of them, and the satisfaction and pride that follows hard work. I checked for errors, recopied it, and turned it in. The next week the teacher pulled out the stack of essays. She thought it was interesting that 29 essays took the same slant— pride goeth before a fall, a proud man is a foolish man, and the sin of pride versus the virtue of humility. I slowly died inside as she read the one different paper aloud, hoping against hope that she would not read my name as the author. I stared at the window with my eyes open wide so the tears wouldn't spill over onto my cheeks. It was humiliating to be different... or was that pride that I should have been feeling? Was it a good thing to have my paper singled out? Looking back, I choose to say yes. There must have been something there worth sharing.

During my first semester as a freshman on the big University of Arkansas campus in the big city of Fayetteville, Arkansas, I was a little girl from the country who just wanted to blend in with the crowd. Surely to stand out in any way could not be good.

My Composition II teacher went over the importance of grammar and mechanics in our writing (sigh . . .). Commas seemed to be particularly important. One comma out of place could cost a letter grade on an assignment. Luckily, I'd had plenty of training with comma rules. One of the first assignments required was to write an essay on a controversial topic— "Abortion." Well, for goodness sake, I was from a conservative little town in Polk County, Arkansas where no one even talked about that, and here it was written on the chalkboard for everyone to see!! How could I possibly write three pages about that? After agonizing and staring at a blank page for a while, I decided to set aside my personal beliefs and simply focus on writing a convincing essay full of reasons and examples. Two weeks later the teacher stated that he thought it was interesting that almost all the essays were written from the same perspective—only one was different. I sat as still as possible and concentrated on the blocks in the floor so that I could keep breathing normally. Was it possible to die of embarrassment? I was filled with shame that someone might figure out that the paper was mine . . . or was that a sense of winning a round of debate that I should have felt? Again, I look back and search my memory for the reason my paper was read aloud. Mechanics can only be seen on the paper, but content and style are the two domains of writing that can be heard. Whether good or bad, my content or style must have been strong—at least worth reading aloud.

By the time I was an upper classman I began to wonder if the sole purpose of writing was to prove skills in grammar, usage, and mechanics. Those were the errors marked on papers of friends and classmates. Those were the easily-explained reasons for grades written in red at the tops of papers.

On a dreary, cold, stormy morning, I set across campus for my final essay in Junior English. The wind was whipping the bottom of my raincoat—I can still picture it, bright green and plastic. Water was pouring off its hood into my face and down my neck. My jeans were soaked from the thighs down. We entered the classroom, wrung ourselves out, and saw the assignment on the board: "Write an essay." That was it. There was no topic or guidance. Students pleaded with the teacher for some help in choosing what to write about. He seemed to think infinite choice should make the assignment something we'd enjoy. I was freezing, wet, and generally in a foul mood for writing. I thought to myself, "Fine. You want me to pick the topic. I'll write about the dumbest thing I can think of. Right now that is raincoats." So, I proceeded to pour out my rage and fury on the paper—tying it all together under the topic of raincoats. (I wish I could see that paper now. I wonder what I said. I wonder if I made analogies. I wonder if raincoats was really the topic or if there was a deeper, more meaningful, topic under that.) A few days later I went to check my grade. In those days, we'd go to the teacher's office where grades were posted by social security number—for security reasons (my how times have changed) so that no one would know who got what grade. There it was, right beside my social security number—A. I checked the list. There were a couple of Bs, a lot of Cs, and a few Ds and Fs, but there wasn't another A. Why was that? What had I written that had made it stand out from the rest? I began to wonder what makes a piece of writing good? Surely it wasn't simply the topic chosen. Surely there was more to it than the grammar, sentence formation, and mechanics. What made the difference? That paper and that grade made me think—to begin my search for good writing. (It would be nearly two decades later before I'd discover the domains of content and style.)

I began teaching in the mid 1980s, and I had a belief that writing should be something the kids would want to do. It should be like art—a treat, something to share and keep.

Writing, according to the curriculum, meant forming letters correctly. English, according to the curriculum, meant recognizing nouns, capitalizing correctly, and matching the right verb to the right subject. So, that's how I taught it—grammar, usage, mechanics, copying sentences—the same way I'd been taught. I still had a desire to do writing that meant something, so I had the kids write "My News." It was a weekly opportunity for the kids to write about their own lives. I saved all of those, and at the end of the year, each child had a treasure—a written personal record of the year. I also had a desire to do writing that was fun. We did this through story starters or class stories. These would end up giving us a springboard for Friday afternoon art to make illustrations. Or, they would be made into booklets and given as gifts. For example: A story starter about a dinosaur in the music teacher's piano would result in 25 short stories. The kids could hardly wait until their music day so they could share with the music teacher. I never gave any kind of grade for these other than a check mark. I never gave any feedback for these other than a "good job" at the top of the page. I didn't know there was a way to assess writing. There seemed to be something missing. I just didn't know what.

During my middle years of teaching, the 1990s, I went back to college to get a graduate degree. I did plenty of my own writing through research papers, but I also began to examine my teaching of writing. These were years of questioning, experimenting, and discovery. Writing takes time, and I was expected to have grades for the grade book. Can writing be graded? I discovered rubrics—grading writing can be objective and points can be assigned. If a product could be graded, I could afford the class time to spend on it. Can writing in the classroom serve a purpose? This question set me on the path toward the integration of writing into other subjects. Writing could enhance the learning of content material because writing involves higher level thinking. Writing is a way to organize thoughts and concepts. It also serves as a way to share information from research projects or individual studies. Can writing be a part of everyday life? Journals could be meaningful personally as well as a means to develop writing fluency. Reading logs, math and science logs—individual writing means individual participation. I tried a lot of things that didn't work out or that I couldn't keep up with. I tried a lot of things that ended up changing my style of teaching. All in all, I think good things were evolving.

Then in 1998, two things happened that helped me define the process of writing and my role as a teacher of writing. The first was that our state began testing writing on the state benchmark test. There were plenty of groans, whines, and moans about how awful this was and about how awful our kids did on this style of testing. But good did come from those results. Teachers were given writing goals to work toward and were being forced to teach writing. We were given labels for the different parts of writing—content, style, sentence formation, usage, mechanics—and were taught how to identify traits for each of these domains. This provided a guide for instruction and assessment.

The second thing that happened in 1998 was that I became a part of the National Writing Project. Through the Northwest Arkansas Writing Project Summer Invitational Institute, I discovered the writer within myself. I knew she was there, but I'd never let her out in public, and I certainly hadn't known that there were other people who loved writing for the sake of writing. I discovered that I had peers who felt the same way I did about writing. Through my work in the Writing Project, I developed a deep understanding of each step of the writing process. That was the point where real transformation could happen in my teaching and writing instruction.

During the intensive four-week NWAWP Invitational Summer Institute, I discovered the power of revision. For the first time, I saw revision for what it could be—not merely a step, but an experience. Revision is writing catharsis.

A scheduled part of the Institute's daily routine was to meet in response groups. This was an assigned group of four participants who were to share writing with each other for the purpose of revision. At first the act of reading a rough draft was intimidating and terrifying. But we shared, listened, complimented, questioned, and suggested. In a short time, a trust developed within our tiny writing community. The compliments of peers who found good in our words boosted confidence and made us want to improve. We began to crave the feedback that would push and guide our revision one draft closer to the end result of a polished piece. I know that this process made me a better writer. I could feel it happening.

I also knew that if writing was to be as "real" for my students as it was for me, revision through this feeling of community would be a key element in my classroom. Because I believed that it should be a part of every classroom, I chose to develop my demonstration (all participants of the NWAWP Invitational Summer Institute were required to develop a hands-on writing demonstration to be used for teacher in service) based around revision groups for elementary aged children.

After experiencing the transforming power of revision in the NWAWP Invitational Summer Institute, I quite frankly became a bit obsessed with noticing revision everywhere in life—not reserved only for the process of writing. Revision is a part of scientific experimentation, cooking, decorating, and math problem solving. During a family vacation to Mount Rushmore, I learned that originally Jefferson was carved into the mountain over Washington's right shoulder. The rock wasn't suitable, so the sculptor had to revise—they blasted Jefferson's face off the mountain, and moved him to the other side. Then they had to move Lincoln back. Later they revised again, and added Roosevelt, who wasn't even in the first draft. If revision can be done on the grand scale of Mount Rushmore, then making changes on notebook paper surely shouldn't seem like such a daunting task.

My recent years of teaching writing have been my most satisfying. The 2000s have been a time of defining philosophies and refining strategies. Writing is not simply a subject—it's just what we do.

Rubrics or scoring guides used to be important to my assessment of writing, but they have evolved into something more. Rubrics are no longer just important, they are absolutely essential to authentic writing assessment. At some point I realized that being a teacher who can assess perfectly is of no value or benefit to students of writing if they don't understand how they've been evaluated. Teaching students to understand their assessments leads to writing improvement. The check marks and "good job" comments were meaningless. Rubrics provide students with specific expectations and information as to what elements of writing they are doing successfully as well as which elements need improvement.

Specific individual response to writing is a way to encourage the teacher-student relationship to become more of a reader-writer relationship. The philosophy presented by Liner, Latta Kirby, and Kirby in *Inside Out* (2003) is that the writing classroom should be different from all others. It should be a place where as much as possible the teacher-student relationship be more of a reader-writer relationship. By asking questions about a student writing rather than telling that student-writer what to fix or change, the writer remains the one with *authority* over the piece. The writer can be encouraged to discover what needs to be revised in order to make the piece clear for the readers. The teacher in the traditional role might tell the student how to fix the writing. The teacher in the interested reader role might ask questions that guide the writer to discover how to make his or her writing better. Discussion, as well as written responses, is important. Talking is an important part of writing. There must be talking in the writing classroom—sharing, giving feedback, asking questions, making suggestions, pointing out what's right through compliments. Writing doesn't have to be a solitary activity.

Writing is thinking: this philosophy comes from Jim Gray, founder of the National Writing Project. While reading the National Writing Project book *Because Writing Matters* (Nagin & NWP, 2003), I began to fully understand this concept. I decided that the reason that there were so many workshops offering quick fixes to teaching writing was that teaching writing is hard. It involves higher level thinking skills. "Use these colored strips, and your students will have all the necessary sentences in a paragraph." "Use these colored pens, and your students will complete these stages of the process." "Follow this pattern using these transition words, and your students will turn out 5-paragraph essays." None of these programs or strategies are bad, but they are only steps or foundations for guiding students toward the deep thinking required by the writing process. Writing-to-learn strategies foster thinking in all subject areas. In this way writing becomes a part of every area of the curriculum—research in social studies, hypothesis in science, explanation of work in math constructed response—where writing is no longer a subject that stands alone, but an integral part of all learning.

Choice as vital to writing success was my next hurdle to cross. I had always been told what to write about—with the exception of the raincoat fiasco. In turn, I'd assigned my students the topics they'd write about. But students write best when they're writing about what they care about or are interested in. The gurus of writing seem to allow free reign of topic selection, but I haven't reached that level of freedom yet. I need a little bit more structure. I've discovered that choice within boundaries works best for my students and for me.

Probably the most important paradigm shift to which I've evolved would be the understanding of the importance of creating a community of writers where writing is valued and writers are respected. Finished products are displayed or shared, but drafts are celebrated as well. Rough drafts are a springboard. Revision is natural. We know that the work done on a rough draft will make the piece of writing better.

I cannot pinpoint exactly when this corner was rounded, but there are a couple of instances in which I was taken aback by the way I saw my students clearly exhibit the characteristics I'd hoped to instill in them. The first happened the year our school experimented with student-led parent teacher conferences. I sat wide-eyed and proud as I listened to my students talk about their writing processes and accomplishments. "This is my rough draft folder. It shows all the hard work I did." "Everything in my portfolio folder has been polished, so it's all special." "All the things written on this side of the line show what I did right on my prompt. I have to look at that to be sure I do it again. Everything on this side of the line shows what I need to work on. That's where I choose my goal for the next prompt." I was amazed at how little I felt I needed to add to their comments on their own writing.

Another time when I am reminded that the students feel safe in the writing community we've developed is when we meet in revision groups before publishing a piece of writing. The listeners' first job is to listen to the piece. Their second job is to give a compliment for some part of the writing. By the middle of the year, they know what makes writing good, and they know the "writing lingo" to express what was done well. I love looking at the reader's face when a listener says, "I got a good mind picture with your description of the setting." Or, "The dialogue sounded realistic." Or even, "Good vocabulary—gruesome and moldy!" A compliment from a teacher is nice, but there's nothing quite as satisfying as a compliment from a peer.

Once a writer, always a writer—I am compelled to make sure my students believe that they are capable and worthy writers. I want that feeling and belief to last long after the benchmark test at the end of the school year. Even now, I seek out opportunities to write for a purpose and long for feedback from my peers. I have made mention again and again—even perhaps complained—of how much emphasis was placed on the mechanical, rather than the creative, side of writing when I was a student; however, it has served me well. As an editor of a book on quick writes, *Spark the Brain, Ignite the Pen: Quick Writes for Kindergarten through High School Teachers and Beyond* (Totten, Eaton, Dirst, & Lesieur, 2003), I got to put those skills to good use. And as the lead editor of another NWAWP project, I worked to instill that feeling of a writing community within the teacher consultants who submitted, revised, and saw their words published in *The Flavor of Our Words* (Eaton, Totten, Wince, & Terell, 2006). Young or old, when a writer sees his or her name under the title of a piece that has been through the process of writing, the emotions crash together like colors in a kaleidoscope—satisfaction, contentment, surprise, and of course, pride.

Living the Process of Writing

I used to think that the writing process was a rigid series of steps to follow in order to turn out a quality piece of writing. The heading of each step should appear in order in the lesson plan book—one step per day, then, *voila,* a great piece of writing! But somewhere along the way, the writing itself became the focus rather than the process of checking of each step in order—prewrite, draft, revise, edit, publish, stop. When that change happens, the writing becomes real, and the recursive nature of the process becomes natural.

Prewriting sets the foundation for the content of the piece. It can be as simple as closing your eyes and thinking about a topic to get your thoughts together. There are countless types of graphic organizers that can help to organize those thoughts. Some examples are the Venn diagram for comparisons, webs and clusters for organizing similar thoughts or facts, story maps for plotting setting, character, and plot development. The old fashioned outline still works to keep supporting details with main ideas. (It's what I used for this piece.) Library research that involves note cards, illustrations on a storyboard, or an interview where answers to questions are recorded are other ways to gather information to be used in writing. But prewriting doesn't have to happen with pen and paper. Viewing a video, reading a book, watching a play, listening to music, or having a discussion can all be ways a writer can gather thoughts and ideas for writing. Anything that sparks the brain can ignite the pen.

Drafting is simply the act of getting thoughts on paper. It seems that drafting would follow prewriting, but perhaps some drafting begins to happen during the prewriting stages. It's even possible that the free flow of writing a draft could be the prewriting for another piece. I don't think a writer can reach the full potential of a rough draft until it is fully realized that it is okay for the rough draft to be . . . rough—even bad. It's a starting point for the something better it will become. To be painfully metaphoric, a beautiful butterfly has to go through the ugly caterpillar stage first. I first truly understood that concept while doing some assigned reading for the NWAWP Invitational Summer Institute—a chapter from Anne Lamont's book, *Bird by Bird* (1994). Not only is the rough draft allowed to be less than perfect, it is expected to be so. Once the true meaning of rough draft is understood, the writer can relax and write.

Revision is the heart and soul of the process of writing as far as I'm concerned. Traditionally, revision has been assigned to the position of following the drafting stage; however, so often revision happens throughout prewriting and during drafting. It's wherever the writing begins to become real—wherever the author rethinks. Conferencing through sharing and discussing is a springboard for revision. For me, it's a vindication from all those "I will not talk in class" sentences I'd written so long ago. I think revision once had the reputation of the most dreaded part of the process. Maybe this is because it has been labeled as the "fix and recopy" stage. Revision is looking again—looking for what's already good and making it better. If you don't C.A.R.E about a piece of writing, then it isn't worth revising. Revision shows it's worth Changing, Adding, Rearranging, and Eliminating. It shows you C.A.R.E. enough to make it better.

Editing, on the other hand, is looking for what's wrong and fixing it. It may be the English teacher's only comfort zone as he or she begins the transformation into becoming a teacher of writing. Editing is something we teachers are comfortable with. The red pen emerges—needs a comma here, this should be capital, spell this correctly. For some reason, there are those who believe that revision and editing are one in the same. The scenario goes like this. A rough draft is turned in. The teacher edits it or points out every mistake. The student then revises it, or rewrites it correctly. What? How did this way of thinking come about? I believe it happens because true revision takes time and effort and critical thinking—in other words, it's hard work. It makes sense that editing would be the final stage of the process before the final copy is made. It is, but that isn't the only place it happens. Writers fix mistakes all along the way, in every stage. Some writers cannot leave a misspelled word in a draft. Others want to get the thoughts down and not be bothered with the technicalities until later. Either way, editing plays such a vital role that we mustn't let it be the stage that makes students lose confidence in or feel badly about their work. I go back to that essay on the importance of pride I wrote so many years ago. When a student-writer has worked and worked so hard to make a piece of writing good, it should be the best it can be. There should be a desire to make it right, to fix whatever may be wrong so that it's something to be proud of. There's no need for the dread of the bleeding essay—one that's been marked in red by the teacher and handed back. If revisions are written in different colors on the draft, what's another color added to the mix by an edit pen? Editing doesn't have to be the step where the teacher takes over. If the student takes part in the activity, it will be meaningful rather than painful. Whenever editing can be done in a conference style so that errors are explained, skills can be reinforced. It's simply what a writer needs to do to make the piece as perfect as it can be. Editing is putting grammar, usage, and mechanics to use in a meaningful way.

Publishing—ah, the reason for it all! A piece ready to share! There's no feeling quite like pressing that print button for the last time, like seeing your name under a title, or reading your finished product to your peers. Publishing can take many forms and use many mediums, but the ultimate reason for taking a piece through the process of writing is to share it in some way.

So, is it over once a piece is finished? I think that a finished product leads to the beginning of another, and that is where assessment comes in. Assessment is more than counting errors and assigning a grade. Assessment should be an opportunity for the student to see what was done well so that he or she knows to continue doing it. It should also provide the chance to learn specifically what can be improved in future writing. A student who understands how a grade letter or number was reached will better understand what makes good writing. A student who understands what good writing is will be more likely to do more good writing and even better writing. In the end, isn't that the goal?

References

Eaton, H., Totten, S., Wince, M., & Terell, L. (2006). *The flavor of our words.* Fayetteville, AR: Northwest Arkansas Writing Project.

Lamott, A. (1994). *Bird by bird: Some instructions on writing and life.* New York: Random House.

Liner, T., Latta Kirby, D. & Kirby, D. (2003). *Inside out: Strategies for teaching writing* (3rd ed.). Portsmouth, NH: Heinemann Publishers.

Nagin, C. & NWP. (2003). *Because writing matters: Improving student writing in our schools.* San Fransisco, CA: Jossey-Bass.

Totten, S., Eaton, H., Dirst, S., & Lesieur, C. (2006). *Spark the brain, ignite the pen: Quick writes for kindergarten through high school teachers and beyond.* Charlotte, NC: Information Age Publishing.

Wilder, L.I. (1932). *Little house in the big woods.* New York: HarperCollins Publishers.

To Write Is To Know

Jessica Fragale

The hardest thing about writing is writing. Even writing this chapter fills me with anxiety, loss of confidence, and fear of people reading my words and judging my intelligence by them. If, after all these years, these emotions still occur, then imagine what our students must feel like. Yet I also have a deep love for writing. It is this love that I try to pass along to my students.

The Past

My passion for writing started at a very early stage. Growing up on a small farm did not allow for many neighborhood games or social groups. Mixing up potions from wild plants, playing with kittens, building tree houses and various forts, and reading books provided my entertainment. Some of my earliest memories are of heading to the local library to check out the "read along" books that came in scratched up Ziploc bags with cassette tapes. I learned to read through those books (very whole language), and I learned how to get lost in the story. It was that time in my life that I came to appreciate a story as a method of escape, adventure, and excitement.

I began to dabble in writing at home and found myself most excited by homework that involved writing stories. I was given a lot of choice and was led to believe that I was good at it. Reading my story in front of the class to

Getting It in Writing, pages 73–92

the laughter of the teacher was like winning an Oscar. When my 3rd grade teacher asked if she could keep a poem I had written for her refrigerator, I was on cloud nine. My first grade teacher had each student take home a Curious George stuffed animal and then write about their experiences with George. She then assembled these into hard cover books for each student. I couldn't wait to get home and read my story to my parents. I still have that book today and still get a sense of pride when I read it even now. Writing was an area where I received praise for my ideas and creativity. It was more than a regurgitation of facts or analysis of someone else's work. It came from me and it was mine. That sense of ownership was crucial in my development and continued passion for writing.

In 5th grade I met my school bus nemesis, Amy. It was rumored that she was a black belt in karate, and I, of course, believed her because logical dates and age requirements didn't matter much when there was a 6th grader about to beat me up. Every morning I would get on the bus and my legs would wobble for fear of what Amy would do that day. If I was quiet she teased me. If I was loud she made fun of my laugh, told jokes about me to the other kids, or threatened me with a karate beat down. The ride home was even worse. But nothing compared to the fear and contempt I felt in the lunchroom. Random apples hit my head. Amy and her ugly group of cronies would look at me and laugh, then sneer when they caught my attention. It was a child's version of hell. To make matters worse, I was terrified to tell my father because then I would have been beat up for sure! My only escape was writing.

My poetry started as a joke and ended as an emotional outlet. I sat in my room writing poems about these girls to make myself feel better and more in control of the situation. Eventually my girlfriends joined in on the fun and, to this day, I have an index card box filled with classics like "Little Bug-Eyed Laura, God I wish you were a-dyin." So I wasn't Keats, but I had cadence, rhyme, description, and a great message. My poems were real. They captured my innermost fears, desires, and wishes. They meant something to me beyond a normal writing assignment or prompt. They may not have represented greatness to the world, but they were integral to the development of my own personal microcosm.

Not to leave my readers in suspense . . . After two years of bus and lunchtime torture, Amy did finally confront me outside of the Junior High. Everyone stopped and stared. There was nowhere to run or hide and I couldn't have moved if I tried. I was immobilized except for the backs of my legs, which were shaking uncontrollably. My mouth went bone dry. Sound and light narrowed into a pinpoint focused on her face. The entire scene was surreal and I thought it was the end. Just as I closed my eyes, awaiting the feel of her karate chop across my face, the principal approached us. Under threat of suspension, she left me alone. That night I told my father about my evil nemesis. I never heard a peep from Amy again.

I often tell my students that story. It is a great catalyst for discussions about bullying and facing our fears, but it also a way for students to see me not as just a teacher, but as a person who has real feelings too and who sometimes sorts those feelings out through writing. After these discussions, students open up more in their own stories. Inevitably, students can't wait to tell me about their own similar experience with a bully, and when I say, "you should write that down" they can't get the pencil facing in the correct direction fast enough. It is real to them. They are reliving the emotions as they write about it. The pencil and paper are no longer the tools used in classrooms but wands of magic they can control.

With Amy out of the way, I could concentrate on the next crisis to come into my life, boys. Does he like me? He is in love with my best friend? Firsts. Lasts. Envy. Lust. Betrayal. My emotions deepened, as did my writing. Instead of poems on index cards, I wrote songs and played them on my Casio keyboard. Instead of funny stories, I wrote of the drama and difficulties of life. It was teen angst to the highest degree and writing got me through it. Writing was how I knew to express myself and deal with complicated feelings.

By high school I signed up for every extra writing class my high school offered. Partly because it was an easy A for me, and partly because I was blown away by my 10th grade English Teacher, Mr. James. He was hard. He demanded perfection. He loved the classics like Frost and Thoreau. He pushed me as a writer. He placed outstanding stories into a glass case outside of the main office. He found small details within someone's writing and read it to class as an example of greatness.

There are many lessons I learned from Mr. James that I try to pass on to my own students. He was the first teacher to value publishing and the visual aesthetics of a written piece. As computers were just becoming mainstream in schools, I spent hours fixing margins, using a space bar to meet Mr. James's expectations. This taught me perseverance, how to go beyond what had already been done, and the principles of Murphy's Law before any major assignment is due.

He was the first teacher to not only create, but to cherish a writing portfolio, which I still have to this day and show my students as well. He always said, "From quantity comes quality." He didn't mean throw everything together and it will be great. He told us time and time again that the only way to become a great writer was to write, all the time. Be it a journal, music, notes, research papers, creative writing, journalism, just write. It is with practice that a writer discovers his or her voice.

Mr. James also said, "Write what you know." This was hard to accept at first. Why couldn't I write about a fairy living in Chicago? What was wrong with fantasy, science fiction, and horror? His answer was always the same. "Write what you know." It really wasn't until years later that I could grasp the meaningfulness behind this statement. In order to be an effective writer, you must truly believe in what you are saying. A character's emotions must be realistic. A setting must be able to be seen by the reader, and thus the writer. He wasn't saying skip the fantasy stories; he was saying do not write about it until it has become alive for you. Robert Frost was legendary because he knew those woods like the back of his hand. Netherland was just as real to J.M. Barry as the Shire was to J.R. Tolkien because they wholeheartedly stepped into those worlds. So many of the great writers were political reformists, underground, homosexuals living in secrecy, the heartbroken, the dying, or just vivid dreamers. No matter how varied the genre and writing style, they all have one thing in common: they all put their experiences and imaginations onto paper for others to bear witness to their truth.

This concept is often difficult to translate for elementary students; however, when I really dig into their imagination and ask them to "get lost" inside their stories, they never disappoint me. It takes time to culture this kind of visualization. It takes patience on the part of the teacher and desire on part of the student. To me, write what you know means write from the heart. Use your past experiences, people in your lives, difficult situations to capture the reader as the memory has captured you. This type of writing does not come from a test released writing prompt. This kind of writing comes from open-ended discussions, sharing related stories, and freedom. Skilled writing does not come from beautiful penmanship, perfect grammar, or multisyllabic vocabulary. Skilled writing comes from the development of a strong and clear message. It is my opinion that a poem written and read through tears of a third grader who lost a brother to cancer is just as powerful as Emily Dickinson or Elizabeth Barrett Browning's analysis of death.

My education continued; however, inspirational writing classes did not. College was filled with essays, reports, and deadlines that didn't promote creativity for me anymore. I became involved with the Film Department and turned my attention to creating stories through moving pictures. I wrote scripts instead of narratives. Music videos replaced poetry. The idea was the same, but the technology changed everything.

The Present

So how does the past affect the present? When I sit down with my myriad of teacher resources I am immediately overwhelmed by the amount of "things" I am trying to teach to my students. By nature, we, as teachers, try to do too much in too short of time because we want to give our students everything we possibly can. We know this, yet we do it every year, every unit, and every day. I've come to the conclusion that this is just who I am as a teacher. Therefore, to combat the overwhelming list of state standards and grade level goals, I thought back over my own history as a writer and tried to pull out the most essential themes that made writing enjoyable and successful for me as a learner. These will be the foundation for my writing workshop throughout the year.

Currently, I am a third, fourth, and fifth grade multiage teacher at a charter school in Hollywood. For clarification purposes, this is not the glamorous "Hollywood" one might imagine. There is no application or selection process. The school serves the students in the neighborhood, which is mostly comprised of first and second generation immigrants from Mexico, El Salvador, Guatemala, and Armenia. The families are struggling financially and their income is considered far below the poverty line. All but one of my students speaks Spanish at home.

The school was a Los Angeles Unified School that became a charter school because we hoped to utilize different curriculums to better reach the students. LA Unified is the second largest district in the nation. By turning into a charter school, we have reduced the amount of anonymity and bureaucracy that goes along with such a vast district. Being a charter school also means that we, as teachers, have opinions that are respected and decisions that are made by us as a collective. It also means that we have to outperform the state test scores of neighboring schools in order to keep our charter alive. What we've ended up with are very dedicated teachers who are always trying to make things better for our students.

Being a multiage teacher is much easier than one might think. The basic philosophy is that kids learn best from kids and that age shouldn't dictate how and when a student learns. My students are between the ages of eight and eleven, though one would never know it based on my groupings. I have fifth graders who are reading at a third grade level, and I have third graders reading at a fifth grade level. Whatever reading, writing, English speaking level they are, I aim to move them up as individuals rather than as a grade. I differentiate where needed, group when necessary, and move about constantly. We switch our students for math and rotate science and social studies curriculum on a three-year cycle. The students have me as their teacher for three years; we are a family.

The opportunity for trial and change has been crucial in the expansion and utilization of the key concepts I value so much. The following Key Concepts of Writing Workshop is my philosophy of teaching writing based on my past teaching experiences and the readings of: *Literacy For The 21st Century: A Balanced Approach* by Gail Tompkins (2003); Irene C. Fountas and Gay Su Pinnell's *Guiding Readers and Writers, Grades Three through Six: Teaching Comprehension, Genre, and Content Literacy* (2001); and *When Kids Can't Read: What Teachers Can Do: A Guide for Teachers 6–12* by Kylene Beers. These resources, along with workshops and experimentation, helped me develop these ever-evolving concepts.

Key Concepts of Writing Workshop

1. As a reader, appreciate a good story in front of the students as a method of escape, adventure, and excitement.
2. Provide choice, freedom, and independence. The best writing comes from the heart, not a textbook prompt. Encourage the students to write for themselves, not the grade.
3. Make students feel good about their writing, and give lots of praise. Students have to feel good about themselves and their skill in order to want to make it any better.
4. Create ownership of writing. Students must have something to look back on with pride and feel that they created it all by themselves. This has to be tangible, with all major decisions left up to the student.
5. Use writing as an emotional outlet.
6. Use writing as a way for students to express themselves as individuals. No topic is too menial or trendy to the author who took the time to write it, even when it's the 100th story about *A Day at the Park*. If I do find myself bored, then I know it is time to ask the right questions to draw out more about the story to make it interesting.
7. Find details within the students' writing to share with the class as an example of greatness. Be specific about what it is that you find great, give credit to the author, and be genuinely impressed with what you are presenting.
8. From quantity comes quality; write, write, write, then make time to write some more. Your students won't think it is important unless you make it important within your daily schedule.

9. Write what you know, your truth. Don't be afraid to use difficult situations.

10. Technology continues to change us as writers; integrate that.

As teachers we can utilize technology in ways that promote writing as it once did for me. The school had just built a computer lab when I entered high school. Mr. James was all about this computer lab. Every assignment had specific publishing criteria. Hours were spent in that computer lab trying to center the words "by Jessica Fragale" exactly halfway down the page and centered perfectly when the paper was folded. This was a new challenge to writing that excited me. Pictures could be added to my poetry. Borders surrounded my stories. Everything I created just felt more official. My portfolio was not only a display of my writing, but of my digital skills as well.

I had sat through typing classes, but typing my own stories is what really taught me computer skills. The same was true of layout design, problem solving, and the desire to learn more about computers. The same has been true for my students. The time spent learning about computers to build a project or portfolio piece has been far more impactful than my direct instruction lessons attempting to teach the same things. In this way technology has been a tool, not another curriculum piece to cover by June.

Technology doesn't just mean computers. Almost everyone, including the poorest of the poor, seems to have a TV. This is a fabulous tool for teaching the literary elements of reading and writing. Unconsciously, we take in information from the *mise-en-cine,* or what is put into a scene, that allows us to draw conclusions, make connections and inferences, and comprehend better. These are the same strategies we try to teach in reading. I often use television and movies to teach these strategies and skills to my students so that they can later "paint me the picture" of what is happening in their stories, elaborating on those elements. Here are some quick examples that have worked for me so far:

- Ask students how they know when a scary part is coming up in a movie. They mention things like it's dark out, there is scary music, it's at night, and you hear breathing or thumping. We brainstorm this list and I write it on the board. From there I ask how an author would let you know it was scary, using their examples and translating them into phrases rather than visual images. They then write their own scary story with extra points if I can feel scared before I even get to the scary part. Students are engaged, clear expectations have been set, and I walk around the room offering advice and assistance to those who ask for it. When we are finished we share the stories at author's chair.

▪ Bring in a flashlight and discuss the various moods created in a movie based on where the light is shining. Show how when the light comes from behind a person it looks like an angel or magical. When the light comes from under a person's face it looks menacing. When a light comes from directly above the person looks like they are in trouble or being scrutinized like an interrogation room. When the light comes from a high angle the person looks smaller, a low angle and the person looks taller. Cinematographers use these details to create a mood. Students are trying to create a mood with their pencil. Even though they recognize and deduct information visually, they often need help recreating it linguistically. We look for examples where authors used lighting or angles to create mood. We then brainstorm how this would look in our own writing.

▪ One of my favorite activities is to pause a movie whenever we meet a new character. I ask questions such as, "What can you already tell me about this character just by looking at him/her?" "Why do you think the director wanted this character to look like that?" "Who can make a prediction about this character?" These are inferential questions that cause subconscious thoughts to come forward into conscious ones. Thoughts students can then replicate when they are creating their own characters in their stories. I also do this with setting, genre, sequence, and author's point of view and perspective.

Logistics

Students walk into a classroom and judge a teacher's respect level by their classroom space. We do it as adults; we did it as kids too. A messy space doesn't send the message that "this is a place of respectful learning where you will push yourself and walk away a better person." I have tried many different types of organization for writer's workshop and find that I still change it every year.

The Writing Workshop Bulletin Board is an interactive bulletin board that has been broken down into the five writing process steps: Pre-write, Draft, Revising, Proofreading, Publishing. Each step has a space for clothespins, Popsicle sticks, cards, or whatever, to mark where each student is in the writing process. This is a visual organizer for me to know where my students are as well as a way to promote ownership for the students. They "move their clip" as they progress through the writing process as a tactile reminder that writing is a process rather than a start and stop procedure. (I put revising before proofreading because who takes the time to check for periods before all thoughts and ideas are organized correctly? I don't understand why it is listed in most textbooks in reverse order, so I did what make sense to me.) The students are explicitly taught how to manage this bulletin board for the first month of school. After that it is a self-run writing machine with teacher energy spent on conferencing rather than disciplining.

Another space saving and organizational tool I use is the Imagination Closet. The students are in charge of this closet from day one. Inside there are dictionaries, thesauruses, books about writing, sample portfolios from previous students, my portfolio from high school, white lined paper, computer paper, fancy paper for publishing, calendar pictures and other visual prompts, art books, student writing folders, and student portfolios. I line the inside of the doors with pictures and words that invoke creativity. The outside of the closet doors hosts a few writing posters and informational texts. When the doors to that closet open, the classroom takes on a different ambience. They know that I love this part of the day, and they get one hour to dive into their imagination uninterrupted. When the items in the closet get messy I simply say, "Oh, no, what happened to your imagination closet?" or "Wow, look at your dictionaries, did an earthquake hit?" A few students always rush over to straighten it out because it's theirs. (I've tried scolding, re-teaching, bargaining, and threatening. All of them take too much out of me and don't work. A simple statement and leaving it up to them seems to be the key.) It is also a direction for students to head when they feel the "I don't have anything to write about" syndrome coming on. Sometimes just the physical act of getting up and walking over to the closet inspires an idea. It also makes writer's block the student's problem to be solved independently.

I wish I had some heroic tale of how random ideas, such as the imagination closet, came about. In reality, however, I needed more space, things were everywhere in my classroom, and writing was getting left to the last item of the day, which meant the first thing to be pushed aside when I ran out of time. My mother used to say, "You need more elbow grease," when a stain wouldn't come out of the floor. I find myself transferring elbow grease to imagination, and the rule still applies for me. Sometimes I have to force myself to be creative in order to "get the spots out."

Writing Portfolios and Writing Folders are two separate things. It is important to keep them separate because I want students to understand that writing is a process and a production. The folder is where everything is kept organized during the process. The portfolio is the final production of items to be proud of. Two separate folders create two separate mindsets. I feel that the students value their portfolio more when it isn't clustered with drafts, pre-writes, and notes. We teach this organization explicitly so that students will continue it subconsciously.

My multiage team and I have all tried various methods of organization for the Writing Folder. Nicky's Folders is a company (www.nickysfolders. com) that offers Writing Folders with six or eight slots to slip paper into. It's expensive but very sturdy. Two folders stapled back-to-back works as well. I have also used a manila folder with items stapled on each side. This works if you have many students or they are old enough to be organized independently; however, get the kid who just shoves things in a folder and the whole lot of it will be a crumpled mess. The writing folder has a pocket for each stage of the writing process.

The Writing Portfolio is the published copy of the student's best work, as decided by the teacher and student during teacher conferences. Mr. James put such an emphasis on portfolios that its importance is still ingrained in me. My high school portfolio was a three-ring binder with plastic sheets to slip papers into. My students had to have the same once they saw mine. I have also used folders, envelopes, and bulletin boards to compile the work. Whatever display, make sure the student chooses the work, is proud and in awe of the final product, and has the opportunity to share the portfolio with parents or other classrooms at some point.

My students walk their parents through their portfolio during parent teacher conferences. I was having a really hard time explaining to parents, in Spanish, about their children's achievements. I started to require students to accompany their parents as translation assistants. One day I asked a student to go and get his portfolio to show Mom. Ever since, it has been an integral part of our conferences. Even when their parents can't read one word of it, you can see the pride in the student's face, which transfers to the parent's face as well. A symbiotic relationship among teacher, student, and parent is created.

Author's Chair has gone from painful to amazing throughout Writer's Workshop. I have nodded off, spent the whole fifteen minutes disciplining, given pages of notes on what was wrong with a story, and dreaded it for a long time. Every year a simple change was made, and it is evolving into my students' favorite part of workshop time. Most teacher books explain to share out at the end of Writer's Workshop. I have found that by having Author's Chair to start Writer's Workshop, the students have more patience and energy, are more enthusiastic to get to work writing their own stories, and are more eager to share what they've written a day before. I am not sure if it is lack of confidence or fatigue that dampens the end of the day Author's Chair, but it is definitely not as effective in my class.

We start off with two authors. I bring my students to the rug to keep them close to the speaker. The author sits in a special chair that only I sit in when reading aloud. The author may or may not read the whole piece, may or may not show illustrations, and may or may not be finished with his or her writing. Writers, myself included, get bored with certain stories. Without committing to the whole story, more students want to share and get input on their story before continuing. It is metacognition and reflection at work.

The first author reads his or her story. The audience then gets to ask two questions, which the author answers and makes note of any additional information to be added later. The audience then gets to make two compliments. This takes training, as the students think "I liked your story," is helpful. We have to teach, model, then praise those students who make specific comments like, "I like how you described what you were hearing and smelling in that passage." "I thought you wrote a detailed description of the setting so it was easier for me to picture it in my mind." It sounds silly, but it is really contagious. Lastly, audience gives two comments. Notice these are not critiques because at this age that seems to shut them off completely. Instead these are ideas that they author may or may not use. The author is instructed to say thank you, no matter what his or her opinion is of the idea, and then to make any notes for himself or herself. At the end we all clap and the author receives an index card from me, the teacher. The index card is filled with specific examples of great words, strategies, skills the author used in the story. Sometimes these comments are hard to find, but every student has done something right just by showing up and trying. One idea or suggestion is written, but I've learned to stay away from the negative. We have plenty of time to find out all the things we can't or don't do right in life. In order to love writing, you must feel successful at it, which will intrinsically motivate you to improve and continue working at it. I find that a card full of positives goes a lot farther and produces better writers than a star and a wish or similar pattern.

That is not to say stay away from rubrics. Rubrics are essential for setting clear expectations and taking the guesswork out of grading for students. However, rubrics should never be associated with Author's Chair unless the public speaking aspect is what is being graded, and even then, keep it separate from the content that was written. Rubrics should be attached to final drafts. Students will only improve if they are given time to redo and fix the mistakes they have made. A rubric for the sake of a grade on a report card takes up 100% teacher time and is 0% effective. Yet, creating a rubric with students, establishing points or percentages of value with students, then asking students to grade students is 0% teacher time and 100% effective. Create a rubric with the class, specific to each writing assignment, with points assigned to various aspects. For example, a very simple persuasive writing rubric might look like this:

	Points	Peer Editor 1	Peer Editor 2	Teacher
Is Persuasive	50			
Has a logical organization	20			
Correct Grammar	10			
Correct Punctuation	10			
Correct Spelling	10			
TOTAL	100			

Even when I have a goal in mind, I let the students believe they are creating the rubric. We brainstorm the items that were covered and emphasized for the assignment on the board. Then I ask the students which of the topics was the most important. This hasn't failed me yet, but I am prepared to "influence" their decision when that time comes. We continue on, evaluating the importance and weight of each item until we have created our list. This is written on chart paper and posted as well as typed and attached to final drafts. I require students to have another student grade them before handing their work into me. This helps improve the grade, and it helps the grader, who is really looking for specific things. The student takes back her paper, corrects it, then repeats the process with a second partner. By the time the paper reaches me, I already have a very good idea of where the strengths and weaknesses of the student are.

For years I created rubrics, went over them in class, asked students to grade themselves and each other, and essentially wasted our time. It never seemed to improve the students' writing. Then I had to make up a rubric quickly, so I did it as a whole group. I decided to let them make scoring guides as well. The students were so excited to score another student's work. They were also very lenient. Struggling writers were getting 80% and higher. I realized three things. One, I was giving bad grades to those who couldn't write, which had meant lots of spelling and grammar mistakes, even though they had followed a structure and accomplished the objective. Two, my "great" writers were those who could spell, but couldn't necessarily summarize or persuade. And three, when students create it they care much more about it. I had students asking me if they could grade each other with the next assignment. It has been in place ever since, though I am still perfecting *when* to make the rubric. Of course I have students who are in a hurry, don't get it, or don't care, and just write down scores on rubrics. When I see that I call the editor in question into My Office.

The office is the place in the room where students can always find me during teacher conferences. They love it when they see that the "Office is Open," "There is currently no waiting at the office," or "Office is closing in five minutes." They also get a kick out of being shooed away because "I have someone in my office right now and can they come back later." Fifth graders get very serious about this. I have even caught students putting up their own handmade office signs on their desk so as not to be disturbed. It is the beginning of the attempt to claim some space where an adolescent can feel in control and independent. (Remember your bedroom when you were a teenager? Try living with a family of six in a studio apartment. You can imagine why delegated space is so important to my students.)

Once the editor has been brought into my office we talk about how his or her editing job is going. I show them the differences between my scores and theirs and we talk through it. I have never had to have a second talk with students because they take it seriously. Anyone who can't work as a peer editor or is playing around during my office hours is simply "Fired." They are told to return to their desk and they are not allowed to write. Then, between conferences, I will speak with the student and rehire them as long as they can explain what was going wrong and what will go right this time. I know this might sound silly, to play like this with the students, but go ahead and be silly. I know many teachers are thinking, yeah try that in my class. I have tried this with 32 students, all of whom were English Language Learners who had no desire to write because it was too hard for them. The play aspect was what made the writing relevant to them. If you can't have fun while teaching, it's time to get out of the classroom, for even play has a purpose.

My first roll out of Writer's Workshop was scary. It was a little bit chaotic; I organized too much but didn't have enough of a system of accountability. September started with one writing system, and by January there was another. It has been, and will continue to be, an evolution. The trials and tribulations that have yielded the best results for me are the following:

- ▪ I find something I loved to write about or read about and share it as a kick off to Writer's Workshop. I share the stories I wrote as a child. I then ask students if they ever get lost in a movie and forget that they are sitting in the seat. I relate this to books and then let them start creative writing.

- I get students excited about writing workshop by unveiling the Writer's Workshop bulletin board and telling them that they will be able to write stories about whatever they want.

- I go through each step in the writing process and model a funny story with the whole class.

- I introduce Author's Chair and require everyone to read one story before opening it up to volunteers. I let students choose their stories but also have an assignment finished so that everyone has something to read. I also try to pick something very sad or very exciting so that the students have an emotional connection to the entire Author's Chair process. From then on, I encourage shyer students and regulate the ones who want to read every day.

- In the beginning of the year, I give students free reign to start writing so that the vibe in the classroom is one of serious concentration and respect for fellow writers. I do not introduce computer publishing or peer editing until the classroom remains in a workshop atmosphere for at least thirty minutes. (I've often sat in my office writing so that students see I'm serious and won't be running around managing them. It takes about two or three days for the atmosphere to remain buzzing with creativity, and not off task noise.) At this point students can take as long as they need in any step of the writing process.

- I try very hard to praise all the hard work and creative writing going on. I provide students with a piece of paper and tell them I am going to time them for two minutes. In that time they are to write down every story idea they might be interested in writing about this year. At the end of two minutes, I tell them to stop and put pencils down. They then have to share their ideas with three people around the room. This gets them up, gets blood into the brain, and they get to hear new ideas. I then time them for two more minutes so they can add any new ideas to their list. I repeat this until students give me the "this is getting old" look and then I move on. This activity has been beneficial because it gets them excited about new ideas, gets them talking to each other as authors, and provides them with a list of topics to return to at any point in the year when they are stuck for ideas. I usually conclude this activity with a spin of the globe and tell them I will write a story about wherever I put my finger, or open a book and write about whatever character I find, or pull an idea from an idea box (box with strips of paper with words like evil dentist, red balloon, burping turtle as story starters).

- Then I let them write.

During my teacher conference a student must come with a specific question or questions. They cannot say, "Can you read this and tell me if it's good." They can talk about portfolio or publishing options. They can come to discuss some ideas if they get stuck. I am a help desk for them.

Publishing is the bane of my existence because there are never enough computers. I have assigned students to specific computers, but fast typists get stuck behind slow ones and everyone loses. I have tried a running sign-up list but it takes forever. I have assigned computer groups where specific students are typing for the week, no matter what, but then some are ready and some are not and if a student doesn't finish typing his story that week, he has to wait a month. The laptop cart is an option for short stories and poetry, if the whole class is ready to type. I would be a liar to say I've figured this out well, so my advice is to ask your students how they want to do it and improve it as necessary.

License to Compute

I was getting frustrated by the one or two students who always got stuck on the computer and would interrupt my conferences to come and help them print a page or save a file. I created a test that students have to pass in order to get their license. Once a student passes the test and gets a license, he or she is free to move about the publishing signups. If they misuse their computer usage in any way, students are "fined" by time in which their license is suspended. Again, they love the DMV analogy and it makes classroom management so much more entertaining for all participants.

Once Writer's Workshop is moving smoothly, I integrate specific types of writing, such as persuasive, expository, or poetry. After a lesson about the structure and a class made example, students return to Writer's Workshop with all elements of choice. However, I give a deadline for which something that they have written will meet the requirement.

I try to show the students that writing has power by sending a beautiful story to the school newsletter or paper, or framing a poem and putting it by the door. I've listened to their persuasive essays and then made a change they suggested but never thought possible. I tell them to write down their feelings of some injustice happening on the schoolyard and give it to the principal. I've read a book because they recommended it in a letter or book report and then talked to them about my thoughts in a letter or book report back to them. When I ask them to read their stories out loud to me I close my eyes. When they are done, I describe the world I saw and see if it is like they imagined. When a student at our school was murdered, we wrote about it. Only through our written words did the tears come out. Writing can be so powerful and real. It can cause us to have knots in our stomach, bouncy legs, sleepy eyes, squeezed tight fists, lumps in our throats, and make us laugh out loud. Once we point that out to students and show them how writing affects us, they will understand that power as well.

Ways to Integrate Writing

Writer's Workshop is not the only time to encourage the use of writing. I often use Quick Writes to jot down feelings and emotions during sensitive times in the classroom. Students are asked to write anything they want onto a piece of paper for a set duration of time, such as seven minutes. During this time there is silence except for the sound of pencils swooshing. No student may "be done" before the time is up. I make it very clear before the activity that the object is to get as many ideas and thoughts down as possible, and spelling and grammar do not count. When they think they are finished they should write some more until time is called. This forces early finishers to continue on and not distract other students. Sometimes I ask students to share their writing out loud, sometimes they walk around the classroom and share with a partner, and sometimes I tell them to put it in their pocket and take it home. The idea is that the writing itself helped the student to focus their feelings; the end product doesn't matter.

For example, one day my students entered the classroom to learn that half of the students would be wearing an orange band around their arm. I refused to explain this orange band; however, as the day progressed, the students quickly inferred that those students with the orange band were not going to have a good day. Orange banded students had to stay in during recess and help me clean the classroom. They were not allowed to use the water faucet. They could not speak to any student in the room that did not have an orange band. They were not allowed to raise their hand and answer the teacher's questions. By lunchtime I had tears and threats of a mutiny. My apartheid simulation had gone far enough. Even though I had a Magic Circle for my students to discuss their feelings, even though I explained what I was demonstrating and why, even though "Nelson Mandela" (my Teacher's Assistant) came and cut off their orange bands to end the apartheid, they were mad! The fifth grade girls were crying and telling me I could have taught them the same lesson in a different way. The younger boys were eager to get out of the room because they weren't used to this version of me as their teacher. The younger girls grouped into clicks and gave me the evil eye. It was real to them. So, I had them do a Quick Write. I told them I wanted them to write down everything they wanted to say to me, even if it was yelling. I wasn't going to read it and they weren't going to share it. You could hear the resentment and frustration in the pencil lead as it dented the paper. After seven minutes I asked the class to finish their thought and to make a decision. They could rip up their paper and throw it into the trash, give their paper to me, or put it in their pocket and take it home. They looked at me confused. I wanted them to realize that they were writing for themselves, not for me. They were writing to channel a strong emotion, not get a grade. The writing was a therapeutic activity in and of itself. Only one student gave me his paper. Most ripped it up, as that was a chance they didn't hear often. The rest took it home. My current fifth graders who were then third graders still comment about that day.

The Apartheid simulation was part of a larger simulation going on in my classroom at that time. We were learning about Africa using the Scottish Storyline Method (Creswell, 1997). Storyline is an amazing methodology of teaching that I recommend to any and all teachers, especially for writing. During Storyline, the students create a setting within the classroom in the form of a frieze (large 3-D bulletin board). They then create characters and act out a real world situation through a series of incidents that are inspired by the teacher. During this time the teacher has an agenda of standards and topics to be covered; however, it is the students and the various aspects of their characters they created that drive the story. The teacher acts as a facilitator and provides key questions that help to keep the story direction. The control of the teacher is referred to as the teacher's rope, as they are more wranglers of ideas then providers of information. In the instance of the Apartheid we had built an African Travel Agency. The Apartheid was an incident in that storyline.

I have used Storyline to teach about the pioneers and Oregon Trail. Student created characters kept journals about their trials and tribulations as we travelled in our story. We've created a moon colony as a futuristic approach to simulate the colonization of the Americas. While learning about the history, students were reliving the conflicts and resolutions of establishing a new home. Students wrote from the point of view of their characters as well as the local inhabitants of the moon whose home we were invading. In a storyline about a News Station, students researched their local neighborhood and wrote scripts and news reports that were filmed in their "studio." Our last storyline was the creation of a Magazine Publishing Company, complete with editors, designers, and writers. The students wrote the articles, chose pieces for the magazine, published the magazine, and then sold copies to students on the schoolyard to raise money for their science camp. Storyline is a great way to reach students who are resistant to typical writing assignments, are English Language Learners, or are just plain bored with school. It is real world application, engaging, hands on, motivational, and real learning at its best.

Because we are in the charter school family, other charter schools have been nice enough to open their doors to share best practices and ideas. Open Charter School invited a group of teachers from my school to come and learn about some programs and activities that have been successful for their students. I couldn't wait to go and was not disappointed. It was there that I learned about Author's Study.

The teachers use writer's workshop, then take the students work to the next level of publishing by creating hard cover books. In Author's Study, each student selects a children's author to study, understand both the writing and artistic style, and then to emulate through the creation of his or her own book. I thought this was going to be a bust with my struggling grade readers; however, it was some of the best work they have every produced.

Aram, a struggling third grader who rarely turned in assignments, missed a lot of school, and struggled with attention was one such student. I took the students to the library with a list of common authors. They had to choose an author based on the books they liked, and then check out three books by that author. The list contained names like Dr. Seuss, Mercer Mayer, Steven Kellogg, Leo Lionni, Beatrix Potter, and Ezra Jack Keats. Aram chose Eric Carle. The first step was for students to read the books many times and to note any patterns they saw in the writing. The second step was to research the art medium used. The next two steps involved writing a biography of the author, and writing a summary of each of the three books chosen. Of course, Aram struggled with this. Then it came time for the students to write their own stories in the likes of their authors. I explained the process of creating a dummy book and couldn't believe it when Aram was the first student to have his completed. He received the first set of real pages and got to work. While I normally had to refocus his attention every ten minutes or so, he was off in the corner working with tissue paper. While other students were punching holes for the binding, he was covering cereal boxes with paper to make the cover. His story, *Ten Little Rubber Duckies* is still one of my favorites in my classroom. He was first to finish and share his story to the class in Author's Chair. The students were blown away and this motivated him further.

Over the last few days of the project, Aram was very quiet over at the computers. I let him be, figuring that he wasn't bothering anyone, so why bother him. I collected all the books for grading and was pleasantly surprised when I opened Aram's. Inside was an incredibly misspelled, crookedly glued biography of Eric Carle that he had written, and it was good.

Although grammatically incorrect, in the back were summaries of each of the three books he had read.

Creating a real book takes the writing experience to another level. Students have a tangible piece of evidence to share with their peers and they are just so proud of it. I have asked students to write tall tales during the Pioneer Storyline. Students have written their own stories about any topic. The options are endless and the time spent is well worth it.

At the beginning of the year, I read one student-written book a day as the read aloud. The fourth and fifth graders light up when it is their book that has been chosen. The third graders sit in awe that a student wrote what the teacher was reading and couldn't wait to make their own. I even go so far as to write up an index card full of literary analysis terms and questions that I can incorporate into a discussion after the reading, which made the author feel even more authentic.

The writing in my classroom was greatly inspired by Marilyn Burns and the National Teachers of Mathematics Council Annual Conference. Every year my colleagues and I headed to Palm Springs for the math conference, only to end up with ideas for every subject of the day. Cindy Neuschwande spoke about the stories she writes about mathematics and how to get students writing their own math stories. I took that session and ran with it. Students create math books that are placed in my library, about math topics. Through writing these stories, the math is fun for the students, they get the chance to feel like the teacher, and through their writing process, the math concepts become more imbedded. Then, of course, the other math students love reading what previous math students wrote, which is like free advertising for me.

The Future

Success and failures have their own momentums.
—Dr. Yoram Sagher

I love writing, even when it scares me. I want my students to love writing, even when it scares them. Writing is about letting out a part of you. It's about making someone laugh or cry. Writing is about being honest with yourself and converting your imagination to words. The mechanics of writing are just that, mechanics, which need to be practiced and re-taught throughout a writer's life. Writing, however, is telling an interesting story. It is a journey that doesn't stop. If I can get this message out to my students before they leave my classroom walls, then I consider myself on the way to becoming a successful writing teacher.

References

Beers, K. (2002). *When kids can't read: What teachers can do: A guide for teachers 6–12.* Portsmouth, NH: Heinemann Publishing.

Creswell, J. (1997). *Creating worlds, constructing meaning: The Scottish storyline method.* Portsmouth, NH: Heinemann Publishing.

Fountas, I. & Pinnell, G.S. (2001). *Guiding readers and writers: Teaching comprehension, genre, and content literacy.* Portsmouth, NH: Heinemann Publishing.

Tompkins, G. (2003). *Literacy for the 21st century* (3rd ed.). Upper Saddle River, NJ: Prentice Hall.

The Journey

Gary French

*The important thing is not so much that every child should be taught
as that every child should be given the wish to learn.*
—John Lubbock, 1887

*My new crop of eighth-grade students stares in disbelief. It is the beginning of
my first class of the year. After they are seated, nothing is said. I look at them.
They look at me. With a welcome smile, I stand in purposeful silence. They
wonder what in the hell is going on. We have begun.*

Many teachers work much too quickly to alleviate this first-day nervous
tension with their eighth-grade classes. These cynical seniors of middle school
know the routine, and these first moments with them are critical. Although
I will not win them or lose them here, I will hit them with the idea that this
class will be different. And disbelief and wonder are a good start. My goal is to
grab their attention, show them sincerity, and demonstrate an openness and
vulnerability, much like a performer with his or her audience.

Three years ago at the age of forty, I began my certified teaching career.
In this short career, I have decided that one of the most overlooked talents
of a middle school teacher is acting, not necessarily the kind that is boister-
ous and does pratfalls—though my students do readily relate and respond
to these abilities—but the kind of acting that is truly able to communicate

Getting It in Writing, pages 93–104
Copyright © 2011 by Information Age Publishing
All rights of reproduction in any form reserved.

to everyone in the room the sincerity of one's inner self. Luckily, one of my former passions was theater.

It is hard for me to know when I first showed my desire to perform in front of people. My childhood, a forgettable swirling anxious nebula of fatefully far-reaching future consequences, required some releases. In the early teens, mine were music and athletics. I loved music; it was an escape from all the things I couldn't control in life. Any sort of sustained note seemed to soothe my soul. I could practice all day long, imitating singers on the radio. My dad, on the other hand, was a working man. And he was just a little bit uncomfortable with my inclinations toward the emotional realms. I don't think he ever said, "Art is for sissies;" nonetheless, real men did not sing unless they wore a cowboy hat. In seventh-grade choir, we wore no cowboy hats; they weren't allowed in school. I did, however, happen to have a deeply caring and generously giving teacher. She taught two subjects: Choir and German. Both would have unanticipated and enduring consequences on my life.

Being new to the school in that seventh-grade year, I had few friends. One of them saw choir as an opportunity for a little bit of freedom from the daily routines. To impress my new friend, I had to conceal my love for singing by only appearing to sing because the teacher said we had to.

So one day, I was in choir with my friend, making trouble and definitely not showing my true enjoyment of choir or that I loved to practice singing, even if it was cheesy musical numbers like *Godspell*, when on my way out of class my teacher called me over. "What did I do now?" I thought as my mind ran through several options for excuses, depending on the scenario.

She tried to reassure me that I was not in trouble, but you always have to be on your toes. Like when you're talking to cops and they say to you, "just be straight with us and we'll help you out." Then you show them the evidence, and nine times out of ten they use that very same evidence to hang you. Needless to say, I was hesitant. She was throwing these words at me that I didn't understand completely: octaves, rehearse, lisp, and Winthrop. I wasn't in trouble.

She asked me to step into a small practice room, just big enough for a piano and two people. She asked me to sing with the notes she played, and I did. I was informed that my range was two and a half octaves, which was good. Little did I realize that I had just auditioned for the role of Winthrop in the high school play *The Music Man*. She offered me my first official role.

After she explained what it entailed, I accepted. This turned out to be one of the greatest experiences in all my schooling. I met and made a lot of friends, who initiated me into the teenage world that included, among other things, beautiful women. The acting group from the school was filled with people who were a lot different from most of the people I knew; they had fresh, open, and unique points of view.

As a teacher now, I realize my students may feel they are forced to act in ways contrary to their inner voice. It is critical that I always remember this. That inner voice is not the class; that inner voice is each one of these particular individuals that happen to be in this group of students, which I am now presently striving to make wonder.

Slight giggles and uneasy smiles propel me to begin my search for the moment. I take in the atmosphere of the room. When will it be? What will I say? Searching, I begin to pace. They wonder "Am I in the right place?" "Is this guy for real?" "Will we have to endure this the whole year?" I sense a little tension beginning to build.

For some mysterious reason tension resides in that space in between, and just like a good musician knows, a capable actor knows the value of a pause. Like the reader of a captivating story, a student's attention is drawn into a lesson by building tension. Yet holding this tension is no small matter. Self consciousness destroys the sense of spontaneous fun and unpredictability that is the gift of the pause.

Many of my actor friends think me strange, even for an actor, because I hate to go to the theater—well, most theater. I hate to go to most theater because it is, for the most part, boring and predictable. And I'm not talking about the storylines or the words; I am talking about the emotional choices, which at the community theater level of performance, ultimately comes down to the director. For example, in life when someone is truly happy, really and truly ecstatic, she often doesn't smile and laugh. Smiling and laughing are the predictable choice. Have you ever seen, perhaps on TV, someone's expression when they win the lottery or, for that matter, a prize on the "Price is Right?" These people well up with an emotion that forces itself out in spite of the prodigious effort to hold it back. Your average director will not only inhibit these raw and unpredictable feelings of dramatic happiness from an actor, but will ban them as well; these emotions take up too much time and are much too difficult to work with on a schedule. The amateur director's inner dialogue goes something like, "I am responsible for getting this show up on time. I cannot be bothered with this search for emotional truth!" To which I would respond, "There is no show without it!"

Standing before a class of eighth-graders has the potential to be somewhat intimidating. But actors know a secret. Always focus your attention outward on the other actors or props and never on yourself. I focus my concentration on them, on really seeing my new eighth-graders, not as a class but as twenty-eight individual people. Like a good story line, the tension builds. I do my best to continue to hold the pause.

As a teacher in the 21st century, this pause is one of the most important things I can give to my students. Students spend much of their lives in the midst of noise: blaring TV, nagging parents, and senseless video games. In a noisy world, one of the most valuable lessons may be the appreciation or reverence of silence.

I learned the importance of collective silence from a Quaker meeting I attended in Monteverdi, Costa Rica in 1986. Raised a Baptist, I had never had a spiritual experience in any formal church. So when my college professor asked me to attend, I reluctantly agreed.

On Sunday morning, we began the steep, muddy hike up to the church. Through the fog, dodging wet leaves and branches, we arrived at a doorless, windowless log cabin. Thinking this cabin the preacher's home, I wondered when we will get to the church. But I soon discovered that Quakers don't have churches. This log cabin was their "meeting house."

Inside were rough-hewn half logs set in two concentric circles. No pews. No pulpit. Small groups and families sat without speaking. Others from the community trickled in. Most wore jeans. Some had no shoes. My professor and I chose our seats. No one spoke. The preacher appeared to be late.

Listening to the silence, feeling the cool moisture of the fog, I sat. Fifteen minutes passed, which when sitting quietly can seem like an eternity. What was happening? I should have partaken in less copious amounts of the Saturday night town spirit. And where was that God-damned preacher?

But something was happening. It is difficult to put into words. I began to relax. A sensation of calmness slowly warmed my insides. Sitting in silence with other people for extended periods of time was not only extremely foreign to my experience but verged on the extraterrestrial. And just as I was getting acquainted with this alien practice, a soft but startling voice shook me from my newfound place of peace. One of the congregation, a barefoot woman wearing a well worn muumuu, told a simple story about an epiphany she had this past week. She spoke of realizing what a miracle it was for an acorn to grow into a giant oak. An acorn knows it will be an oak; something inside knows. This has become my understanding of true faith: a deep uncensored knowing; knowing things will get done; knowing that I will complete this chapter that I am presently trying to write; knowing I am who I am.

*We need faith; my students need faith. I will need to show them this faith
in the future. Continuing the search for the first words, knowing there will
be the right time, I will demonstrate to them the vibrancy of improvisation.
Somewhere inside the acorn knows.*

My most dependable baby sitter glowed radiantly throughout much
of my youth. The television bewitched me with an array of favorite shows:
*Popeye, Spiderman, Fat Albert, Lassie, Mayberry RFD, MASH, All in the Family,
Chips, The Six Million Dollar Man* and *The Bionic Woman....* But my favorite,
all-time show was *Kung Fu.* Like most young boys, I loved to watch action
heroes fight the bad guys. Although the hero, Kwai Chang Kane, fought
and defeated many bad guys, I liked him and the show for other reasons.

The young Kane is an orphan. Kane desires something more than the
other orphans, who fight each other for food and water. He seeks to enter
the Shaolin monastery, renowned for its teachers. One cannot, however,
simply knock on the door and be welcomed in. Neither can the aspiring
student's parents fill out a form and pay a fee. The student must show that
he is ready. One of the most poignant moments in the whole series comes
at the beginning of the original *Kung Fu* movie.

At the gate of the great temple, the young Kwai Chang Kane stands with
two other children eager to gain entrance. Vulnerable to the elements for
what appears to be several days, through hunger and thirst, the three wait
to be admitted. It is here that Kane begins to demonstrate his superior will.
Unbeknownst to them, the master is watching. When tired, the two others
sleep. When it rains, the others seek shelter. Kane, however, simply stands
and waits. After several days, the master opens the gate, and the three hungry, thirsty, and tired boys are let in. At last, after all the waiting, they have
succeeded and are accepted into the great temple. Or so they think.

The master brings them into a warm room and sets three cups of hot
tea in front of them. Immediately, the cold, hungry, tired, and thirsty boys
gulp down the long awaited cups of glorious tea—except for Kwai Chang
Kane. Exhibiting a discipline and restraint far beyond his years, the cold,
tired, and thirsty Kane politely waits for the master's permission. Kane's two
companions are eventually led out, never to return; Kane is accepted into
the prestigious monastery.

This story has affected my whole life. As far back as I can remember, I
wanted to be Kwai Chang Kane. I deeply desired to find the great master, the
great teacher, to train me for life: "To always expect the unexpected," to have
worked harder than ever I thought possible, to gain all the skills to make me

a master of life and, finally, to "snatch the pebble" from his hand when it was my time to leave. How hungry I was to learn. Where was this master?

I will break the silence soon and am looking for just the right place in this precious time to introduce myself. But I will try to hold the quiet an additional moment or two longer.

Thirteen and fourteen years old may arguably be the most difficult era of life. During this period in my life, my family moved from the exurbs to a small town that was in the process of becoming industrialized. The backdrop of my childhood was to continuously observe the beauty of the open woodlands around my home being torn up, burned, and converted into pavement and buildings. Then there was a new school to contend with. The first day, first hour, first minute of which was as an unpleasant experience as I can remember. When the bus stopped at my house to pick me up and I boarded, it was full of students. I asked several to let me sit in their seats, but all refused. The bus driver couldn't move the bus until I was seated. She repeatedly asked me to sit down until finally she was yelling. I had heard of the saying "between a rock and a hard place" before, but I had never understood it to the extent that I did that morning. With no place to go and completely overwhelmed, I began to cry; twelve-year-old guys don't ever cry.

Even at that age, I was aware that I was making an important first impression at school. The students on the bus laughed at me as I struggled to hold back the torrent of tears and prayed for a crumb of grace. The bus driver yelled even louder. Finally, someone—I don't remember who...yes, I do— she was, what I would later find out, the toughest girl in the school—made some kids slide over in her seat so that I could sit down. I felt like the hunchback of Notre Dame when the beautiful Esmeralda ignored the taunting mob and brought the parched Quasi Moto water. When he is released from the stockade, he goes to the bell tower and ecstatically shouts out, "She gave me water! Water! She gave me water!" She gave me space to sit.

Thus I arrived at my first day in the new school completely humiliated. Although traumatic, this experience left no lasting scar. The same cannot be said for my three minute talk from eighth-grade English.

The time is now. Like an early morning plunge into a chilly Vermont lake, I jump in: "Good morning! My name is Mr. French!"

Sitting in the back of a plane, the four of us barely knew each other. We had trained for eight hours and were keenly aware of every possible thing that could go wrong, and at one time or another—had gone fatally wrong.

I drew number two. Though I'd thought I was not too bothered by heights, I was definitely wrong. Jeff was not coming back. And, now, my turn. I couldn't get the door open. The pilot looked at me with that come-on-already, you're-gonna-go-sooner-or-later look. Then he leaned over, flicked the door handle, opened it up, and ordered me to stand on the peg. Just like Jeff before me, I climbed out the door and was gone, never to return.

The first thing you're supposed to do when the chute opens is check to make sure the lines aren't tangled. You could be falling faster than you realize and hit the ground much harder than anticipated. But the day was too beautiful to check lines: clear sky, warm, and miles upon miles of visibility. How glorious it was just to hang there, with no other sound but the wind, suspended from the heavens like a god.

"What did I just do?"

My mom and I used to practice magic tricks. We started simply with one of my favorite tricks, "The French Drop." I liked it not only because of the family name in the title, but because it was sleight of hand: a trick without tricks. Those were always my favorite; they were more real; they relied on practiced skill; they had integrity.

Mom, on the other hand, liked the elaborate set-ups. She would take days building and preparing secret compartments for a trick that she had read about in "Magic Magazine." Looking back on it now, I think she wanted me to be some sort of magical entertainer. My mom loved the movie, "Houdini," and it is still etched in my memory, especially the end, where he coughs up blood from the combination of being unexpectedly punched in the stomach by a fan and, unbeknownst to him, appendicitis. I used to let people punch me in the stomach, and later, I even contracted appendicitis.

"What did I just do? Would anyone like to guess?" My students look at each other with uncomfortable smiles. I stand quietly again before them, letting a thoughtful silence settle over them, encouraging them to search for an answer.

I was terrified of the day I would have to give my Three-Minute Talk— only three minutes. But my teacher had emphasized that three minutes can be a very long time in front of the class, and that we needed to prepare very thoroughly for it. The subject of our talk could be anything we wanted. I decided on magic.

When the dreaded time for my turn came, I vowed to, as always, give it my best shot. I read from my note cards and performed a few tricks. Two of the tricks were made by my mom, with hidden compartments and support wires, which I knew I would not be able to conceal from the class, and I said so in my presentation.

Two minutes and twenty-three seconds later, I finished. After a lengthy pause, my teacher began by saying, "You just stood there for two minutes and twenty-three seconds mumbling about why we shouldn't like your presentation." Pause. "That was ridiculous. Give me ten." He was also the junior high basketball coach.

"What?"

"Make it twenty."

"Now?"

"If you don't give me twenty-five now..."

Many of the deepest scars from growing up were the wounds from sincerely trying to do what was right and then being punished for it.

"What did I do?"

A young man in the back corner of the room raises his hand timidly but with a hint of a smirk.

"You said, 'Hello."

"Yes! Excellent! I said, 'Hello!'"

How old were Romeo and Juliet when they fell in love, thirteen or fourteen? Not yet old enough to drive a car, bikes are freedom at this age. I spent hours riding around the trails, woods, and back-roads of our town, sometimes with my younger brother or a friend, but mostly alone. I was new to the area and there were lots of new things to see.

Some kids even have horses, but I had never known anyone personally that did. Yet, on this fateful day, I would. I was riding up a hill on a new road, and as I crested the top, I saw someone riding a horse. As I approached, I saw she had long jet-black straight hair. I didn't want to startle the horse so I gave a wide berth to pass, glancing back to say hello. And there it is.

You never know when or where it will strike, usually when you are not looking for it and you least expect it. Young teenagers are especially conductive to its life altering force. I couldn't stop thinking about her. I had only said hello. I began riding my bike every day in that same area desperately hoping to catch just one more glimpse of her.

One day, I saw her on her horse, and after she assured me that the horse wouldn't spook, we began to talk as we rode, she on her horse and me on my bike. It was glorious! This magnificent being was spending time with me! I was filled with all kinds of powerful emotions that encouraged me to do things that I normally would never do, like register to take German during my eighth-grade year. She wouldn't even be in the class, but it was a class that *she* had taken. Now, I would have to choose between woodshop and metal fabrication for my other elective. Additionally, I signed up for cross-country, although I hated long distance running and had therefore, never ran longer than a lap around the track. That girl with the black hair on the horse inspired me to do many right and good things. Under this trance of love, we created a list of three things we wanted to accomplish in our lives: graduate from college (no small feat since no one in my family, on either side, had done so); run an Ironman triathlon (I ran a smaller version called a Tin-man when I was a sophomore in college); and write a book, which I didn't think I would ever accomplish, but as I write this now...

"A first impression is important! What makes a good introduction?"

My new students already seem more focused, and since I was so enthusiastic about the answer to the first question, they are beginning to open up. A student with braces, pony tail, and a sharp glint in her eye raises her hand.

"Yes, ma'am, what do you like when someone introduces himself to you?"

"To look me in the eye."

"Excellent! Yes! Good eye contact." I then mimic meeting someone, mumbling hello while looking at the ground and giving no eye contact.

Laughter.

My parents accepted C's on my report card. D's were the warning signal. A's and B's were great, if they happened to show up. My dad remains ambiguous about the value of education. He's old-school: a self taught, take responsibility, get-the-job-done, and skeptical-of-professionals kind of man. He believes, without question, he can do anything he puts his mind to better than the next guy.

During most of my youth, dad was superintendent of greens at a private country club. Ever since I turned fourteen, the legal working age in Ohio, I worked my summers on the golf course. Much of the work was menial and mindless. For example, when I started my first assignment, I was to trim around every tree on the course, up one fairway and down the next. Some days I would finish a couple of fairways; other days, I would finish only part of one, depending on the number of trees, bushes, and small objects like fences and the sprinkler control boxes. And by the time I finished all eighteen holes, it would be time to start again.

The older and more experienced I became, the more the tasks became varied and interesting. One summer, I was in charge of sand traps—big holes with sand in them. Or so I thought. When it rained the sand would wash down from the top sides of the trap to a big pile in the bottom. I and my crew would head out and put some sand back to the tops.

One day, I was finishing up a trap near the eighteenth hole, when my dad came over and observed what I was doing. He was not happy. "Making beautiful traps is an art; there is an art to everything, even digging ditches." And I knew he believed it. "The finished trap needs to be like a bowl. Sand must flow from all sides gracefully and blend smoothly into each other, leaving an equal amount of sand throughout." I picked up the shovel and began moving the sand, not really seeing what he meant.

There was yet another art form I needed to learn first—proper shoveling. That day I watched my dad, the boss, come down into the sand trap, wearing a board-meeting suit, and show me how to correctly grasp the shovel and throw sand efficiently. He made it seem effortlessly efficient, throwing twice as much sand accurately to where it needed to be with much less time and effort. There was definitely a reason he was the boss.

Somewhere inside there is a powerful yearning to know. How many simple things do I take for granted? A student who appears to be insubordinate or insolent may, simply, have never been shown.

"What next? Good eye contact and?" No pause.

"A handshake," says a bright-eyed, mischievous girl from the back.

"What kind of handshake?"

A guy in the front who has been trying to show everyone that he is not paying attention speaks out sharply: "What do you mean what kind of handshake? A handshake's a handshake and that's that!"

"Would you please step up here for a moment?"

Thinking he is in some kind of trouble for suddenly speaking out, "I don't want to."

Before I can assure him that he is not in trouble, the girl from the back steps up. As she arrives at the front of the class, I look at the floor, reach out a very weak and limp looking hand, and mumble a good morning to the floor.

"Have you ever had that happen to you? It's the worst! What do you think? What's a better way?"

After we come up with ideas as a class, we narrow them down to four important steps to a good introduction: eye contact, firm handshake, speak clearly, and listen—really listen—to the other person.

I had walked past the college auditorium twice yesterday, once pacing for almost half an hour, a great fear mixed with a great desire. Today is the final day—do or die. This is the time I have been waiting for.

Mostly, I got into college because of a generous scholarship. Yet there were so many who helped me along the way, like the teacher who said I would be successful some day, the girl who inspired me to take German, and the guidance counselor who worked with me to turn my academic direction from the industrial arts into college prep during my junior year because I had panicked and had thought that if I didn't change my direction drastically, I would be trapped forever in my small dysfunctional town with limited options.

I suppose many of my teachers thought that I shouldn't go to college, especially an expensive liberal arts school, since my grades were just a little better than average. My acceptance into the school hinged more on entrance interviews and recommendations than on GPA and tests. In addition, I had to agree to take a remedial English course as well.

I knew little about what college was about, what studying something meant. It didn't seem legitimate. You didn't dig anything, build or fix anything, or physically accomplish anything at all. What did it mean to major in literature, philosophy, psychology, or sociology? I had no idea. On the other hand, something about the whole thing was enormously exciting, an adventure that somehow felt right.

There is a reason my college is known to be a "teaching school." I never knew anything like it before: high quality people completely dedicated to their students' success. The student to teacher ratio might have been bigger, but it felt like ten to one. Often students were invited to dinner, or to professors' homes, or on walks, and I am forever grateful for these professors' enthusiasm, intelligence, and depth of commitment to the success of their students.

Desperately pacing in front of the auditorium, I had read the script through two full times; it pulled me along like a sail on the wind. It's as if Ibsen had some sort of direct communication with me, and I knew—really knew—who the main character Gregors Werle was. I don't know how I knew, but I knew him inside and out. I had no college acting experience, yet I opened the door and walked in.

Many of the auditioners in the theater had head shots and several page resumes. At this time, I only knew a head shot as a good way to kill a deer with a 22 caliber rifle, and my only play had been *The Music Man* in seventh grade. Although it was my fifth year in college—all of which I spent auditing literature classes—I had no college theater experience. And today was the final day of auditions. I read for the parts of the grandfather and the friend. I did not get to read for Gregors. Although I passionately wanted the chance to perform the part, I was somewhat relieved since it would entail being on stage for most of the three-hour production.

Two weeks later, the cast list was posted. I was Gregors Werle.

"Everybody out!"

Again the stunned silence and confounded looks of "Is this guy serious? Is he for real?"

"Outside. Let's go!"

I am for real. And I'm very serious.

"One big line outside the door. One at a time. Each of you will introduce yourselves to me." Each of you . . . Individual . . . Marvelous . . . Exceptional . . . Filled with potential . . .

And I ask myself the most important question a teacher can ask: "Would I want to be a student in my own classroom?"

At least for today, I answer "Yes!"

To Be a Good Writer

Anne Smith Gleason

"To be a good writer, you should be writing every day." My heart sank at my professor's words. I certainly didn't write every day. "You should write about what you know." Again, I thought I just might be dead in the water, as I was a 40-year-old woman, back in school to be a teacher. I could write about raising four children but was sure that wasn't going to help me teach writing. "Your students should see you writing." This just wasn't a promising start. My BS in Biology was rusty and out-of-date. I only wrote occasional letters, emails and papers for college. I didn't see how my background would be useful in helping me teach writing to elementary school students. As a person who demands a lot from herself, I was worried.

The undergraduate Writing Methods class I was attending was filled with young kids (20-year-olds). Many of these students just wanted the syllabus and wanted to know what they had to do get an "A" in the class. My concern was how to teach writing. Could you teach writing?? Didn't writers have an innate burning desire to tell a story? How could you teach that? I read my own children's writing over the years and realized they were much better writers than I ever had been. I was not confident in my ability as a writer or as a teacher of writing.

This writing course proved to be pivotal in developing my attitudes toward teaching writing. The foundations laid and methods taught in that

Getting It in Writing, pages 105–113

class still form my teaching today. A critical component of the course was working with an actual student to give practical and hands-on experience in teaching writing. Each college student in the Writing Methods class was assigned a sixth grade student from a nearby elementary school. We communicated with our students by email. As the sixth grade students were assigned writing projects, they emailed their college "student teacher" their planning page, rough draft, revisions and final copy. I was assigned a student and we started emailing right away, him from school and me from home. I was required to analyze all parts of the writing assignments—everything from word choice, organization, conclusions, writing paragraphs, sentence structure, details, strong introductions, voice and audience. This seemed very murky to me. It wasn't as natural for me as teaching math or science. Those subjects would be easy to measure growth and progress. Better word choice? Voice? How would I teach and assess that??

As we began emailing back and forth, I started to understand how to communicate with my student about writing. I had strict parameters on critiquing my student's work. When analyzing my student's work, I could make one suggestion for every three positive comments. I found it difficult to find lots of good things to say about my student's rough drafts and to limit my "negative" comments. Often a writing piece barely covered the front of a loose-leaf piece of paper! I learned to be very detailed in giving advice. For example, I might write, "Can you think of another word for 'fun' in the third sentence of your third paragraph? You have used the word 'fun' three times in this piece." I had to design a rubric for each writing piece and explain it to my student. I had never even heard the word "rubric" before this class. I learned to ignore minor (and not so minor) grammatical errors and focus on the writing. By learning to give very specific feedback, tailored to one writing skill, I began to see how to growth and progress in writing could be monitored.

One challenge for me was giving comments and suggestions by email without seeing my student's reactions to my ideas. I felt like I was the blind leading the blind. One of my strengths is developing a rapport with each student. Without a face to face meeting, I had to rely on the written word. About two-thirds of the way through the course, all the college students met their sixth grade writing buddies. While awkward, it was fun to meet "my" student and it seemed that he was even more responsive to my suggestions after we had met.

In the beginning, I had no idea what to expect from a sixth grader and thought my student's writing was weak and undeveloped. As the class progressed, I realized he was bright and a better than average student. At first, my student just copied my suggestions and put them in his writing. When I brought this concern to my professor, he said I should model what

I expect in a piece of my own writing. Then my student could work on his own piece without copying my words. I felt this would be a very sophisticated skill and wasn't sure a student could see a model and apply it to his own writing. Sure enough, my student could do it. Modeling became an important part of my pedagogy.

Another challenge for me was to give concrete specific suggestions about one writing skill at a time. I was very holistic in my approach, and wanted to help with all aspects of writing in every writing piece. I learned to be very concrete and explicit in giving suggestions. Getting specific and clear feedback helped my student become a better writer. By the end of the course, my beliefs about teaching writing solidified, with only a few modifications over the past 11 years. These beliefs are to give clear expectations and directions for each writing piece, to model what I expect, to have a one-on-one conference with each student, and to create and to explain a specific rubric so students know how they will earn their grade. Because of my science background, I was very analytical and nit-picky about grammar and the structural parts of writing. It was more of my own style. Even though I had learned a lot about teaching writing, I still had a lot to learn about appreciating writing. My third graders would teach me this important lesson.

When I started teaching third grade eleven years ago, I followed the intensive model I practiced when I had one student. I expected a lot from every student. I had a one-on-one conference with every student. I wrote very specific and detailed suggestions to students. Each writing piece followed the Writing Process—brainstorm, rough draft, revise and edit, final copy. The other third grade teachers expected one good paragraph from their students, with a topic sentence, three to four detail sentences and an ending sentence. I expected two or three paragraphs! I also had children write revisions when necessary. It seems this wasn't done because it was too laborious for eight- and nine-year-olds. Truly, the way I taught writing was very laborious for me! Classroom management became an issue. When I had one sixth grade student's writing to analyze, I was able to give precise, clear directions and encouragement. The reality was that I was teaching third graders with classes ranging from twenty to twenty-four students. I had to plan what the other students would be doing while I was conferencing with a student. It never seemed to go well. Yet, while it was laborious, I felt my students improved tremendously throughout the school year and worked to their potential. Yes, I demanded a lot, but my students received a lot of support. The pedagogy that I had learned in undergraduate school felt right. I did not want to lower my expectations.

The first year I taught, I felt that teaching writing was exhausting. I taught all subjects and had an inclusion class. I was very ambitious and idealistic. I was determined that my students wouldn't suffer from my lack of experience. Every student would improve. As a result, I constantly checked with my colleagues to see what they were assigning their students in writing. Everything any other teacher assigned, my students did as well. Everything! And almost every piece of writing went through the writing process. On any given day, half the class was waiting for a conference with me. Every part of the writing process involved teaching and modeling. Brainstorming was a group process before they worked on their own brainstorming. I made a different graphic organizer for each writing piece. Before they could write a rough draft, I had to teach them how to use loose-leaf paper. Most of my students came to third grade knowing how to circle words they thought were misspelled. Revising and editing were foreign concepts. They were stunned when I asked them to rewrite something. Final copies were tricky as well, because of using loose-leaf paper. One of the most challenging concepts to teach was paragraphing. Not a single student knew what a paragraph was—in their own writing or in stories they were reading. My students had never heard the word rubric. I taught a lesson on what a rubric was and how to use one. Peer editing was a new process; again, a lesson and modeling on peer editing. Most third grade students knew how to alphabetize but couldn't use the dictionary. That was another lesson.

I encouraged, praised, and made suggestions. I made charts with the children's names on them to keep track of where each student was in the writing process. I asked other teachers how they managed writing in their classroom, and they said it was difficult. One suggestion I heard was to have the students read their independent books while waiting for conferences. I immediately put that into practice but wasn't satisfied with that as a solution. It seemed my top students, who already were the better readers and writers, had more time to read than my weaker readers, who needed to read more but never had the time. As that time, my school district's writing curriculum included general outcomes but didn't delineate specific writing assignments children should master or develop. As the year progressed, my students really did improve in writing, despite my frustrations.

I constantly evaluated my classroom techniques. Was I clear in what I expected? Did I expect too much? Did I give too much help? I didn't have any major insights. I didn't know or trust any other way to teach writing. And as I taught all content areas, I was going through the same evaluation process towards all my teaching. My first year of teaching ended in a whirl of energy, and I started graduate school that summer.

My first year was also tough because I didn't know the routine of a public school. I had never done any student teaching or substitute teaching. I had never seen a Teacher Manual in any content area. I had taught preschool part-time for ten years. As a preschool teacher, I felt like a fraud because my college degree was in science and I had no educational background. In order to feel more professional and less like a mom who was good at managing children, I attended many seminars and workshops. The job grew into a five-day-a-week job—a part-time preschool teacher and part-time director of the preschool. I began to read books about teaching preschoolers. I learned what prewriting skills my preschoolers needed. Preschool hours were short, with two and a half hours per session. After ten years in this environment, I was truly terrified when I was hired to teach third grade. I was hired immediately upon receiving my teaching certificate. I walked into my classroom for the first time in July to get my room ready for September. The only things in my room were a teacher's desk and chair. That was it. I went home and told my husband that they hired the wrong person because there weren't any books, pencils, manuals, desks, chairs, chalk . . . nothing. I didn't even know where to start. I reminded myself that I didn't know how to be a preschool teacher and ended up doing a good job at that, so I could definitely do this.

During my second year of teaching, writing was still the most difficult content area to teach. Science and math seemed easier to teach than reading and writing. Math and science are concrete—"hard" sciences—objective facts and data. I was naturally interested in these subjects, as well as social studies. I am a voracious reader, yet it was my weakest subject in high school. I didn't do well with inferential thinking or understanding metaphors or allegories. Creative writing? I couldn't do it at all. I didn't have stories waiting to be written floating around in my head. Poems? No way. For some reason, I always associated "writing" with creative writing. I discounted technical writing, essay writing, letter writing, or any nonfiction writing as real writing. Where did this bias come from?? I started working on my Master's degree in Curriculum and Instruction. I would not be a specialist in Literacy. I felt that teaching Reading and Writing was amorphous and too subjective, and I was never sure that what I was doing was the best way to teach these subjects.

As I continued to teach third grade, I monitored my expectations for writing. I started to learn that not every piece of writing had to go through the writing process. Each piece of writing that went through the writing process took approximately two weeks. Friendly letters and journal reflections didn't have to go through this process. I added "quick writes" to my curriculum. Quick writes were three to four minute writing pieces in response to a prompt. I usually connected the quick write to another content area. Sometimes, quick writes would be summaries of what the students had just learned. Other times, quick writes would be predictions about what a story would be about. I also added a mailbox to my classroom. Any student could write to me and I would write back. The students loved getting hand written notes from me and I could model sentence structure, word choice and spelling. Another part of writing was writing in response to reading. Students come to third grade barely writing in complete sentences. By the end of third grade, students are expected to write answers to comprehension questions in complete sentences and use details to support their answers. Teaching students how to write this type of answer was an ongoing process. I taught students how to restate questions, how to answer all parts of the question, and use specifics from the story to support an answer.

The longer I taught, the more I began to realize *all* writing is writing. I know, it seems obvious, but I thought only the writing assignments that went through the writing process were "real" writing. I was compartmentalizing writing into a rigid box, despite the fact that my students were writing all day long, and in all content areas. I was trying too hard.

I decided that I would use a more global approach to writing. My writing curriculum would include: writing process pieces, less formal pieces, writing for enjoyment, free choice writing, poetry writing, writing in response to reading, journal writing and writing in content areas. I would work on classroom management techniques during student conferencing times.

By my fifth or sixth year of teaching, classroom management during conference time, while remaining a challenge, became more routine. I was clear in my expectations in what waiting students would be doing. Often students had choices. I listed what students should be doing on the board. Some of their choices included: work on a creative writing piece of your choice, finish corrections, write a letter, finish other work, or read. Included in my literacy program are two activities that students can work on any time they have free time: Reading Response Journals and Reader's Workshop. Reader's Workshop is a three-to-four week assignment that children complete independently. Each Reader's Workshop centers around a genre such as mysteries, biographies, or nonfiction. I pick out books from all reading levels. The students read a required number of books and then complete a different activity for each book. All activities involve writing and work on applying reading strategies. Reading Response Journals are letters students write to me about a self-selected book. Every two to three weeks, students are required to hand in a letter to me, following a "recipe"—four paragraphs which must include narrative elements, connections, thinking and predictions. I write back to each student. With all this in place, classroom management has become easier. Another activity students can work on during writing/waiting time is their "Book Talks." Students read a self-selected book and write a quick summary, read a paragraph from their book to the class and design and draw a book cover for their book. They then think of two open-ended questions to ask the class. This activity is many students' favorite independent work. I usually introduce book talks in the spring, after the other parts of independent work are well established. Do students still talk too much or lose focus during this time? Yes, but re-direction is easier and expectations are clear. There are plenty of writing/reading activities to keep students engaged and writing during the time they have to wait for a one-on-one conference.

Another area of growth for me as a teacher is in modeling. When I started, I would model the whole writing process. I learned to be careful in what I modeled, because students used my ideas in their own writing. Now, students are not allowed to use my ideas in their own writing. As time went on, I began sharing my thinking and brainstorming processes by talking out loud. I would write on the board. For each writing process assignment, I start a rough draft—cross out words, add words, ask for suggestions from the students, and write quickly and messily. Students soon recognized when I was thinking. I asked my class how they know when I am thinking and they've said that I "get a look in my eyes," I "stare," I get "very excited," and I "stop talking for a minute." I want my students to feel excited about the creative process of writing and hopefully I model that for them. I now have a "wired" classroom, a SmartBoard, and an Elmo, which makes it much easier to share my writing and show how I change my writing as I go along. I usually model the beginning to every writing assignment, but don't always model a piece to completion. I found that my enthusiasm helps most students get started on their own writing. They didn't need to see my finished product. Also, my model can limit students' thinking because students who are very procedure oriented will try to make their writing like mine. Occasionally, I have a student model for them from the basal reading series I use. If a writing assignment lends itself to a specific procedure, I make a "recipe" that the children can follow to meet the minimum requirements for the piece. Using one or more of these techniques seems to be effective in motivating students to write, as well as teaching them what I expect.

My students have taught me many things. Length was not a measure of quality writing. My first few years, I was thrilled with lengthy pieces. I was teaching eight- and nine-year-olds and assumed that anything more than a paragraph was excellent. As I became more discerning, I realized that many longer pieces written by this age group tended to be very list-like, simple and declarative. And while well written, sometimes these pieces lacked voice. And then I'd read a shorter work, and sometimes, just sometimes, it would be filled with voice, charm and personality. Something else I learned from my students was not to limit their creativity with too many directions and too much modeling. I learned to let them know what I expect, brainstorm whole group, model the beginning, and let them write. I also came to understand that I couldn't predict who would enjoy writing. There have been many times over the years when students with learning disabilities in reading would enjoy writing. Just because they couldn't read on grade level, didn't mean they didn't have ideas for writing in their head. And every so often, a student would write something so profound, sweet, or insightful that it would move me tears. This taught me not to assume anything about a student. Students' personalities are not predictors of good writing. For students with good verbal-linguistic skills, writing can be the best way for them to communicate their ideas.

One basic lesson I had to learn was not to conference with a student so much that I practically wrote the assignment. Because I wanted all students to do well, I would help students with poorly written rough drafts—a lot. It was then hard to assess the student's final copy fairly because I had helped so extensively. As time went on, I began assessing student's rough drafts or revisions and graded them. This is a practice I continue even now. My students understand that I grade their rough drafts or revisions because final copies are the corrected versions of their writing that they write after conferencing with me.

Assessing writing can be difficult. To take the subjectivity out of assessing, I have students grade themselves on a rubric. Each rubric is specific to that writing assignment and to the skills I'm grading. I grade them on the same rubric. Quite often, students are either way too hard on themselves or, conversely, way too easy. My goal is to introduce the concept of self-assessing and being reflective, as most third grade students are not sophisticated enough to really assess themselves. I feel much of what I teach in writing works at building a strong foundation that students will build on as they mature. I have tried peer editing on and off through my eleven years teaching third grade. Students really enjoy peer editing (they get a special pen to use), but I haven't found it to be a very effective technique for improving writing, as the students mostly correct each other's spelling. The students enjoy peer editing (they feel important) and we use this technique a few times a school year. I save all final copies of everything my students write and return them at the end of the school year. They are astonished to see how much their writing has improved since the beginning of the year.

I continue to be holistic in my approach to teaching writing. Because third graders are just starting to write, I usually don't focus on one skill. Students come in September with limited writing ability, often only able to write two or three sentences. There just isn't enough length to their writing to pick it apart and work on specific skills. Some examples would include word choice, lead, voice, length, and topic sentence. Instead I focus on the assignment such as persuasive paragraph, descriptive paragraph, poetry, or letter and work on teaching the form. I teach specific skills, whole group, as they come up. I can also work on specific skills during one-on-one conferences. This approach individualizes my instruction, as I can work on very specific skills with my more mature writers and basic skills with my students who are at a more basic level. However, all levels of writers are responsible for writing the assignment.

A word (or two!) about punctuation—I focus on punctuation in all daily writing but not in rough drafts of writing assignments. Every day my students correct two incorrectly written sentences that are on the board. The sentences have mistakes in spelling words of the week and in the punctuation skill we are working on. I collect the paper at the end of the week and get three grades from that one paper—a spelling grade, a language art grade and a handwriting grade. The class practices specific punctuation skills on worksheets. As I conference with students on their rough drafts, I will work on punctuation skills for that person. If I find a lot of students making the same kinds of punctuation errors, then I will do a mini-lesson on that error.

While teaching writing continues to be "messier" than teaching the other content areas, I have learned to relax and trust the process. I have also learned to trust my students. Seeing students improve in writing from September through June is very gratifying. The simplicity and honesty of eight and nine year olds continues to bring joy to me professionally as well as personally.

My Quest from Personal Journals to Non-Fiction Extravaganza

Kim Kendrick

Bookmark

"Where do you put your bookmark, Mom, where you've already read or where you will start reading?" This was one of many questions proposed by my daughter, Julianne, a first grader who has fallen in love with the printed word this year and writes in her journals every night. Yes, I said journals. She has possession of three. One is her personal that I'm not allowed to read and another is laid on my nightstand when she is finished. It is passed back and forth, growing in maturity as fast as her vocabulary. Her third one is for drawings of her day. My favorite is the one we share between the two of us. When I respond, I use several of her misspelled words. She then reads it back to me before she writes back.

Dear Diary

My first memory of writing was in the sixth grade when I began writing in my five inch by five inch five-year diary. I loved this diary and still have it today. Each page was divided into five sections. It began January 1, 1972

Getting It in Writing, pages 115–122

thru January 1, 1976 on the first page and ended with December 31, 1972 thru December 31, 1976 on the last page. Each section on each page was one inch by five inches in size. It was heart wrenching to try to squeeze all my thoughts over an entire day into this miniature space, but being the rule follower that I was, I tried to write as small as possible. Eventually, I just couldn't stand it, so I cheated and stole space from the next day, and so on, completing an entire year by May. This broke my heart. When I share this story with my students, looking into their solemn faces, I promise I will never limit their journal space. Cheers, raised fists and high-fives fill the air.

Classroom Journals

Our classroom journals consist of three. One is our Personal Journal in which we write about anything we want, but their all time favorite activity is "Magazine Day." Parents help me tear out all mature advertising before we begin. Magazines are spread out on the floor as students get their scissors, glue sticks, markers, and pencils ready. Writers cut pictures from the magazines and attach to their journals followed by their thoughts. One of my favorites is the picture of high heels joined by a list of the ten best reasons to own a pair of high heels.

Another is our Starting Points Journal. My personal favorite. We write in these with a lead, sentence starter, or picture prompt. In the book *Hatchet* by Gary Paulsen (2006), Brian has many "First Days" as he recalls them. We come up with some of our own: first accident; first experience with a loss of pet, family member, place, or thing; first purse/wallet; first favorite cereal; first bike; first smell of baking cookies; first time being patient, or not being patient.

The third is our Reading Response Journal. This stays with us when we read. We use these to record sparkle words from our stories, cool passages or phrases, or an interesting plot or character quality: personality, appearance, likes/hobbies, or dislikes. Journals are a great way to get to know shy students. Even low kids can draw pictures in their journals to compliment their writing.

Personal Letters

My second memory of writing was when I experienced a loss. When I was 30 years old my dad passed away due to a sudden heart attack. Nature did not allow me to say my good-bye, so it was imperative for me to write him a letter. For three days, I wrote. On the day of his funeral as I sat next to his coffin writing as fast as my fingers could move (void of all punctuation if I remember correctly), someone brought me a chair and told me they needed to take him away soon. I told them not until my letter was finished. My sweat was dripping down my forehead joining the tears on my cheeks. I could no longer feel my fingers. Finishing before they took him away was a must, so I pressed on (doubting now that it was readable by anybody but him). When finally finished, I shoved it into the layers of fabric where no one else could find it. It was finished. I shared all my regrets, apologies, and praises that I couldn't open my mouth and share with him even through prayer without an audible blubbery bawl that made no sense to even me. During other times of sadness, I have written letters that I never sent. I threw them away. Just writing them helped me work through my feelings. Because of this experience, on occasion I give my students journal leads pertaining to a loss or a regret. A mini lesson could include a picture book to prompt memories of their own. In this way, your students may gain closure just as I did.

Personal Journals

After my dad passed away, I began writing in a journal and felt so successful that I numbered my journals on the back. They had to be spiral bound, so they laid flat. This attempt to gain some sense of who I was and where I was going lead to my first writing survival kit in an organized area on my nightstand right next to my pile of reading material. My writing survival kit included mechanical pencils, markers, pens, stickers, tape (now glue stick), and magazines. This entire bedtime routine took about an hour.

Refracting Light

As Abigail Thomas (2008) writes, "we do better when we're not trying too hard—there is nothing more deadening to creativity than the grim determination to write" (p. 5). This leads me to the gloomy reality of having to teach the dreaded research paper. "Non-fiction Extravaganza" is how we kick this off.

I begin by pointing out that even fiction has evidence of research to make it more believable. In chapter 13 of *Hatchet,* Brian tries desperately to spear fish in the lake and continues to miss until he remembers a science lesson on refracting light to help him master this task. Without this detail, many realistic animal conflicts and hunting for edible food, this story would lack realism that makes it an award-winning novel.

There are so many interesting people, places, and things to read about. I know a lot of people who have either been on a vacation or wanted to go on one, or has a sweet memory of a person, place, or thing. There you go—another journal topic to kick off your research paper.

My non-fiction section of my library is separated out, books and magazines, and then charts for each class are displayed on the wall. Small one-centimeter horizontal squares are across from each researcher's name. They are on a mission to read as many non-fiction books as possible in three weeks during our reading workshop time, as well as at home.

Five different types of book report forms are set out for them to choose from. Some are better for biographies, some for memoirs, and some for science/history books. As they turn in their reports, I pass out two to four stickers per report as I glance over the detail, occasionally asking my students questions. They place these stickers on their chart by their names.

Finally, each child has a Research Portfolio, a collection of various research ideas to last them several years. To make things interesting, I require my researchers to choose one topic from their Research Portfolio that deserves to be on a U.S. postage stamp, design a new stamp, add USA and current postage rate, and tell me why this person, place, or thing deserves to be on a stamp using two additional resources (three in all) and a minimum of three paragraphs in block form or indented paragraph form. Papers will include an introduction, topic sentences with supporting detail, and finally a concluding paragraph. An outline is provided. I act excited about these new stamps and show the kids how I will display them. Their reaction to the assignment is positive.

The once dreaded research paper is now a stimulating writing activity even for my low readers. Copies of their final papers and stamps are placed in clear views in a class three-ring binder and housed in our classroom library.

Addressing Fear

My most recent personal writing experience (other than grant writing) was when I was invited to attend the Northwest Arkansas Writing Project with Dr. Samuel Totten at the University of Arkansas in Fayetteville. My journey was an opportunity for me to advance from journal writing to other genres. Most importantly, I was given time to become one with my writing, just as Brian from *Hatchet* became one with nature. Brian recalls one of his teacher's words of wisdom, "You are your most valuable asset." I learned that every student, no matter how few experiences they feel they have had, have enough rich writing material right within themselves if they know where to look. Brian held onto these words as he survived the plane crash alone in the Canadian wilderness. He found out fear can be helpful and harmful as did I that summer. Helpful because it helped me realize that my weaknesses and fears could be some of my best writing material. Fear can also be harmful when I allow it to paralyze me. Self-doubt can take over. Here are a few of my personal favorites: "Why did I think I could do this?" "Who was I kidding?" "I don't have time for this." "Who really cares what I do or have done?" By reaching out to our students at an early age, we can rescue them from these words of self-pity. My most cherished "gold nugget" I took with me from my Writing Project experience is to write with my students. I sit up higher than them, so they can all see me writing. I often write on overhead transparency paper, so they can see how I draw lines through unnecessary information instead of erasing it and insert sparkle words. After I share my draft, I ask them for help on the lead and closing. I let them see how I morph their ideas into my own paper.

Note to Self

In *Hatchet*, Brian keeps mental notes because he has no other way to record his experiences, and even in his dire situation, he knew it was important for him to remember. I model for my students how to jot notes to self when they hear or see something memorable, even if they have to scribble on a napkin. I personally bring the napkin in and tape it to my journal right in front of them. Brian has flash backs during his adventure. I refer to this as memoir, modeling for these young writers that our memories are jumping off points for other genres. By taking the "Ten Best Reasons to Own a Pair of High Heels" and turning it into poetry, they are able to see this evolution right before their eyes.

Virtues

Willpower, patience, hope, courage, and trust are the virtues that saved Brian's life. These are ingredients to the recipe of life as a writer. Willpower is necessary because it takes discipline to make time to write. Patience because sometimes you're on a roll and other times you draw a blank. Kids need to be given hope and hear about your experiences or an author's experiences with this, so they don't quit or give up. Brian explored new terrain, which was extremely uncomfortable for him, but it was how he learned to connect with nature that he felt reborn as the new Brian. It is through experiencing courage with various writing experiences—some successes and some we consider failures—that eventually gives us that confidence we want for all of our students. When Brian had to land the plane with no previous flying lessons, so too will our students be asked to write on topics or in genre they don't have previous experience with, but through picture books, personal stories by us or their peers, and novels, we can build their confidence, so they feel capable rather than incapable. It is through trust in their teacher that they will allow themselves to put words on paper, conference with him or her, and produce a piece they are proud of. Their first draft like Brian's plane may crash and sink, but their experiences in polishing the pieces will layer to build a stronger writer in the end.

Visualization

In Writer's Workshop, picture an item from a story—draw it if you can, or ask a student to, and then link parts of it with your lesson. For example: Brian's hatchet, his only tool, is made of steel (a strong material) with a rubber handgrip and attaches to his belt. While reading this novel, I hung a diagram of this hatchet on our classroom wall. Next to the steel part, I put "Compliments." Next to the rubber handle, I put "Don't throw anything away." Next to the belt loop hook, I put "We won't let you fall." In order to gain their trust, I model how to ask questions during writing conferences and give specific compliments. I choose what I call "gold nuggets" from their pieces, place them on overhead transparencies and share these well-written sentences or passages with the class. These compliments make my writers strong like steel. Like the rubber handgrip, which helps the hatchet not fly loose when it is swung, I ask them not to give up on a piece of writing and not throw it away. Instead, I ask them to set it aside if they need to. They may decide to come back to it later. Finally, like the hatchet's belt loop hook, I let them know that they can rely on myself and their classmates to hold on tight to them and not let them fail/fall.

For Vocabulary Building I use 3-column notes: 1. Write word. 2. Use it in a sentence. 3. Draw a picture or symbol, which will help them remember its meaning. I do this activity using my overhead projector, so the kids can follow along. Vocabulary words are chosen from our stories, so they see or hear them in context. For difficult words, post them around the room along with several students' pictures. Cartoons are another way for students to remember new words. Ask a volunteer to draw a single cartoon in a square demonstrating the meaning of the word. Copy it to transparency paper, and show the class. Then post it in the classroom. Use your Word Wall space if you have one.

Get Motivated

To fight depression, Brian would tell himself to get motivated. I tell the kids that this is our job as a team. I motivate them, and they motivate each other. Brian also recalls using positive self-talk at crucial moments to survive, so I make sure the kids are given time to compliment their own work aloud or in writing by asking, "What do you like best about this piece?" A favorite book of mine that I have reread more than any other book is called *How to Talk so Kids will Listen . . . and How to Listen so Kids will Talk* by Adele Faber and Elaine Mazlish (1999). When conferencing with young writers, I use the methods shared in this book. I repeat back what they wrote in order to gain more detail. "So you were afraid?" They always respond with more detail that can be used to replace the word afraid in their writing. When they write on every other line it is so much easier for them to add information. By modeling, I'm able to show them how important it is to listen to each other and their environment. "Don't Touch that Pencil!" is an exercise in which they verbally share their ideas to a writing prompt and listen to each other. I, too, enjoy sharing my personal experiences. Having taught in many different environments from Hawaii to the country to inner city to a children's shelter, I share stories and books that include settings much different from their own, to broaden their background knowledge.

Naturalist

Inspired by my son, Jacob, who enjoys the outdoors as much as I do, My Nature Journal was designed for children with the most overlooked intelligence of all the multiple intelligences—the naturalist—the child who is out digging in dirt for bugs during recess. It is designed to be carried in an outdoor type of bag with pencils, various kinds of paper, markers, binoculars (I purchase these from Oriental Trading Company), and a book of ideas for writing topics in the great outdoors, in backyards, front yards, porches, patios, in tree houses, on swing sets, in trees, over ant hills, in garden. It is passed on from child to child. The more you have, the quicker each child will get to take one home for the night. We leave no stone unturned in our outdoor writing classroom.

Bookmarks

My quest to becoming a master writing teacher begins and ends with me being a writer myself. Not a perfect or even great writer, but one who enjoys the craft or art of writing. One who recognizes writing as work and as a process in which mastery requires willpower, patience, hope, courage, and trust. I encourage all of you to become writers and readers with your students and place your bookmark behind your reading or in front of it, wherever you choose.

References

Faber, A. & Mazlish, E. (1999). *How to talk so kids will listen . . . and how to listen so kids will talk.* New York: Harper Collins.

Paulsen, G. (2006). *Hatchet.* Riverside, NJ: Simon & Schuster.

Thomas, A. (2008). *Thinking about memoir.* New York: Sterling.

Revolution and Evolution

My Career as Writer and Teacher

Sharla Keen-Mills

When I was three or four years old, there was a drawer in the kitchen filled with lined stenographer pads, pieces of deckled letter paper, yellow legal pads, and Big Chief tablets that, along with a variety of pens and pencils, most stamped with the logos of hardware stores, gas stations, and insurance companies, made up our household writing supplies. My contribution was a box of 64 Crayola crayons and a variety of stubby colored pencils. My love of pen and paper probably started when I did tracings on the variety of papers in that drawer. Even at age four, I was fascinated by the handwriting of both of my parents; I thought it was artistic and beautiful. Ever the bossy little princess, I demanded to be taught how to write. To satisfy me, my mother wrote my name several times on a sheet of paper in pencil, then I traced the words in pen. She provided me with page after page of family and pet names, addresses, and nursery rhymes to trace. At the bottom of each page was space for me to try the letters and words on my own.

I have no idea how my first grade teacher handled a student who wrote cursive letters before learning to print, but I do remember enjoying making the large rounded Zaner-Bloser alphabet on multiple-lined writing tablets with a fat red pencil. Perky Mrs. Hall, dressed in straight wool skirts and

Getting It in Writing, pages 123–144
Copyright © 2011 by Information Age Publishing

pastel cardigans, went beyond teaching me to print letters; she taught me to read, and to make up a story. I doubt we wrote much of the story down, but we learned to express a narrative. The catalyst was a life-size papier mâ-ché Shetland pony that we created in class from wood scraps, chicken wire, balloons, newspaper strips, and buckets of flour paste. The black and white Tempura painted pony came alive in our imaginations, and the first graders of Washington Elementary school told story after story with either the pony or one of us as the main character.

This experience, coupled with my father's penchant for spinning a fanciful story, especially a funny one, sparked my desire to communicate any event as either thorough or entertaining, but did I consider myself a writer? Never. Not even when I wrote stories for my junior high school newspaper and was made editor. Not even when I was standing on a stage winning an Arkansas Scholastic Press Association award for a humorous feature article I had written. I was not encouraged to write anything during my school years except for the school newspaper and sentences copied from the end of a textbook chapter along with reports summarized from encyclopedias.

Then along came a middle-aged dark-haired woman teacher whose ninth grade English class I will never forget. We spent 95% of our time diagramming sentences and underlining adverbs and prepositions from exercises in the back of a grammar book, but on a few golden days, we were encouraged to write. On one of these rare days, the teacher walked around the room at the beginning of class with photographs she'd gleaned from a variety of calendars. She handed me the image of a gray tabby kitten posed with a basket spilling out small yellow mums. I connected this photo to a Disney movie about a cat with three lives named Thomasina (Disney, 1963). I immediately began scribbling away about a cat who managed to have more than nine lives; she'd just started her tenth. It has been almost forty years since the day I held that calendar photo in my hand, but the way I felt when I wrote that day continues to fuel my need and desire to write. We did not share our writing with others in class, but I shared with friends and family, who were sufficiently impressed, but I didn't really need that. My own sense of personal satisfaction and enjoyment was enough. To my teacher's credit, I did not receive the paper back with red marks all over it, just a few words of encouragement. Shortly after this I wrote a poem during Algebra class (oh well...) that I thought was psychedelic enough to fit into my 1969 world. Even though the most exotic substance I'd imbibed by the tender age of fourteen was a Kool menthol cigarette, my poem has lines influenced by the peyote-induced lyrics of Jim Morrison and was filled with just enough teen angst and dark wishes to appeal to other adolescents. I brought my poem proudly to my English teacher, who put it up on a bulletin board of student accomplishments. For the first time, I had published something outside of the newspaper. Even if no other student took the time to read the poem, I passed it with satisfaction every day on my way out of the classroom.

I wish I could say that the English teachers that followed me through high school encouraged and guided my desire to write, but they did not. I diagrammed more sentences, labeled clauses, and tried to unravel the mysteries of comma use. I wrote a research paper on the Mayan civilization from carefully numbered index cards that I had lost interest in long before the due date. Thankfully, I had neat handwriting and was a good speller, or I would have been subjected to many more miles of red ink than I saw.

Despite this lack of encouragement at school, I wrote. I wrote reams of notes to friends at school. I kept a pink diary with a flimsy lock hidden under my mattress, and I wrote letters, hundreds of letters. Long distance phone calls were expensive and generally forbidden to me. My cousin and favorite confidante, Rhonda, lived sixty miles away, so we wrote weekly and vied with each other for the "cutest" stationery. I collected beautiful writing papers and pens the way my own children collect CDs and MP3s. Even now, the stationery aisle of any store calls to me. Rhonda's brother Herb was drafted away to Vietnam, so I always made sure I wrote to him. Onionskin envelopes with red, white, and blue air mail stickers from overseas in the mailbox were a special delight, especially since Herb was four years older than I. I wrote to guys I met when I visited Rhonda or my step sisters in their small towns. I wrote to my grandparents, great aunts, and my father who no longer lived with us. I honed my skills as a story teller and relayer of accurate information in the letters I wrote as a teen. And, unlike my e-mail files, I still have many of those letters tied with ribbons and stored at the top of my closet in a floral paper-covered box, so I can get them down on rainy days and go back to my girlhood. I wonder, do text messages and e-mails hold the same delight for today's kids as those multicolored envelopes I found in my mailbox after school each day? When I see the excited reactions of my own students to the music or chimes that alert them to their latest text messages, I tend to think so.

In college, I wrote research paper after research paper, essay after essay, *ad nauseum*, until the day came for me to provide a writing sample sufficient enough to allow me to bypass Junior English Composition. The humorous essay I wrote from the prompt "Gardens I Have Known," comparing my neighbors' personalities to their gardens and how they cared for them was the most enjoyable test I have taken. I didn't have the opportunity to actually select my own writing topic until I took an essay writing class from a professor who gave me positive comments on my writing along with suggestions for improvement. Her feedback encouraged me to continue to tinker with a piece of writing until I was satisfied with it instead of just glancing at my grade and throwing the paper away.

Unfortunately, this experience is in vivid contrast with the writing wasteland that was my teacher training. Although my teaching certification is secondary English and social studies, perhaps the most absurd aspect of my college career is the complete lack of any training whatsoever from my college of education in the teaching of writing. My methods teachers used the buzz words "writing across the curriculum," yet made no effort whatsoever to model the concept or to train me to teach writing. I had infinite opportunities to write research papers, but never on the subject of teaching writing to adolescents, never any exploration of myself as a writer.

Then I met Mona, Betsy, Rose, and Carol. I was hired over twenty years ago by Mona Briggs, a former English teacher and voracious reader of cutting-edge professional research and ideas, for my first teaching assignment: seventh-grade geography with no room of my own. The Fifties-era building was bursting with students and was under construction, so I shared quarters with three other teachers that first year. I soon learned that the building was the least important aspect of the school's reconstruction. It was 1989, and I had dropped into a milieu of reformation spearheaded by four feisty divas who put a copy of the Carnegie Council Adolescent Task Force's *Turning Points: Preparing American Youth for the 21st Century* into my hands and welcomed me into their circle of change (Carnegie Council 1989). Willingly, I followed them down a path strewn with interdisciplinary teams, writing to learn, flexible scheduling, and portfolios, my head filled with Peter Elbow, Donald Graves, and Lucy Calkins in an effort to "recapture millions of youth adrift" (Calkins, 1986; Carnegie, p. 8 ; Elbow, 1980; Elbow & Belanoff, 1981; Graves, 1983).

I had plunked myself into an atmosphere of rebellion against poor standards, minimum performance tests, and grammar worksheets. It was a heady, frustrating time filled with setbacks and recalcitrant colleagues. I learned early that teachers have to fight for what they know is best for their students. One of our biggest battles with colleagues and parents was over heterogeneous grouping. We'd read and were convinced by the work of Robert Slavin and others on the problems with ability grouping (Braddack, 1990; Mills, 1997; Slavin, 1990). *Turning Points* also recommended the grouping of middle level students heterogeneously whenever possible (Carnegie, 1989). Our administration finally allowed us to have no seventh or eighth grade ability grouped classes in all of the core subjects except mathematics as long as we differentiated instruction, which we were already doing; however, this little elitist monster continues to raise its head to this day.

After this little victory, we managed to convince some science teachers to join us, and we formed two interdisciplinary teams of English, geography, and science. Students evaluated their own work and wrote reflectively about their learning. Much of this metacognition was based on the training we had given them based on their personal learning styles. Shelves were built in a storage room to house student portfolios that would follow them to the next grade. We took over 300 seventh-graders to a zoo to study and write about biomes, created units with several differentiated levels of instruction, and even created our own award-winning economic system in our classrooms of moveable walls and blocked schedules. We were in demand as presenters on teaming, interdisciplinary instruction, and writing to learn across the state, the region, and the nation.

Even today, when I am frustrated with the lack of progress in writing instruction, I think of a presentation Betsy and I did in 1998 in a small town near Memphis. The teachers were agreeable and remarkably cooperative for a full two-day writing-to-learn inservice in August right before they had to have their rooms ready for school to begin. However, on the second day during a presentation of an interdisciplinary unit involving state history, the Civil War, and cotton production, I handed out a packet of materials and put the rubric for the unit on an overhead transparency. Just as I had started to explain the rubric, the room became instantly silent; not a paper rustled or chair squeaked. Betsy's eyes met my own anxious ones. What had we done? Had we stepped on someone's Southern sensibilities in this Mississippi Delta town whose residents still grew a little cotton along with the soybeans? Had I slipped and used an inappropriate curse word? Had my underwear fallen to my ankles? Finally, a mild-looking fortyish woman near the back of the room raised the handout I had just given her into the air and asked, "Now, did you say this is called a rubric?"

"Yes," I said, "Or you can call it a scoring guide if you wish."

"Well, Missy, this thing here is worth more than all of the workshops I've had in twenty years!" The room erupted into a discussion of this remarkable tool that actually allowed children to know how their work was to be evaluated before they even turned it in. The science and health and shop teachers who were so uncomfortable teaching and evaluating writing realized this rubric could be designed so they could actually do so with confidence.

It was 1998 and no one in this entire faculty had ever seen a rubric. Betsy and I were stunned. What kind of professional development had they been getting? Did they ever read their professional journals? Were their administrators living in caves? Under these circumstances, we would have expected stubborn resistance to anything outside rote learning, but in truth, the teachers in that small school were eager—no, starving—for better ways to teach. They knew the same-old-same-old wasn't working. They were as dissatisfied as the cadre of teachers in my school were when we started shaking things up in our district. They embraced what we had shared with them and begged us to come back and teach them more of these "new" ways of doing things that reached the upper levels of Bloom's Taxonomy.

The excitement of those Delta teachers re-energized me, but I soon learned that change and the constant battle for best practice can exhaust even the most dedicated teachers if reform is carried on their backs alone. They cannot sustain restructuring without adequate support. Our district was willing to allow flexible scheduling, but not reduced class size. Top administrators agreed to our new curriculum proposals, but would not or could not give us the paid time to write a vertically and horizontally aligned curriculum. I think Rose, Betsy, Carol, and I quit four times in as many years, our resignations ignored by Mrs. Briggs.

We soon settled into routines we could manage with limited resources, and directed our attention to Nancie Atwell's *In the Middle* (1987). We, like thousands of other teachers out there, were forced to make our "revolutionary" changes inside our classrooms behind closed doors, one student at a time. Blessed with an insightful and forward thinking English curriculum coordinator, Judy Gregson, who coordinated a study group for those of us in the district interested in better ways to teach writing and in becoming better writers ourselves, we met once a week to discuss the realities of implementing reading/writing workshops in classrooms of 25 to 30 children that met for only 45 minutes a day. One teacher in the district, in our building, managed to convince administration to let her teach three ninety-minute reading/writing workshops a day, but for the class to pass our state's scrutiny, it was English Language Arts plus Reading as an elective. In addition, she had up to 27 students in each class. Unfortunately, a new district superintendent was hired who knew about creating the fewest number of full-time equivalents (FTE's) but nothing about the research-based teaching methods we were trying to implement, and not only did the ninety-minute reading/writing workshops die, but so did our interdisciplinary teams and block schedules. Interdisciplinary student portfolios were no longer supported, their closet commandeered to hold boxes of paper. We were tiring of the fight.

Disheartened, Betsy, my co-teacher, dearest friend, and mentor, moved into the corporate world and, after just winning Arkansas Teacher of the Year and the Milken Award, Rosemary left teaching. Mona was lured away to be a principal to the children of celebrities in an exciting progressive school in the Rocky Mountains. Deeply disappointed, but refusing to give up, Carol and I stayed and were allowed to work as an eighth-grade social studies/English team with me as the English, not the social studies member as I had been before. I moved into the void left by Rosemary—no easy act to follow. Fortunately, I had Rosemary's daily support via e-mail as I tried to fill her gifted and capable shoes. Carol and I did not have blocked classes that we taught together. We each had six classes with 25 students in a class. They were scheduled so that I could keep the same 25 for two class periods for a certain time period, three weeks for example. Then we would switch students and reteach the unit we'd taught the first set of students. These blocks of time allowed my students to really dig into a writing workshop or a history project, but they still had the same amount of instructional time, not the double class periods needed for an ideal reading/writing workshop.

Nevertheless, these were my halcyon days as a writing teacher. The children and I wrote together, conferenced, and wowed their parents. I took mini-lessons and activities Rosemary had used and made them my own. Even though I had about 25 students per class, I managed to conference with my students individually at least twice as they completed a piece of writing because I had plenty of time for long workshops built around the idea that the writing process is recursive, not linear. For a song genre unit, I taught students how to "steal" someone else's music and write their own song lyrics matching the rhythm. On the day we performed our songs, parents and other family members came to sing with their children, garage bands set up in the classroom and everyone in the building felt the bass. My students and their parents beamed with pride. I had managed to begin the year working on creating a safe place for my students to write and share their writing.

I shared my own sometimes convoluted writing process with them: prewrite in the shower, forget prewriting, procrastinate, draft, edit while revising, draft some more, go back and revise, edit, find a stopping place and put the piece away for at least three days, revisit the piece, hoping for new inspiration and better organization. Finally, I make the decision to finally leave the thing alone, but some pieces call to me years later, yearning for more revision. The crafting of chunks, sentences, and words during revision is the fun part of writing for me, so I often shared this part of my messy writing business with my students in hopes my enthusiasm would be contagious. I became very close to the students I came to know during this honeymoon year as a writing teacher, and I still sorely miss them. It was the best year of my teaching career to date—the year before the barrage of standardized tests.

That year was the pilot benchmark test for our state, and my students averaged 98% on the writing part of the exam, but I quickly realized something had been missing, as they scored an average of only 73% on the reading open-response section. I had poorly integrating reading with the writing we had done. My students had written responses to literature, but I certainly hadn't taught them timed reading test strategies. Instead, I had used every available teaching day, bell to bell, just to accomplish the writing workshop. Students were encouraged to self-select their own reading, but very little class time was devoted to either the reading itself or responding to it in writing. I prided myself on writing all of my lessons and never using a text book, not even a literature book. We had learned the elements of fiction through some short stories, and I had combined the obligatory poetry unit with my song-writing workshop, but that was the extent of any reading/writing integration.

My other serious failing was teaching grammar in context. I didn't go so far as to not teach any grammar at all, but my attempts outside conferences with students were few and far between. I knew from reading Constance Weaver, George Hillocks, and others that ninety years of research has found little transfer from isolated grammar exercises to authentic writing and that teaching selected aspects of grammar in context of student's own writing is more productive (Hillocks & Smith, 1991; Weaver, 1986a, 1986b). But I constantly asked myself, "Just what is context anyway?" I understood it conceptually but not practically. I tried Atwell's individual proofreading lists for kids, but did not make them effective (Atwell, 1987). I found Don Killgallon's book on sentence composing, but discovered this to be in just as much isolation as the sentences to parse in a grammar book (Killgallon, 1987). William Strong's sentence combining looked promising, but I was never satisfied with the results and found it difficult to plan a course of lessons for the year (Strong, 1986). Once I even pulled out some grammar worksheets in the sorely misguided notion that I could make up for not teaching much grammar "in context." Fortunately, the writers of our state assessment knew enough of the research about that and students were not asked to parse sentences or identify verbals on a test. However, even that was soon to change, but for then, student control of usage and mechanics were assessed on the timed writing part of the test. My students always did very well on this, but I still didn't feel as if I'd prepared them for a discussion of adverbial clauses in high school even though I was confidant high schoolers didn't sit around at lunch asking, "How 'bout them participles?"

In addition, I had the low reading open-response scores to consider. I took what I'd learned about reading test strategies in Advanced Placement training and applied it to our state tests. I devised a sequence of strategies to help students tackle these timed test items and took three weeks of instructional time for students to apply and practice them. By this time I had been made English department chair for our building, so I taught the strategies to the other teachers in my building. The results were three-fold: our building had the highest literacy test scores in the state, I found myself to be a district trainer for the state tests I despised so much, and the beloved song unit was replaced by test writing practice. I struggled balancing product and process writing because during the state Benchmark tests students write in an artificial timed situation in which they produce zero drafts, editing and revising on the fly. These tests are the antithesis of process writing, brushing aside all research data and regressing one hundred years. "Nancie," I wailed, "how did this happen?"

For me and my students, the year 2001 of the No Child Left Behind Act (NCLB) was the final unraveling of all we had achieved with restructuring ten years earlier. In response to the accountability in NCLB, my district responded with even more tests. Before our state standards assessment test had been implemented, our district gave standardized tests such as the MAT every other year to assess our students. These were increased to years K–9 and given in addition to the state assessment test. Then came the push for TOTAL HORIZONTAL ALIGNMENT and tests every quarter to make sure students were not only learning, but all learning the same thing at the same time. By the end of 2004, my eighth-graders were tested a total of 25 days: five weeks of instructional time. The test scores in the district have improved every year, but not, in my opinion, because of this additional top-down mandated testing which teachers and parents strongly protested. We had indeed improved literacy by improving teaching, but we had also managed to train a generation of good test-takers.

Ironically, further disintegration of our earlier progress was the class size reduction we'd wanted for so long. The grant we finally got to support this meant that Carol and I could no longer block our classes because only English classes were reduced, not social studies. Even though Carol and I did not teach in the same room, we still collaborated and connected our reading and writing lessons to both history and English. Now, with the exception of the people in my English department, I collaborated with no one, and Carol, my long time friend and one of the original "divas," moved on to another school. I was flying solo for the first time in eleven years.

I turned my attention that year to obtaining Professional Early Adolescence/English Language Arts certification from the National Board of Teaching Standards (NBPTS). Rita Caver, a colleague and friend from our town's high school who was a Teacher Consultant for the National Writing Project, had long tried to recruit me to attend the Summer Invitational

Institute of our local writing project, but I'd put her off saying I'd do it after I earned NBPTS certification. Clearly frustrated, she told me getting certified would be ten times easier if I would get National Writing Project training first, but she called my bluff and agreed to get NBPTS certification as well. Only one or two people had become certified in our town, and our district was only marginally supportive, but our state had started offering some incentives, so Rita and I became our own support group. I had always reflected on my work, forever making changes, some for the better, many for the worse, but this was the year I crawled completely inside my head and took my students with me.

The portfolio process forced me to take my teaching practice apart and look at the realities. What had I learned to improve instruction in twelve years of attending and giving workshops, taking graduate courses, reading professional literature, talking with colleagues, and spending some 20,000 hours with over 2200 young teens? No, it wasn't so much what I'd learned—what I knew was effective instruction—but what I was actually doing.

I was scrambling to reinvent my writing workshops into my new time frame: 50 minutes a day. My new class sizes seemed promising. Even though I was still teaching six sections a day, 114 students was better than 150. With no more than seventeen students per class, I should be able to do more individual conferencing without the other students tearing down the walls; I could evaluate even more writing. More, more, more. I thought I could compensate for the loss of teaching days due to testing by teaching smarter and leaner, but I found I had little left to cut, and I lost more student adjustment time (come in, sit down, sharpen a pencil, locate my agenda, write down today's assignments, find my homework, locate my writing notebook, etc.) when I wasn't blocking two periods in a row, even though I had always provided several opportunities for students to move around in the longer classes. I took stock of where I was and found the following:

- Literature circles—successful
- Increased self-selected student reading and authentic responses to literature—mediocre
- Reading logs—too time-consuming; I loathed reading most of them
- Sustained time in class for reading—sporadic; my students couldn't count on the time; very small classroom library
- Grammar instruction—still evolving and frustrating, the students still hated it
- Spelling—essentially nonexistent

- Vocabulary logs using deep processing methods, words based on student reading—mildly successful student-torture devices that made me cringe when I stared at those notebooks to be graded
- Writing notebooks—difficult to get students to not only use, but value; frequently lost
- Mini-lessons—usually took most of a class period and could not really be applied until the next few days
- Peer conferences—still a work in progress, but modeling for the class really helped
- Writing workshops as a whole—just so-so, usually student choice within a genre specified by me; lack of computer access hinders time spent writing, especially for my strugglers
- Test-writing—aggravating, I tried to incorporate throughout the year rather than the "Benchmark Boot Camp" approach right before testing, but I still resented the time it took to practice timed writing. Overall, my students were very successful on state and national assessments. Much of this was because they had several years of good instruction before they came to me.
- Writing assessment—just okay, rubrics based on state writing standards, still more product rather than process oriented, but students still maintained writing portfolios, reflecting on and evaluating their own writing. I had managed to get permission to use these as final semester exams rather than a multiple-choice-bubble-the-dots test.

Clearly, there was room for improvement. After reading over twenty books, much humming-and-hawing, and list-making, I went to the experts: my students. After a series of class meetings, the kids and I reorganized my classes, so they could learn the state standards and do well on tests but also learn what they wanted to learn about reading and writing in my class. We kept literature circles but expanded the reading choices. I agreed to dedicate one class period a week to student reading and eliminate reading logs, but the students agreed to increase the number of books they were expected to read every school year to 25. Accountability for reading these books were short responses to literature that taught them College Board Advanced Placement skills (primarily to support an assertion with evidence from the text) and improved their ability to take state and national standardized tests. We kept a modified version of vocabulary logs and added a spelling component.

We changed procedures in writing workshop as well. Instead of putting all writing information in student writing notebooks (à la Nancie Atwell and rolls of tape), we created dividers in student notebooks that created a text of sorts for the class (Atwell, 1998). This way, students could leave their writing notebooks in the class in their writing folders. No more missing notebooks. I accepted the reality that the small percentage of my students who were what I call "scribblers" by nature would carry a notebook with them everywhere and have journals or diaries at home whether I asked them to or not, and the rest of my students would write primarily in class or at home on their computers. I also gave up the idea of writing any more than quick writes with my students during writing workshop. After all, my job was to support them during that short time we had together, not polish my own prose. I still wrote the pieces I assigned to my students and shared my successes and failures with them, but I wrote outside of class, so I could be more available to my students during class.

My students helped me create a written form to improve peer response groups, and I agreed to help out with particularly recalcitrant, difficult, or uncooperative students by creating a response group in which I was one of their peers. In the past I had moved from response group to response group, participating and modeling each time, and in some classes I was still able to do so if no particularly prickly situations arose. It was another way I could give a personal response to a student on his or her writing. Both my students and I found "state-of-the-class" meetings helpful, but time-consuming. They helped me determine who might need a personal conference, and it provided a good venue for accountability and any quick advice I could give. The students and I agreed to allow me to call these short meetings whenever I thought best (usually when we were deciding on topics and especially when I thought most everyone should have at least one draft and be ready for revision or crafting mini-lessons to apply). I also tried to schedule computer lab days within a writing workshop. At that time, probably only half of my students had computers at home and even fewer had access to the Internet.

The one bugaboo for us was grammar. They agreed they liked when I used student sentences as models, to determine why the student writers punctuated them the way they had or why they used a phrase at the beginning instead of in the middle of the sentence. I also did some Think Alouds with them on either my own choices or another writer's choices. My students were most interested in the models of other eighth-graders than those from the books they were reading (I always get permission from a student before using his or her work as a model). I had been unable to meet and conference with my students often enough for them to create their own proofreading lists based on their personal mistakes. This idea from Atwell (1987) and Linda Reif (1992) and others sounded great, but I wasn't making it work. Instead, I devised a proofreading checklist with models and examples based on our standards called "Get your Ducks in a Row" that I copied on bright yellow paper, so students could find it easily in their binders and use it to edit their own and others' work. I also tried some twice-weekly short editing practices in which students labeled the parts of speech in sentences and then went through a process via a series of questions to find sentence patterns such as S-AV-DO or S-LV-PN because the state assessment test had started to include these types of questions. I never graded the accuracy of this practice, and I tried to make it as much fun as possible, but my students still found it intimidating. It also wasn't in context of their own writing, and no matter how many times they found subordinate clauses in sentences, they still didn't put a comma in a compound sentence, nor did they put one after an introductory element. If it hadn't worked for the last two hundred years, why did I think it would work now?

During this year when I managed to get my NBPTS certification, our department of education began an initiative to improve literacy instruction across the state, particularly reading instruction, and they financed some intensive training called Literacy Lab. Ken Stamatis, a consultant at a small parochial college, had assembled the latest and most telling research on the teaching of reading and writing, especially to elementary and middle level students, and packaged it in a form that was initially very successful and is still a viable project (Literacy Lab, 2008). Stamatis insisted that administrators be part of the training and that the state or school districts provide research and materials for the participants. My current principal went to one of these early training sessions along with a few of the teachers in our English department. I was grateful to Mr. Stamatis because he helped make sure my principal, the other English teachers in the building, and I were all on the same page. Upon returning from one of these sessions, my principal said excitedly, "I've got to tell you about Nancie Atwell!" I admit it was with wicked satisfaction that I gave her a short history lesson about what had occurred in her building some ten years earlier.

Because of Stamatis and his convincing research data, our principal helped us build good classroom libraries, and she no longer sneered that we were wasting time when our children were "just" reading in class. When the more-testing demons try to descend on us yet again, she stands with us. Despite extreme pressure from parents and some members of the administration, she avidly supports maintaining our heterogeneously grouped classes where all children learn pre-AP strategies. She advocates writing to learn in all classes, and actively recruits teachers for training from our local National Writing Project site. This is the power of educating administrators with hard research they can appreciate. Administrator knowledge and support is vital for change in instruction to occur.

I was the first teacher in our building to become a member of the National Writing Project (NWP) since my team mate Betsy left years earlier, but with my principal's help, five other teachers in the building have become NWP Teacher Consultants in just as many years. After creating my NBPTS portfolio, I knew how much I needed the NWP to help me improve what my students and I could not. Rita had been right all along of course. At the risk of sounding like a zealot: it changed my life, or, as we like to say at the Northwest Arkansas Writing Project (NWAWP), "It changed my DNA." I had certainly benefited from the work done by the NWP in my teaching career via other members' books, articles, and advice. I felt just like those teachers in the Delta who had just discovered a rubric for evaluating writing. The National Writing Project has been in existence since 1974 and the NWAWP had been in existence since 1998. What had taken me so long?

I live in one of those "artsy" places in the world. Like Asheville, North Carolina or Santa Fe, New Mexico, Northwest Arkansas is one of those places where universal creative forces must intersect or something because the area attracts creative people: writers, artists, performers, and craftsmen. However, this creative juju was lost on me. The only writing I had done since college was academic (graduate school research papers, usually about the lack of instruction on how to teach writing in colleges of education) and professional (workshops and my NBPTS portfolio) with the exception of some sporadic bouts of journaling and the writing I did along with my students. I rarely wrote or received handwritten letters. I e-mailed, called, or texted. I had ideas about pieces I might write, but teaching consumed every extra minute. When I could, I worked at a small real-estate investment company I had created. Who had time for writing? Not only did the NWP give me an excellent research-based model for improving my writing instruction, but it provided the opportunity and engendered the desire to create my own writing. When I shared my writing, other people laughed and cried in all of the right places. My fellows encouraged, wheedled, and teased out the best of what I wanted to articulate. I got that feeling back I had when I looked at my poem on the bulletin board in that English class of long ago: I was tapping into the juju, and my students could tell.

After I became a Teacher Consultant, I presented teaching demonstrations at our writing project's mini-conferences for teachers in the area, open-enrollment institutes, and regional professional development, but co-directing the month-long summer invitational institute was my greatest joy. Being surrounded by the best and the brightest educators local districts had to offer, learning from them, and coaching them is the profoundest of enriching experiences for a teacher like me.

The first change I implemented at school was to create an elective course called Art of Writing that is blocked with a journalism class taught by a colleague. We switch students at semester much like Carol and I had switched our English and history students during our interdisciplinary block. The course is based on a process writing model. The students have a few projects, but the rest of the time is writing workshop for independent writing. They have response groups that the students and I work very hard to make sure feel responsible for the work of every group member. I get feedback from the students and, based on their needs and desires, provide craft and genre lessons and quick writes on most class days, then students write or conference as needed. One of the students' projects is to research markets that publish work by teens. They are required to submit at least one piece for publication as part of their final assessment. Several have been accepted in publications such as *Teen Voices, Teen Ink,* and *Cicada.* We publish an anthology of selected works from the semester course and celebrate with the Journalism class at the end of the year. My hope is that once they get the bug, they'll be hooked as writers for life, published or not.

If I weren't active in my local writing project, I would not write as much as I do now. Northwest Arkansas Writing Project events force me to carve out the time to write, to write for myself and any audience I choose. Indeed, the project sponsors a venue for local authors and teacher writers to read from their work for an audience. In addition, we regularly read our writing at the local arts festival. Steering committee meetings and spring and fall writing retreats provide more opportunities to write and share with my peers. One of my earliest opportunities to be published was in a book edited by NWAWP members, which is a collection of stories about the importance of food in our lives, complete with recipes (Eaton, Totten, & Terrell, 2006).

These personal writing successes notwithstanding, the NWP's main business is writing education based on solid research. Dr. Samuel Totten, the founder and director of the Northwest Arkansas Writing Project, strongly encouraged us to write professionally, especially about the teaching and learning of writing. I'd written a research article about the need for high quality staff development on writing instruction for teachers and administrators as part of the requirements to become a Teacher Consultant for the NWP, but I got bogged down in it and set it aside. I have to admit that underneath my disinterest was the belief that I couldn't actually get published in a juried journal. Then Dr. Totten and other members of NWAWP edited a book of quick writes for all disciplines grades K–12 to which I contributed

(Totten, Eaton, & Dirst, 2006). Having articles published in a professional book was encouraging. I had also written some other articles in graduate school that I had set aside in a file folder, but there was one that nagged at me to revise it. I knew the idea was unique, but I was intimidated by my perception of the "snooty" editors of literary journals, so the article languished in a lateral file. Then one of my fellow Teacher Consultants told me about her experience at the National Writing Project Professional Writing Retreat and encouraged me to apply. The NWP hosts twenty Teacher Consultants from across the country in an intense week-long seminar on writing for a professional audience. It sounded like the encouragement and support I needed to pursue one or more of those articles I'd put away, so I plucked up my courage and applied.

I was accepted! Laptop clutched to my chest, I walked into an adobe building south of Santa Fe, New Mexico filled with people with which I felt an almost instant rapport. With the support of the three other members in my response group, writing project leaders, and Art Peterson, senior editor of *The Quarterly*, I drew on the Santa Fe juju and managed to knock out a twenty-page draft by the time my plane landed back at home a week later.

So where am I now and where do I want to be? My creative writing class continues to evolve and improve as I give more of it over to the students. I continue to get their input, and now they are providing some of the writing opportunities to "grease the wheel" during writing workshop. I learned about "justwrites" from Melissa Krut, a member of my response group at the NWP Professional Writing Retreat. The subject of the article she developed at the retreat, justwrites are timed ten-minute freewriting exercises that begin with a two or three word starter and can take the writer into some of the unknown places in their brains. Sometimes they result in stream of consciousness compositions, but other times they result in inspired poetry as well as prose. I have a large class jar sitting next to a pad of paper in my classroom. Art of Writing students are invited to write the starters. On the days we have justwrites, I draw from the jar and write the starter on the board. "Pretend parades," "Rapidfire perspiration," and "By the time..." are a few examples (Krut, 2008). I start a ten-minute timer, and we all write without stopping until it rings. Students are not as reluctant to share these as they are some of the writing that results from quick writes, possibly because they often include some incoherent rambling, which my young writers find very amusing. I use justwrites to illustrate cutting prose to the bone to produce a poem, and my students produce some interesting poetry when they apply it to their own prose, justwrites or other pieces.

I tested a new strategy in the writing class response groups that I now use in my English classes. I assign response group members based on personality and ability, and I've found that three is the best number in a group for eighth-graders, but sometimes the class size dictates some groups of four. I first show videos of response groups (some with students and some with teachers), then I model a response group with two student volunteers. From the beginning, I stress group responsibility for every member's writing as well as personal responsibility to the group to have drafts ready and to be an active responder on group response days. Based on the NWP model I learned (I have also read similar procedures in Linda Reif's *Seeking Diversity: Language Arts with Adolescents,* 1992), I model and teach students to listen carefully as the writer reads his or her piece aloud. The responders take careful and very specific notes under three categories: strong aspects, questions, and suggestions. Strong aspects are specific. "Dew sparkled like diamonds on the spider's web" not "good description." "Rattled and bounced" not "good verbs." "Lead has character in action that grabs" not "I liked your lead." Questions can be anything that occurs to the listener, but especially helpful to the writer are the clarifying questions that help the writer make sure he or she has elaborated enough or is coherent. Students are taught not to couch criticism into questions: "Have you thought about throwing away that first page and starting over?" Suggestions are given as "I" statements: "I'd like to hear more about your relationship with Uncle Barry," or "I'd like slower pacing, so I can see that ball coming over the plate toward your head." Otherwise, students lapse into "You should" or "You need to . . . " which strips some of the ownership of the piece from the writer.

These response sheets are kept by the writer to assist with his or her revision. In addition to peer response sheets, each group must complete a Peer Response Group Responsibility chart and turn it in to me before they leave for the day. When I tested these charts with my writing class, I found it reinforced the concept of group responsibility for each member and enhanced the support for the individuals. Each chart identifies the piece read by each writer that day or if the writer didn't bring his or her piece. Suggestions for revision are recorded for each session. I use the charts to help me as I make notes about daily writing workshop scores, which are best primarily on "good faith participation," which includes behaviors such as diligent thinking, drafting, responding, and active revising, utilizes time well, contributes to a non-distracting and productive environment. Sometimes I put questions or comments on the forms, and I return them on the next day the entire group meets. Here they record what changes were actually made to each writing piece as well as further suggestions for improvement. I can compare these charts to all of the drafts and the peer responses of a student's polished piece. This helps me track each student's process on a given piece of writing. I have found that thinking through the elements that go on the chart, which is completed by the group as a whole, reinforces revision, especially with the students in my English classes who do not have enough interest in writing to take it as an elective. During a writing workshop, students may meet with a partner any time they want a response, but I set aside days for the response groups to meet, so students know when they can expect this feedback.

On these days, I rotate through the response groups, adding myself as a member, until I have participated in at least one meeting of each group. I listen and respond just as the other members do. If there is time, I share one of my pieces as well and get student feedback. This allows me to hear and respond to almost every piece being worked on at a given time. I usually make arrangements for individual peer conferences following these group meetings. They are another way I decide who needs my time the most if I do not manage to conference with every student as many times as I would like. My participation in the groups also reinforces specific, helpful feedback as well as how the group should be conducted.

My writing workshops are still centered around genre studies. First I immerse my classes in the genre. We read at least twenty various examples, including those of professional authors and my former students as well as my own pieces (good and bad). Then we decide in small groups and the class as a whole, what makes the most effective pieces. I compile these elements from all classes and provide a synthesis for each class to modify and ultimately approve. In the years since I have used student-created rubrics, the students have generated almost exactly the same list of attributes that make a particular genre effective. In fact, if there was more educational jargon in the student lists, they would almost match our state rubric exactly, with the exception of the state's litany of usage and mechanics skills.

For usage and mechanics, my students are more interested in how much these errors interfere with meaning relative to the length and complexity of a piece. At this stage in their development as writers, I tend to agree. It is tempting to just pull out the same list of criteria generated by past students and skip these few genre analysis days in the interest of cramming in more teaching time, but so far I've resisted. I have seen the power of student ownership and self-evaluation. Because I must assign grades, the students and I evaluate their work based on daily workshop "good faith participation," quality of the piece based on the rubric they have generated, usage and mechanics, and the quality of the reflective writing they do when they finish each piece describing the "history" of the piece from how they got their ideas to polishing strategies. Early in the year, we look at examples of reflective writing and generate a rubric for this genre just as we do the others. Once the students have produced the elements on which they want to be evaluated, I create a rubric and give a copy to each student as they are just getting their ideas. When I can manage the wall space, I make a large poster listing the criteria. I'm learning that this information on the wall, as long as it is easy to locate and is not cluttered, is a valuable reteaching and reinforcing tool. It is certainly more accessible to students than digging through their binders for the copy of the rubric. When the time comes for final assessment, I assign grades based on the student assessment and my assessment equally. I have learned that as long as students understand the elements of the rubric (and they do if they create it), then they almost always evaluate their work just as I would. I like that this is another step toward making them independent writers. In an effort to reinforce the process rather than the product, the rubric is more heavily weighted on the process items than quality or usage and mechanics.

Grammar continues to be one of my gremlins, along with too much testing and too little time. However, I am hopeful. The work of Jeff Anderson (*Mechanically Inclined*, 2005 and *Everyday Editing*, 2007) has finally gotten through to me. He provides enjoyable ways to teach grammar that will improve student writing and address their most common errors. At the beginning of a school year, I always get a sample of student writing to assess what areas I need to address in their writing. In the last few years, the list of grammatical errors I've compiled hasn't changed much: inconsistent shift in point of view, no commas after introductory elements or in compound sentences, and problems with pronoun case and pronoun-antecedent agreement. Jeff Anderson has devised lessons and methods that help me address my students' problems in a relatively painless way, and we continue to look at grammatical constructions that help students with style. Similar to the work of Killgallon and Strong, Anderson invites students to notice and then to imitate model sentences or paragraphs, but the inclusion of current popular songs, hands-on activities, and visual scaffolds in the classroom make his methods more successful for me. Even more important, they are always followed by applying what they've learned to a piece of writing. The biggest challenge I have is to not get sucked into being she-who-spouts-big-grammatical-terms-and-shows-off, especially when a student asks a question about a construction we aren't currently learning. Giving my eighth-graders just enough information is the key. I have a friend who insists on discussing the intricacies of a video game with me that I have never seen. It's as if he is speaking a foreign language, so I shut down and just nod. My students do the same thing if I spout present *progressive tense*, *subordination*, or *gerund* at them.

My students also shut down if I mention state testing, but I have some hope there as well. Our district leadership has recently found and shared Tony Wagner's *The Global Achievement Gap* (2008), which makes sound arguments against over-testing, teaching to a test, and the focus on the College Board's Advanced Placement Program. My administrator told us that as long as we don't get into "trouble" with low test scores, she would much prefer that we go "deep rather than wide" when we design our curriculum. Our entire district including parents and other community leaders are dialoguing about the ideas in Wagner's book, and I see some positive change coming, not only with excessive testing, but also time for teaching and time for collaboration with peers.

As for my own writing, I had the courage to create this piece of professional writing and submit it to an editor, but I have to admit, I am still refining the article I wrote for the NWP Professional Writer's Retreat. My goal is to apply the final ribbons and bows and put the thing out there after I grade the upcoming semester writing portfolios. Snooty editors, here it comes! My own writing continues to inform my teaching. My students need to see my struggles and failures along with my successes to help demystify the whole "writing thing." My writing workshops, and especially my creative writing class are set up similarly to workshops in which I have personally participated. My eighth-graders know I am part of a community of writers, that I have peers who support me just as their own response groups, friends, and family support them. I am also a member of their writing community. When I am stuck or have a problem with part of a piece of writing, I will go to them and get their opinion. I trust their instincts, and I want them to know that. They begin to see both my writing and their writing as a lifelong journey, not just as single, isolated projects. Since I am writing at home just like they are (homework), it helps build our community. Besides, the more I learn about teaching writing, the better writer I become.

Not long ago, I complained to a colleague, Thomas Cochran, about not finding the time for my personal writing. Tom taught part-time and wrote part-time when he authored a young adult novel, *Roughnecks*. However, personal circumstances took him away from his writing for eight years. It gives me hope to know he recently finished his second novel, *Running the Dogs*. He said, "You'll find the time if you really want it." This is true of anything I suppose. I am so dedicated to teaching I often work ten to twelve hour days, yet two years ago I made up my mind to do something for me. My yoga classes and practice force me to leave the school building by 5:00 P.M. almost every day. At first I was surprised to learn that my teaching didn't suffer but actually improved. My yoga practice also helps me deal with my ego. I have a reputation for excellent teaching, and I'm afraid of losing it. Slowly, albeit painfully, I'm learning to let go of it, to let go of competing with other teachers, and to focus just on my students, one class period at a time.

Of course, in a perfect world, I'd write daily on an open lanai awash in ocean breezes, or on a small terrace overlooking the narrow Parisian streets of Montmartre and the dome of Sacré-Coeur, or even on a screened porch facing Carolina tidal marshes and passing shrimp boats. In reality, I find myself taking the advice I so often give to my students to "just sit down and start tapping the keys" in my tiny office adjacent to my kitchen. When I take the time to actually look away from the computer screen, as I did this morning, I might see a doe and her young fawn walk warily through the trees that skirt my house. Writing here on this Ozark mountain, while not a daily practice, isn't a bad thing, not bad at all.

References

Anderson, J. (2005). *Mechanically inclined.* Portland, ME: Stenhouse Publishers.

Anderson, J. (2007). *Everyday editing.* Portland, ME: Stenhouse Publishers.

Atwell, N. (1987). *In the middle: Writing, reading, and learning with adolescents.* Portsmouth, NH: Boynton/Cook Publishers, Inc.

Atwell, N. (1998). *In the middle: New understandings about writing, reading, and learning* (2nd ed.). Portsmouth, NH: Boynton/Cook Publishers, Inc.

Braddock, J. H. (1990). Tracking the middle grades: National patterns of grouping for instruction. *Phi Delta Kappan, 72,* 445–449.

Calkins, L. (1986). *The art of teaching writing.* Portsmouth, NH: Heinemann.

Carnegie Council on Adolescent Development. Task Force on Education of Young Adolescents. (1989). *Turning points: Preparing American youth for the 21st century.* New York: Author.

Disney, W. (Producer) & Chaffey, D. (Director). (1963). *The Three Lives of Thomasina* [Motion picture]. Burbank, CA: Warner Brothers Television.

Eaton, H., Totten, S., & Terrell, L. (Eds.). (2006). *The flavor of our words.* Fayetteville, AR: Northwest Arkansas Writing Project.

Elbow, P. (1980). *Writing without teachers.* Cary, NC: Oxford University Press.

Elbow, P. & Belanoff, P. (1981). *Writing With Power: Techniques for mastering the writing process.* Cary, NC: Oxford University Press.

Graves, D. (1983). *Writing: Teachers and children at work.* Portsmouth, NH: Heinemann.

Hillocks, G., & Smith, M. (1991). Grammar and usage. In D. Lapp & D. Fisher (Eds.), *Handbook of research on teaching the English language arts* (pp. 591–603). New York: Macmillian.

Killgallon, D. (1987). *Sentence composing: The complete course.* Portsmouth, NH: Boynton/Cook.

Krut, M. (2008). Get it write: Two strategies for writing teachers. N*WP Professional Writing Retreat Anthology June 2007* (pp. 1–12). Berkeley, CA: National Writing Project.

Literacy Lab: About Literacy Lab. (2008). Retrieved November 25, 2008, from http://www.smartstepliteracylab.org/about.html

Mills, R. (1997). Grouping students for instruction: Issues of equity and effectiveness. In J. L. Irvin (Ed.), *What Current Research Says to the Middle Level Practitioner* (pp. 87–94). Columbus, OH: National Middle School Association.

Reif, L. (1992). *Seeking diversity: Language arts with adolescents.* Portsmouth, NH: Heinemann.

Strong, W. (1986). *Creative approaches to sentence combining.* Urbana, IL: ERIC and the National Council of Teachers of English.

Slavin, R. E. (1990). Achievement effects of ability grouping in secondary schools: A best-evidence synthesis. *Review of Educational Research, 60*(3), 471–499.

Totten, S., Eaton, H., & Dirst, S. (Eds.). (2006). *Spark the brain, ignite the pen: Quick writes for kindergarten through high school teachers and beyond.* Charlotte, NC: Information Age Publishing.

Wagner, T. (2008). *The global achievement gap.* New York: Basic Books.

Weaver, C. (1996a). *Teaching grammar in context.* Portsmouth, NH: Boynton/Cook Publishers, Inc.

Weaver, C. (1996b). Teaching grammar in the context of writing. Retrieved July 6, 2005, from http://www.english.vt.edu/~grammar/GrammarForTeachers/readings/weaver.html

Finding the Writer

Carol Malaquias

I spent many years as a vibrant, motivated fifth grade teacher, all the while having no idea how to teach writing. It seemed a mystery, how one child could get words to flow on a page and another could not. I came from a single "What I Want to Be When I Grow Up" essay a year, at the most. Voracious reading did not make me a fluent writer, nor did my mastery of *Warriner's English Grammar.* I winced my way through Advanced Exposition for my Liberal Arts degree, and my courses for my teaching certification did little to enlighten me.

Norwich, England, 1974: The Blackdale Junior School. I had crossed the Atlantic as a college student to learn their secrets. I marveled at a pyramid of shoeboxes piled and draped artistically in the middle of Richard Whybrow's room, each bearing its own miniature diorama of Shakespeare's *Macbeth,* with bits of writing placed to fill in the gaps. Mrs. Stevens used colored cord to sew her students' finished "best books," which the children had filled with their stories and drawings on the school's current theme or project. The children dutifully wrote in their "jotters" —independent research, accounts of experiments—and then transposed it for display, neatly lettered and illustrated with a black paper frame.

Britain's open, richly-provisioned classroom was the epitome of educational philosophy at the moment. A thematic structure loosely served as the

Getting It in Writing, pages 145–157
Copyright © 2011 by Information Age Publishing
All rights of reproduction in any form reserved.

curriculum: that year it was "Five Hundred Years Ago," an enormous theme that had been webbed with every possible offshoot. We made lino-cuts of illuminated letters to print, baked bread, rubbed gravestones, wrote songs and plays. Child-centered experiences and projects begot writing, and display motivated it. Bruner (1971) wrote that "knowing is a process, not a product" (p. 72). Although display seemed paramount to the British school system, those aforementioned jotters were the instrument of the process of learning through writing.

I returned to a concrete bunker of a school in inner-city Pittsburgh to do my student teaching. It had been built in the early seventies to serve the "open classroom," an educator's utopian dream where students and teachers could be grouped and regrouped according to need. The American teachers' consciousness had not caught up with the vision, and reality built huge dividers via bookcases and even precariously piled up furniture in an effort to block out the incessant din from the neighboring "family group pod." It was self-enclosed in every respect but for the open spaces above the dividers over which the noise ricocheted mercilessly. The children sat in horizontal rows facing the blackboard, where the "chalk and talk" teacher held court.

One large, lone girl sat at a back table, sweat shining on her blown-up cheeks, in a yellowed leopard-spotted fake fur coat that she clutched tightly around her rotund middle. The building was so grossly overheated that I had shed my own sweater as soon as I walked in, so I didn't know why she was wearing such a coat. She was more than reluctant to participate in class and refused to leave her self-imposed prison. The teacher ignored her back there. I was appalled and could not imagine her situation.

"Denita can't bathe or wash her clothes, because her family has no water at home, so she sits back there in her coat to minimize the complaints about the way she stinks," my cooperating teacher whispered unsympathetically when I inquired.

We all spent the day going from workbook to workbook at the sound of the tone. Nothing met with my approval: the classroom was devoid of materials, and the children were accustomed to iron-handed external control. My cooperating teacher very reluctantly allowed me to plan some lessons.

The dichotomy in ability made me cringe as some kept up with the fifth grade work and others were left in the dust. I formed groups for math; I had my "lows" write to explain dividing up real-life objects, because I knew hands-on learning made better connections with the brain. Steve, Eric, and Billy divided up my shells and pink and blue beach pebbles I had acquired beside the North Sea.

Billy wrote, "We share the shells and I have 5 and ever boodie has 5 and ther wear three boys. We share the beach pebbles equally and we all have 2 pebbes thar wear not more let ovr."

I brought in piles of manipulatives and devised task cards based on the five senses as a stimulus to writing. Inexperienced as they were with independent exploration, the children were rowdy but especially willing to get out of their seats. One group went around the school with my tape recorder looking for specific types of sounds; one group went outside to listen. Two groups stayed in the room, one rubbing textures and the other listing favorite foods. The whole class was actively involved as I tentatively guided them in creative discovery. I followed up by having them do a writing piece inspired by their sensory words. Darin finished a story of patching some jeans, with a cutout of jeans and pieces cut from his texture rubbings glued on. I could only encourage "best work," a term I had learned in England, although I didn't know what that was; I was completely accepting of *any* work.

In 1977, I landed a job in my hometown in a suburb of Boston, teaching reading, language arts, and social studies to grade six of an elementary school. The curriculum was a simple list of textbooks on a single sheet. Youth and enthusiasm supplemented my ignorance. Overwhelmed by papers to correct, they piled up interminably around the counters, and I saved the "creative" writing for last. I remember staring at a piece blankly and then correcting only the grammar and mechanics (my personal expertise). Never able to catch up and not really knowing how to affect their writing, I assigned little to none and taught as I had been taught, from a language arts text with follow-up exercises.

I went back to teaching in the nineties, after a hiatus to raise my little daughters to school age. As I finished a Master of Education degree in Curriculum and Instruction at Lesley College in Cambridge, I was hired to teach a fifth grade on Cape Cod, Massachusetts, where we made our home. At the time, whole language strategies from New Zealand were coming to the fore and basal readers were beginning to get dumped. Children were writing as early as kindergarten with invented spelling rampant and, with a dearth of phonics instruction, difficult for the children to outgrow.

I wrote my culminating project for my Master's on "Building a Literature-Based Language Arts Curriculum." I used Regie Routman's (1991) idea of reading response journals to help my fifth graders connect to whole novel texts. My students' struggle to respond in writing to their reading gave me a window into their thinking. I was beginning to value writing as thinking.

I tried valiantly to be a writing model for my students, as Routman prescribes. "We cannot be teachers of writing until we demonstrate the craft ourselves," she cautions in her *Invitations* (Routman, 1991, p. 161). I carefully wrote one piece called "Stairs," about my daughter's insistence that we climb every *duomo*, tower, and set of stairs on a recent trip to Europe. After at least five drafts, I had eked out a page and a half. I had included every member of my family and invited the class to incorporate their family members into their pieces. I got some mileage out of "Stairs" at the beginning of every year, until the complications of their personal family situations began to give my students more angst than the assignment was worth.

For creative writing, I used the pure process approach: self-selected topics, (teacher's) hands-off conferences with the works "owned" by the child. This component of my curriculum held the first murmurs of the writer's craft. Donald Graves' book (1983) helped me to understand the process, and I constructed an enormous floor to ceiling bulletin board in my classroom called "The Road to the Rainbow" with a stone path spelling out the steps: Prewriting, Writing, Revising, Editing, and Publishing. It was simplistic but a place to start. I typed all their stories for them into booklets in order to motivate their finished products and so that they could see the final, edited version.

Prevalent in my district at that time was the John Collins (1985) approach to writing, which I found contrived. The teacher graded an assigned writing piece on three previously chosen "focus corrections." The rest of the writing went unattended. Often these focal points were purely mechanics: complete sentences, proper punctuation, correct use of capital letters. To my mind, the approach made the writing stilted; there was no requisite for the overall growth of a creative writer.

I also utilized Science Learning Logs and a Math Problem of the Week. Again, writing allowed me to open windows into my students' thinking. Had they understood the science experiment or did they get the completely wrong take on it? I purchased a couple of collections of problems of the week (Seymour, 1982, 1984) and the students took turns presenting their thinking, which they had written up in their notebooks, to the class on Fridays. These presentations allowed for many different mathematical strategies to arrive at a correct solution. Marilyn Burns (1987) was also using writing to get children to think about important math concepts. Together with the original stories, this is all termed "real writing." I continued to search for authentic writing opportunities.

In the mid-nineties, my district was beginning to use the latest best practices in education to develop curriculum. The whole language approach to

reading and writing was coming up through the lower grades. My fifth graders were arriving knowing the process of writing. We replaced our outdated
science texts and the archaic information they contained with units in kit
form. With "writing across the curriculum" a somehow new and exciting
innovation, many writing components were included in the new science
units. With some regret, I eschewed using writing to activate knowledge:
those first shared *mis*conceptions, composed at the moment when interest
was at a peak, were too often the only ones remembered.

I found *Storypath* from Everyday Learning (McGuire, 1998), an interactive program in which students create a character and build that character
through writing in response to interactive staged events. We donned mob-
caps and tricorns to sit at town meetings and debate the issues of pre-Revo-
lutionary Boston and followed up with letters telling of our plight to family
members back in Britain or letters of protest to the king and his appointed
governor. Character interpreters brought the experience further to life, as I
cajoled several of the related arts teachers into assuming roles for the class.
Students were in this way involved in living history. They internalized their
social studies material better than ever this way. I gave no test of facts, dates,
and analyses: the dates were at the top of their published letters and the
facts and analyses embedded in my students' accounts of their experiences.
I first utilized the included rubrics to grade their work.

Rubrics altered my perception of grading. Not only did they serve to
give the writer a focus, but they offered a fair evaluation of the result. *Storypath's* rubrics were a departure from the mechanical corrections that John
Collins (1985) and I had made. They specified content (include two aspects
of colonial life) and aspects of the writer's craft (write from your character's
point of view, include your feelings about the event). I graded each item
on the rubric simply check-minus (neglected it), check (good attempt), or
check-plus (got it). It gave me a reasonable idea of how my students were
working on their writing, so it was the first time I felt a writing grade to be
a useful indicator.

I attempted to utilize Writer's Notebooks after reading an article from
Columbia University Teacher's College. The children described in the article wrote for hours and read through their notebooks to discover themes. I
made a few attempts to crack the covers with my students, but since I didn't
keep a writer's notebook myself, they went mostly unused for lack of guidance. Every September, I ordered the black marble composition books, and
every June I sent them home with the majority of the pages empty.

It is the dawning of a new millennium. My class is writing successfully
in every subject of the extant curriculum—science, math, social studies,

and reading. Yet, my district has adopted no writing curriculum for fear it would be too restrictive. To have none seems somewhat nebulous. To serve the new state-wide testing, the fourth graders received training in writing to a prompt. Rubric-graded models showed the students what a high-scoring piece of writing was. In every grade, we had to administer a yearly grade-wide prompt in order to preserve the training for future tests. The teachers gathered to score the writing of students other than their own. The score would somehow indicate the next step. What it did do was place a failing grade on most students. They had no more idea of how to get from a two to a four than I had to get them there.

Luckily, our librarian approached my class as the possible audience for a budding author, ready to publish his first fantasy novel for children. His publisher had required that he obtain some feedback from the age group of his future readers. Immediately, the manuscript changed our read aloud time from primarily receptive to highly participatory. Their opinions were requested, and my fifth graders stood ready to render such. Enraptured, we read the book daily. The usual twenty minutes became forty. They questioned, offered alternative wording and plot, dialogued with each other, critiqued. Their opinions had an audience. When the read aloud time was up they groaned and moaned for more.

After each read aloud session, my students went to their seats to write a page of response in a journal, a simple packet of pages for each chapter. We passed these on to the publisher, along with a tape recording of a Reader's Theater scene. The author appeared in the classroom to a rapt and appreciative audience. Questions about the writing process were flying, in the tangible form of one manuscript. Every answer was meaningful, because they had a voice in it, however small. After the author sent news of acceptance and the approximate date of publication, my class celebrated with an author party. They felt electrified by the successful fruition of an author's journey. My students, being just as likely to gravitate toward video games as books, identified with this author, who grounded them in the authenticity, excitement, and reality of writing a book worth reading. Reading and writing became such cool things to do. Reade Scott Whinnem (2003) acknowledged my class in his *Utten and Plumley* and presented each one (and me!) with a signed copy the following year. Reade visits every year now.

Reade Whinnem also invited me into the Writer's Group he led. Feeling like a nonwriter, I struggled, awkwardly and sometimes painfully, to find my own voice. To my surprise and great satisfaction, I came to call myself a writer, an event which forever changed my perspective on writing and teaching writing.

Now I was tuned in to writing as writers do, not just in word but in deed. I bartered to attend the Mid-Winter Institute at Lesley University, where the cutting-edge experts in the field of writing would be speaking. The theme was The Writer's Notebook. (Remember my perennial empty ones?) This conference at Lesley was pivotal for me as Ralph Fletcher, Sharon Hill, Linda Rief, and Georgia Heard inspired me. My students express themselves from the heart as they "plant seeds" (Heard, 1999), writing for fluency in their marble composition books every homework night. These unfinished pieces are fodder for revision work later: their unfinished nature means I meet with no reluctance when I ask the children to choose one on which to practice a revision strategy (Heard, 2002). They eat up this mini-lesson, try it, share it format. The practice is immediate, often using one of their notebook entries, and the sharing is powerful. With the class circled up on the rug, they identify what they notice about each writer's attempt to embrace the strategy. And most of the students nail the strategy. I post each revision strategy by name, Sharon Hill's idea, with examples of the mentor text alongside student examples, for the remainder of the year as reference (Davis & Hill, 2003).

My subsequent month at the Invitational Summer institute of the Buzzard's Bay Writing Project provided even more painful and important awakenings as my fluency seemed to falter at times. A subsidiary of the National Writing Project, it is a multifaceted program of exposure to writing and writers and daily opportunities to write and share. We are also recognized and paid as Fellows and take turns sharing an inspirational writing lesson of our devise. We participate in writing lessons for kindergarten through high school, and in this community of writing teachers/writers, I began to see the big picture. My students and I are writers, in a writing community, supporting each other in the craft.

With the help of our school's Literacy Coordinator, Dr. Jim McGuinness, also a Lesley University instructor, I train peer conference partners to make one suggestion from a rubric we have crafted together. This serves to differentiate instruction as well as motivate students to further revisit their writing for revision. As a class, we create rubrics specific to each writing project, which the students continually refer to during the peer conference and return to their writing feeling empowered with a revision task. They are able to improve their writing while retaining a strong feeling of ownership, as evidenced by multiple revision drafts.

We begin by defining the genre and relating it to a written example, to make the reading-writing connection. Jim uses the buying a puppy scene from *Ginger Pye* by Eleanor Estes (1951) to illustrate the writing of one scene of a story. We guide the class to notice and discuss elements of the scene: extra description of setting, the characters' dialogue, description of characters, the action. The characters don't leave the setting, and when they do leave, the scene's over.

Then we build a rubric together, using a story scene previously written by the teacher. Notice that the teacher's writing is the bridge between the professional and the student. We invite the students to tell what's good about it, specifically. They might notice interesting action, description of setting, characters, objects, dialogue, word choices, and mechanics: spelling, punctuation, a new paragraph for each speaker. These elements take their position on the rubric.

At this moment, we may notice that the class is deficient in one of the points on the rubric such as dialogue conventions, and we share the pen to practice on a chart. Children assume the roles of characters in a conversation and are responsible for creating the dialogue. The drama and humor of creating writing together makes this type of mini-lesson stick.

As Dr. McGuinness has a flair for the dramatic, he shows the children how to read the rubric in an exciting way, element by element, beginning with a four. Each level of an element gets less exciting and more dejected. We take turns reading and laughing at the performances: the rubric begins to become internalized.

When it's ready, we train two conference partners on each others' writing. We caution them to talk only about the rubric and tell what they like first: "The strongest part of your writing is . . . " They should make every effort to use the author's words in doing this and then give one, and only one, suggestion. They then ask, "Do you know what to do? What?" and have the author repeat their suggestion so that he or she can return to their work, fully armed with a revision task. The final question of the conference is, "How do you feel?" Asking this preserves the integrity of peer conferencing, assuring that the writer has a positive experience.

We may try to train two more conference partners at this point, with all four at the table, using one to train another. To maintain the tone of a workshop, we come up with rules together. Talk in whispers and be polite are often all that is needed if students are motivated to work on their pieces. The teacher's place is at the conference table, listening in. There I might discover the need for mini-lessons such as "show, don't tell" or the use of the thesaurus on two verbs per page.

It is helpful to also train peer editors. I choose those children who have attained a command of the writing conventions. They don't do all the work. If there is no effort to edit in evidence, they simply write, "Needs work" and the date. To edit spelling, we teach them to start at the end and go backwards in order to see each word singly. Then they should read forward, a whole sentence at a time, looking for making sense, verb agreement, and in this case, dialogue punctuation. They should circle any part that is incorrect.

My next foray into peer conferencing was with the nonfiction persuasive essay. The Plate Tectonics science unit suggested the students write one as an alternative assessment. I began with five lessons on ways to support a topic sentence: description, reasons, anecdote, facts, and combining all four. For each mini-lesson, we discussed the teacher-written example. The students went off to try it in their Writer's Notebooks. Gathered on the rug, everyone in the class shared the efforts and noticed successes with the strategy. Meanwhile, during science time, my class was partnering to find and list examples of evidence to support the theory of plate tectonics.

Then I reviewed the structure of a five (or more) paragraph essay:

- The first paragraph is a topic paragraph, which tells reader the purpose of the essay and the thesis statement, or statement of belief.
- There must be at least three separate paragraphs to support the thesis.
- The concluding paragraph restates the thesis but does not bring in any new information.

We built a rubric together, incorporating the basic elements of a well-supported persuasive essay. The class read the rubric in an exciting way, element by element, and got to work on the essays. The conference partners put up their signs when ready, and the children brought their rubric with them. I planned mini-lessons according to need. Editors put up their signs when ready.

One of the wonderful aspects of teaching fifth grade in my district is the week we spend at an environmental education collaborative. My students experience the geology, flora, and fauna of their native Cape Cod through outdoor education. I have always wanted to try teaching nature writing from field notebooks, but once more had not attempted it myself. Through the National Writing Project, I found the definitive guide to teaching nature writing, *The Alphabet of the Trees* (McEwen & Statman, 2000). With it, I was able to plan many opportunities for my class to utilize a field notebook to stimulate nature writing in the classroom. I planned "power spot" experiences (McEwen & Statman, 2000, p. 64) in the schoolyard and the seashore week of nature journaling that follows.

Each evening, the students examined the mentor text and used their field notes and sketches from the day as the stimuli for a poem in that style. The idea of mentor texts is powerful; the successes my students have make me swoon. We share everything each night and publish a booklet of all the poetry in four sections, dedicated to our nature teachers who haul the sketchbooks around in their backpacks for us.

Monday

On the trail: Do a sketch, notice and write notes: colors, shapes, movements, small details, patterns of light, surroundings, feel, smell, listen to it.

Mentor texts: Page from my nature journal and "Young Sycamore" by William Carlos Williams (McEwen & Statman, 2000, p. 118).

At quiet hour: Read poetry examples and use notes to begin to draft a poem.

Brian wrote this amazing poem from his beach walk notes and sketches:

Coastline Dunes
Giant mountains of sand
Held together with long,
Thin blades shooting from
The ground

Blotches of yellow
Blooming, brightening
With leaves, drooping
Like they're sad about
Something

Sticks and poles
Guarding the top
Like electric fences
Around a jail

Rubbery plants
Smooth as a
Rain jacket
Along the bottom

Leaves like teddy bears
With painfully sharp edges
Guarding themselves
Almost like knives

The dune rises high
Covering the blazing sun
Letting animals, plants (and people)
Have relief and rest
There are gashes in
The dunes, pouring
Down an avalanche
Of sand, sliding
Down like a waterfall

One day it will be hidden
From sight, swallowed
By the mighty blue sea.

Tuesday

On the trail: Do a quick sketch with name, physical description, feelings, three metaphors/similes.

Mentor texts: Student examples (McEwen & Statman, 2000, p. 274).

At quiet hour: Simple descriptive poem, with connections if desired.

Kelley was being specific in her poem written from her notes in the white cedar swamp.

Spagnum Moss
Like the back of a turtle,
Like the green rug on which I lie,
The softness of heaven with a color so green you can't compare.
The treasure of the forest,
A friend to all the trees,
Not hard to find.
Here's a clue:
It lies beneath the fallen leaves.

Wednesday

On the trail: Sketching and writing.

Mentor texts: Lines about nature from *The Book of Questions* by Pablo Neruda (McEwen & Statman, 2000, p. 169).

At quiet hour: Make a question list and then a question poem.

Zachary has some deep questions in his poem:

Questions

Why does nature want to take over the trails?
Why might my tree be straight or curvy?
Is my tree old or young?
Do the birds weep for their homes being destroyed?
Does the ocean ever get tired?
How do plants feel that they can't move from place to place?
What does it feel like to be a fish and probably never be in the air?
How could our lives be different if we had predators?

Thursday

On the trail: Sketching and writing.

Mentor texts: "Earth Teach Me" by Nancy Wood (McEwen & Statman, 2000, p. 281).

At quiet hour: Interpret poem, try own in that style.

Thais wrote a powerful one on our last evening:

Earth Teach Me . . .
Earth teach me stillness
like the bat who sleeps in his cave.
Earth teach me freedom
like the polar bear who swims in peace.
Earth teach me caring
as a dog securing her young.
Earth teach me suffering
as the plants that die away.
Earth teach me courage
as the tree who stands alone.

I try to follow a workshop model for writing time and find sharing to be the single most motivating factor, just as it is for me in my personal writing supported by my writers' group. Peer conferencing has been motivating, too, although my trained conference partners would understandably rather work on their own pieces. The class was able to write a persuasive essay on the theory of plate tectonics, what I once considered to be an assignment attainable only by the gifted child who naturally (and mysteriously) had made the reading-writing connection. We do playwriting about historical figures, math writing to explain procedures and thinking, and use flash-drafts (Fletcher, 1993, p. 63–65) to enliven nonfiction writing. Writing impacts every facet of my fifth-grade curriculum now.

It's been a long journey. I'm not there yet, as I still have goals. I want every child to progress in fluency and internalize strategies. I want share time to be immutable and frequent. I want to continue to explore making the reading-writing connection. That I have made the writer-writing connection I believe made all the difference.

References

Burns, M. (1987). *A collection of math lessons.* Sausalito, CA: Math Solutions Publications.

Bruner, J. S. (1971). *Toward a theory of instruction.* Cambridge, MA: Harvard University Press.

Collins, J. (1985). *Cumulative writing folder program.* Andover, MA: Collins Education Associates.

Davis, J. and Hill, S. E. (2003). *The no-nonsense guide to teaching writing.* Portsmouth, NH: Heinemann.

Estes, E. (1951). *Ginger Pye.* Orlando, FL: Harcourt, Inc.

Fletcher, R. (1993). *What a writer needs.* Portsmouth, NH: Heinemann.

Graves, D. H. (1983). *Writing: Teachers & children at work.* Portsmouth, NH: Heinemann.

Heard, G. (1999). *Awakening the heart.* Portsmouth, NH: Heinemann.

Heard, G. (2002). *The revision toolbox.* Portsmouth, NH: Heinemann.

McEwen, C. & Statman, M. (2000). *The alphabet of the trees.* New York: Teachers & Writers Collaborative.

McGuire, M. E. (1998). *Storypath: Colonial Boston and the struggle for independence.* Chicago, IL: Everyday Learning Corp.

Routman, R. (1991). *Invitations.* Portsmouth, NH: Heinemann.

Seymour, D. (1982). *Favorite problems.* Palo Alto, CA: Dale Seymour Publications.

Seymour, D. (1984). *Problem parade.* Palo Alto, CA: Dale Seymour Publications.

Whinnem, R. S. (2003). *Utten and Plumley.* Charlottesville, VA: Hampton Roads Publishing Company, Inc.

Show Me a Cover Story

Forays into Teaching Writing to Reluctant Writers

Faith-Ann McGarrell

"**M**s. M? Did Chris talk to you about his story?" Mrs. Peters approached me, her face flushed with excitement.

"No," I replied, "I have not seen him today."

For the rest of that afternoon I wondered what this particular student could possibly have to say to me. A member of my senior writing class, he seemed to have an excuse for every late writing assignment. I just knew that I would be hearing one of them: "I fell asleep brainstorming ideas and by the time I woke up it was time to catch the bus for school;" "I had it but these guys jumped me on the bus and took my stuff and my paper was with all my stuff;" "Man, Ms. M. That was a hard assignment—I got it in class but when I got home I didn't get it anymore;" and so the stories piled up. It seemed as though after three years of being in my English class he, and most of my students, should have known more about writing than they currently did.

"Hey Ms. M! I been looking all over for you. Guess what? They want me to send a picture for my story!" Chris's voice came from behind and soon his lanky frame stood in front of me, all smiles. "They accepted my

Getting It in Writing, pages 159–173
Copyright © 2011 by Information Age Publishing

story and they want me to send them a picture. My moms is taking me this afternoon to get some done professionally. I mean, it's gonna be a cover picture, you know."

I blinked and backtracked in my mind, "Why is he telling me this? Who accepted his story? When did he write anything?" Then, I remembered the contest.

Each year I encouraged students in English I-IV to enter an international writing contest sponsored by a youth magazine. Contestants were invited to tell their story. For the first time that year, I had incorporated the writing of the entered story as part of the students' in-class writing, and adopted a seminar format. Submission day was a big day in that they filled out their entry forms together, made sure their final drafts were indeed, final, and addressed the entry envelopes for mailing.

Chris was the first to have his story accepted for publication in the magazine. While he did not win the contest, the editors found his story, and the stories of four others, suitable for future publications. All five also received invitations to be featured on the cover. The students were excited and so was I.

A Rough Start

I started teaching writing by default. I studied literature for both my undergraduate and graduate programs, and my ultimate goal was to teach literature—to inspire students, to generate within them the same love for literature that I felt I possessed. When I started my teaching career, however, it was not at the college level, as I had imagined it would be.

Circumstances led me to a seventh and eighth grade language arts classroom. My only experience with teaching writing was a Rhetoric and Composition Seminar which focused primarily on Composition theory, and a two-year stint as a writing tutor at my university's Writing Center, where we were taught to focus on content first, and grammar second. We were told that we could not solve a student's grammatical deficiencies in one session, nor were we being paid to edit student work—a tough line to take, but an understandable one.

My first teaching experience was as a seventh and eighth grade language arts teacher in Florida. We read Lois Lowry's *Number the Stars*. I realized that this task would involve more than just reading and discussing. At some point, my students would have to write. And write they did. Any and everything. I resisted the urge to edit. I resisted the urge to teach grammar. I had no idea how to get them to expand their ideas beyond a mere cursory reading of and response to the prompt questions. I delved back into my Methods of Teaching Literature course notes for some granule of insight, but found little more than a list of great young adult books and ideas for generating discussion. This was resourceful, but what I really needed was insight on how to get my students to communicate legibly in writing.

At the close of that school year, I received an offer to teach English, all levels, in addition to Journalism, Creative Writing, and Public Speaking, as needed, at a small private high school in Illinois. What a great opportunity! I would have my own classroom, and it would be all up to me. Yet, the apprehension niggled at the back of my mind, "I have to teach writing." Surely, this group would be better. After all, these would be high school students at a private institution, exposed to smaller classrooms, and one-on-one instruction.

My first days in Chicago, however, were a reawakening to my inadequacy to address the task without additional instruction for myself. The challenges were the same. Students were unfamiliar with writing beyond the prompt question.

Grammar instruction was required by the school and took the form of filling out worksheets and answering questions from a grammar text. The concept of an essay of any kind was in its nascent stages. In addition, students had not made the connections between writing, speaking, and grammar. Many were not at grade level in reading, and English was not the favorite subject.

They Won't Even Try

Apart from the fact that English was not a favorite subject, what troubled me most about my students was their seeming lack of desire to even try to complete an assignment, regardless of whether it was a reading or a writing assignment. It seemed impossible for me to teach anything if my students were not even willing to make an attempt. At first, I thought it was because I was the new teacher—maybe they were testing me so see how long I would last. I ruled out that theory, however, when I realized that their lack of performance was not limited to my class, but extended to all their classes.

In order for me to succeed, I needed to address the problem in stages. At that time, my concerns rested with the dichotomy between the level at which my students were performing and the level at which they were required to perform. In each grade, I had students who were performing at least three to four grade levels below what was expected. I had ninth graders reading at a sixth grade reading level; tenth graders performing at an eighth grade reading level; and, several eleventh and twelfth graders were at eighth or ninth grade reading levels. Their required texts, however, were one to two grade levels ahead. For example, sections of the ninth and tenth grade literature anthologies were evaluated at a tenth or eleventh grade reading level, and the eleventh and twelfth grade anthologies were at a college level. Reading, then, was frustrating my students.

By extension, writing also proved a challenge. In addition to a literature anthology, each grade level had required a grammar text and a vocabulary workbook. The text outlined parts of speech, usage, sentence structure, diagramming, and paragraph structure, with a highlighted section on the research paper at the end of the book. Each chapter had several practice exercises, and the teacher's edition and resource package provided a bevy of additional practice exercises and worksheets. Writing, at the time I arrived, involved completing and submitting the exercises in the text and the worksheet exercises. The research paper was the longest writing assignment students had written, and this was reserved to the upper grades.

The teacher prior to me lasted one year, but had given students a taste of what they were capable of in terms of creative writing. Their major assignment that year had been to write and dramatize a play. They subsequently took the play "on the road" to several schools in the area and out of state. Yet, even with this exercise fresh on their minds, students had not yet connected the creative exercise to the process of writing. My frustrations rested in finding a way to make reading and writing meaningful, necessary, and doable. I felt strongly that if students realized what they were capable of producing, they would not stop once they started expressing themselves and sharing their thoughts. I also felt strongly that the more they read, the more they would find a way to connect to the world in which they lived.

How I Overcame my Frustrations in the Writing Classroom

Overcoming my frustration in the classroom did not happen in a day, a month, or a year. It took at least two years of trial and error before I found what I thought would be a workable solution to the apathy in my classroom. During that time, I learned to put aside my pride, recognize my need for help, and set about finding out what I could about the nature of my students.

Acknowledging my inadequacy was the first step I took, and it was not an easy one—pride has a way of enabling denial. A steady stream of bad papers, constant student complaints about assignments being "stupid" or "boring," and paragraphs masquerading as papers soon won over my pride, and I realized that I needed help. Help would come from two sources: my colleagues and additional reading.

Recognizing my need for help, I began seeking out my colleagues. There is a seeming silence amongst teachers when things are going wrong. For some reason, there is that misconception that if students aren't learning, then "it must be me—I'm a bad teacher." I made tentative forays into dispelling this myth by talking with one of my colleagues in the science department.

"How are the kids handling your textbook?" I queried one afternoon.

"Why do you ask?" She responded, not directly answering my question.

I proceeded to share my concerns about a few students that I knew we shared. I noted that they were having difficulty with my literature anthology and that it was on grade level and maybe a little above, and that I suspected that these particular students were functioning below grade level. She continued with her lunch, and did not corroborate or deny my suspicions. Feeling like a failure, I left the discussion alone, finished my lunch, and returned to my classroom.

Later that week, my colleague came to my room. School had ended; the students were gone, and the hallways were quiet. She proceeded to unload her concerns about her students' ability to write up their lab reports. "They have no concept of a sentence, paragraph structure, nothing! I am tired of returning papers littered with editorial marks because I know it doesn't mean a thing to them—and it's not as if I want them to correct the paper and turn it back in to me. That would make no sense. It's just that I feel something has to be done, and I don't know what or where to start." At that point, I knew that I was not the only one.

That I had company in my assessment of my students' performance gave me motivation. I began re-reading my writing textbooks and looking for information about the nature of my students and what ultimately would make them successful. I realized that if my students were not learning, it was my responsibility to find out why, and to find out how they learned best. I realized that I needed to start from where they were and move backward— they would have to write what they knew, and then the mechanics of their writing would become more meaningful, and the intent of their writing would be more meaningful as it evolved through a process of writing and re-writing. This was seemingly contrary to what Don Murray (1980) posited when he noted that "The process of making meaning with written language can not be understood by looking backward from a finished page. Process can not be inferred from product any more than a pig can be inferred from a sausage" (p. 3). My process, however, involved trying to understand where I would place the mechanical structures of the language in my instruction. The pedantic, directive method of instruction in grammar was obviously not working, so my students needed another approach. I realized that I did not have to do this by myself. I could get help from my colleagues. If I was concerned about the quality of writing in my classroom, then I am sure they were, too. I began to realize that the problems in my room were not only in mine, but also other teachers, as well, had problems.

"Getting" My Students

Getting to know more about my students also helped me to "get" my students, as much as that is possible from an outsider's perspective. Ninety-percent of my students came from non-traditional family structures where some lived with grandparents or aunts, some lived with one parent with no contact with the other, some were in the foster care system, and some lived in shared custody situations where at any given time they resided with either parent.

Ninety percent lived within the city limits, some never having gone more than ten blocks, north/south or east/west of their home. Most used public transportation to get to school or walked. Most went home to an empty house and remained alone at home sometimes until as late as 11:00 PM. For ninety percent of my students, the hours they were in school, from 7:30 AM until 3:20 PM, were the most supervised hours of their lives.

Their condition was not that different from that of many students living in an inner-city. According to Genevieve Johnson (1997), several factors placed students living in inner cities at risk of not only failing to learn, but of also entering adulthood "illiterate." These factors included those that are familiar: substance abuse, early pregnancy, truancy, lack of motivation, and limited English language competencies for either the students, parents, or both. Having a sibling who dropped out of school was also a risk factor, as well as lack of community involvement in the neighborhood, abandonment by developers, poor facilities, and lack of opportunities and service. Most importantly, Johnson (1997) cited that teacher preconception and prejudice, an unwillingness to modify the curriculum or individualize instruction, and a lack of resources also helped to create a climate where students feared for their safety, could not complete the homework, were unmotivated and bored, and received little support from home. Taken together, these factors described my students to the letter. Sadly, these factors also described me, to some degree.

Realizing that my concerns were shared by several of my colleagues boosted my confidence. In opening the discussion, I began to receive support and generate interest in cross-curricular writing experiences. The science department and the English department collaborated on entering students into a local science competition. The senior level writing students wrote proposals, conducted experiments, and wrote their final reports between the two classes. Three seniors had their proposals and final writing projects selected for the final round of competition—a first for the school.

Seeking to understand my students' lives reinforced in my mind that they needed to write what they knew. My students had a better understanding about the world than they gave themselves credit. In order for them to realize this, they needed a class period that was restructured for their success. Instead of a full ninety-minute session dedicated to grammar and sentence structure, each English course was divided into four distinct sections: a twenty-minute mini reading or writing lesson, followed by a twenty-minute peer conference or teacher directed conference on whatever students were reading and writing at the time. This was followed by a forty-minute open reading/writing session where students worked on individual writing projects. The final ten minutes were reserved for questions, points of clarification, and announcements. It took two months for the system to fall into place and begin to work effectively. Soon, students came to English knowing exactly what they were going to work on for that session. This structure gave me the time to work with students independently, in groups, and as needed.

What Did My Students Need to Succeed?

I realized that my students, in addition to lacking skills, lacked confidence in their ability to contribute to the world they inhabited. In order to adequately address these gaps, I needed a system that would allow for positive talk, rewards, incentives, and one-on-one time; I needed a system that would allow me to incorporate their interests and experiences, and ultimately lead them to a system of self-directed learning and independence.

Motivation had to come from the hallmark of adolescent behavior: the self. I began re-reading the works of several authors who had shaped my theoretical understanding of composition. Stephen Judy in *The Experiential Approach: Inner Worlds to Outer Worlds* (1980) cites several major premises as essential to teaching composition:

1. The best student writing is motivated by personal feelings and experience.
2. Writing from experience takes place in many modes of discourse, including creative forms, but by no means excluding expository and academic modes.

3. Writing from experience often, but not invariably, requires that students write for a readership—often someone other than the instructor.

Judy listed several other factors, but these three spoke directly to the needs in my classroom. In another work, Tchudi and Tchudi (1999) state that "reading, writing, listening, and speaking are learned by doing, not principally by studying abstractions or completing exercises" (p. 11). They further denote that as English teachers, the best way to transmit a love for the language is to provide opportunities for students to use the language. To do this, our classrooms must be language centers, stimulating and motivating students to engage with words.

Erika Lindemann (1987), in *A Rhetoric for Writing Teachers*, provided several connections between Piaget and theories of adolescent learning. For example, we live by extension, vicariously; we think based on experiences; we know more that we are able to verbalize; and we have an innate desire to "know" ourselves and the world in which we live. Above all, from Lindemann's work, I found support in a key idea: "Beginning teachers, however, have not had the opportunity to develop a philosophy of teaching. They remember how they were taught; they read; they listen to others suggest what writing courses ought to do—but evaluating the information is difficult. Until they develop a conceptual framework to help them sort out what they read and hear, they must teach by trial and effort" (p. 3). This offered comfort as I navigated my way through the process of creating more engaged writers.

While a system of reward and incentive would serve as an initial motivation, at some point learners would have to embrace writing as a part of their own experience, regardless of whether or not there was a system of rewards in place. Vygotsky's Zone of Proximal Development came to mind as a way of bringing to the classroom an atmosphere of interdependence and intradependence. Nancy Frey and Douglas Fisher (2006) in their work *Language Arts Workshop: Purpose Reading and Writing Instruction* provide insight on how Vygotsky's Zone becomes essential to reading and writing instruction. Vygotsky defined this Zone as "the distance between the actual developmental level as determined by independent problem solving and the level of potential development as determined through problem solving under adult guidance or in collaboration with a more capable peer" (p. 5). Another way of referring to this is the gradual release of responsibility model, which begins with explicit instruction of a given strategy, then moves on to guided instruction as students try it out on their own, and students assume more responsibility as they work with one another and then independently. This model exemplified what I wanted to happen in my classroom.

Methods that Worked

Collaboration Across the Curriculum

In addition to collaboration across the curriculum with the science department, several disciplines were willing to collaborate with the English department. The art students wrote descriptions for their art work in preparation for city-wide gallery showings; also, application forms, college application essays, and job search information came through the English department. With increased opportunities to focus on different forms of writing, the only useful method that seemed to allow this type of flexibility was the workshop or writing seminar approach.

Writing Workshop and Portfolio Writing

As a result, I adopted the workshop approach to writing instruction and a portfolio approach to provide students with an opportunity to reflect multiple styles of writing. Tchudi and Tchudi (1999) note that while each instructor develops his or her own approach to using the writing workshop method, several factors remain constant: student engagement, student choice, student ownership, and student independence. These factors seemed to work well with the needs of my students at that time.

In order to implement this strategy, I needed to re-organize my classroom to reflect a workshop style. In addition to restructuring how I would use the ninety minute block periods, I also needed to restructure how I presented elements of the curriculum and the physical layout of my classroom. This was a challenge in that I did not have many resources. Glass paneled window panes covered the wall to the east and cupboards covered the wall to the west. Green tiles covered the floor and the walls were a mixture of green and cream paint. Desk chairs that had seen better days, decorated with the names and social affiliations of past students, proved problematic for writing instruction in that they were also small and cramped.

During the first year of implementing the workshop approach, the bulletin board at the back became a message board where opportunities for writing were posted and constantly updated. The bulletin board at the front became a mini-lecture message board where short writing tips were posted. For example, the writing cycle, tips about brainstorming, sentence structure, style, and punctuation trees, were posted. The wall of cupboards became the last bulletin board upon which student work was displayed. Most of the time poetry was displayed on this board. As part of the workshop approach, students were required to keep a daily writing journal, a writing folder which contained items in progress, and a final portfolio folder, which contained items ready for submission and/or publication.

I realized that the effort put into small details often precipitates success overall. Faculty meetings were held in the English room. Over the course of several months, my principal began to ask questions as he noticed that the classroom was begin transformed into a more active space. I shared with him what we were trying to accomplish, but he did not say much.

Returning to school after a semester break, I found that my room was carpeted with a deep royal blue carpet, and two bookshelves appeared, as well as a round table. The desk chairs had been replaced with newer, un-marred blue desk chairs. Finally, the entire room received a fresh coat of paint. The room, transformed by matching furniture and décor, suddenly looked inviting. My principal shared that over the break someone had donated several items, and he remembered the workshop and thought we could do with a few bookshelves and a table. He asked if we could use a few of the word processors that were no longer needed in the computer lab, and I emphatically said, "We certainly could!" The carpeting and the chairs came courtesy of a parent organization that wanted to do something for the entire school, and the English room benefited.

Creating the climate slowly brought about a change in the student response to what the writing workshop sought to accomplish. The components of the writing workshop, as outlined by Lucy Calkins (1994) provided an opportunity for learners to adjust. Mini-lessons, work time consisting of writing and conferring, share sessions, and publication celebrations became staples in our classroom.

What surprised me the most was that students began to, without my prodding, actually read the publication opportunities posted on the bulletin board to the back of the room. I remember the day Kalita came in and said, "Ms. M—Look what came in the mail yesterday!" She handed me a heavily handled letter from the editor of a city-wide publication of student poetry which stated that her poem, created during one of the workshop sessions, had been accepted for publication. It was our first publication for that group, and the excitement was palpable.

I adjusted my expectations of the perfect paper, and created a new expectation. Each student had to write and maintain a writing folder that reflected different types of writing: a narrative, a report, poetry, research, book reviews, and a social issue/current event analysis. During their writing sessions, they were free to write and work on any of their pieces, as long as they were writing.

Students entered writing competitions, submitted entries to local poetry anthologies, magazines, and state writing contests. Students began to see themselves as writers in residence. Were there still grammatical issues and mechanical misunderstandings? Certainly. Were some students still trying to pass off a paragraph for an essay? Definitely. What changed was the overall tone of English class. I had not heard "I'm bored" or "This is stupid" for several months.

Continuing Education

Another way of addressing my frustration came from returning to school in the summer to maintain my teaching certification. As part of the summer session, I attended courses in instruction, reading strategies, the teaching of reading, learning styles, and secondary methods of instruction. Each course provided an opportunity for me to plan how I would implement what was learned that summer into my classroom. These summers away from my students allowed me to talk with other English teachers, many of whom faced the same struggles I did. In sharing our stories and tips about what worked and what did not work, I was able to gain more confidence in my ability to teach my students—to prepare them for not only a working life, but a writing life.

I learned how to use a rubric and how to grade selectively. One challenge I faced was grading the 80 plus papers that would come in on a given day from different classes. Should I read every paper? Would it be cheating my students if I did not read every word of their paper? How would I move students away from the misconception that I needed to correct or edit their paper? Immaculate Kizza (1997) in her essay "Developing Intrinsic Motivation for Students' Writing" notes, "Often, students ignore our very comprehensive comments on their papers and instead focus on the grades, thereby doing very little to improve their writing but succeeding in disheartening us" (p. 277). It was often quite disheartening making changes that sometimes seemed to others as not prescriptive enough.

Focusing student attention on developing intrinsic motivation proved to be a challenge. For several students, this occurred only when they realized that they were responsible for their own portfolios. I taught students to peer conference on specific elements of the paper, and I, too, would read for the same. Final drafts received at least two thorough readings for coherence and content. This greatly adjusted my reading load, and my students became more independent in their ability to critique not only their own papers, but those of their peers.

Rubrics proved to be my salvation. They forced me to clarify what I wanted my students to gain from each formal writing task and at what level I expected them to perform. For my students, it provided an opportunity to focus on specific skills, and it also clarified their ability to look at their own work critically.

Conclusion: Lessons Learned from Colleagues, Readings, and Summer Sessions

During my five years of teaching writing at the high school level, I had several epiphanies. First, share the load. I learned that my frustrations were not unique to me. Several of my colleagues shared similar experiences and were willing to work with me in addressing our common concerns. I also learned that it was important to "get" or understand my student population. In doing so, I was able to identify several factors that needed to be a part of their learning experience if they wanted to continue to a higher level of writing and comprehension.

Second, my students lacked skills and confidence. I needed to provide opportunities that would allow them to develop their skills and build their confidence. Concurrently, I needed to adjust expectations, but at the same time, maintain standards. I needed to demand high standards and expect them. High interest reading paired with writing workshops and portfolio assessments offered motivation and opened the door to student expression. This led to a gradual release of responsibility and more interdependence and independence in the writing classroom.

Lindeman (1987) states that "Learning to write well, then, has value far beyond any power to bring in a paycheck or pass a course. Students will not underestimate the importance of a good salary or a diploma, but they can also come to appreciate acquiring a skill which helps them relate ideas, solve problems, make sense of their experiences, and manipulate a complex symbol system to communicate their thoughts in many voices" (1987, p. 7). This proved true with Chris, the young man whose first publication opened for him a world of confidence and purpose.

Chris, like many young adults, developed a fascination with guns. One afternoon, while simultaneously playing with a handgun and talking on the phone, he accidentally shot himself in the head. The bullet penetrated his left eye, leaving him blind. He entered ninth grade with everyone having heard his story, but not ever talking about his story. Throughout our workshop sessions for three years Chris wrote about everything else—from attempting his own rap lyrics, to poetry, to research writing on the Harlem Renaissance, but never his own story. Our second set of entries into a magazine contest had him frustrated. He did not know what to write and felt conflicted.

"Ms. M?" He said during one of our conference sessions. "Do you think I should write my story?"

I looked at him and he looked at the floor. "Chris, why would you want to write your story?" I asked. It seemed appropriate that he should have a reason for wanting to share something so intensely personal—that a story like his should not be one shared on a whim.

"Well, I never really thought about what happened. It just happened and now I think I want to write about what happened."

"Fine," I replied. "You know, you don't have to submit it as an entry if you don't wish to do so. It can be a portfolio piece."

This gave him an escape, and he took it. The process of writing his story was a strange one. It started with one paragraph that was very factual. It stated what happened, how, the time, and the result. Each workshop session he wrote a little bit more, and his peer writing group prodded some more and he wrote a little more. One afternoon his mother, Mrs. Peters, stopped by the classroom. "Thank you for getting Chris to write his story. He needed to do this, but I was afraid that he would never face his injury." I shared with her that I had nothing to do with Chris writing his story; that was a decision he had made on his own.

As submission day drew closer, Chris decided he would submit his story.

"I don't want to win anything, but I know if I can put it out there, then I can talk about it more."

Talk about it he did. It appeared to me that after our submission day, that was all he talked about. It was as if writing about the experience made it more real to him, and the chip on his shoulder seemed a little less harsh. Several other students had their stories published that year, but for Chris, it was a life changing event. He seemed more energized and began making plans for the future.

Student Success and On-going Performance as Writers and Readers

My students' writing continued long after I left that program. Several moved on to attend two-year colleges and completed their programs. Several more attended four-year colleges and graduated. One, after leaving my program to attend another public high school, became editor of his high school paper and garnered interviews with several high powered community leaders. He eventually earned a college scholarship to study journalism at a university in the southern United States. Every so often, I hear from one of my past students, and they say, "Ms. M, I'm still keeping my journal, you know," and I feel good.

Many of my students, however, left high school before they graduated. Others, while they completed their high school requirements and graduated, did not go beyond high school. It is my hope that the writing life continues for those in this group. Will Fitzhugh (2006) in an article titled "Where's the Content" writes about high school student writing that is "Short on facts. Long on touchy feely" (p. 42). His concern rests in what happens to high school students who are rudely awakened to the rigor of college writing after coming through a secondary program that emphasizes and validates experience.

While his point is valid, the context in which he writes does not address the needs of reluctant writers. As Murray (1980) notes, start from a blank page and move forward. For students whose experiences with writing have been limited to worksheets and sentence structure, the blank page is a daunting but necessary part of their learning experience.

The realization that student success is dependent, to a large extent, on teacher efficacy is one that has remained with me in my teaching. In addition, the understanding that adapting the curriculum and individualizing instruction is helpful to all students, not just those who are at-risk, has empowered my teaching. In order for motivation to last, external sources of motivation must take students to that level where they are interdependent and independent. This allows them to benefit from peer collaboration, but at the same time, take responsibility for their own learning. Finally, the support of colleagues and mentors is invaluable to success in implementing new pedagogy. These four ideals remain with me today and continue to guide my practice.

References

Calkins, L. (1994). *The art of teaching writing*. Portsmouth, NH: Heinemann.
Fitzhugh, W. (2006). Where's the content? *Educational Leadership, 64*(2), 42–46.
Frey, N. & Fisher, D. (2006). *Language arts workshop: Purposeful reading and writing instruction*. Columbus, OH: Pearson Prentice Hall.
Johnson, G. M. (1997). Teachers in the inner city: Experience-based rating of factors that place students at-risk. *Preventing School Failure, 42*(1) 19–26.
Judy, S. (1980). The experiential approach: Inner worlds to outer worlds. In T. R. Donovan and B. W. McClelland (Eds.), *Eight approaches to teaching composition* (pp. 37–51). Urbana, IL: NCTE.

Kizza, I. (1997). Developing intrinsic motivation for students' writing. In S. Tchudi (Ed.), *Alternative to grading student writing*. Urbana, IL: NCTE.

Lindemann, E. (1987). *A rhetoric for writing teachers*. New York: Oxford University Press.

Murray, D. (1980). Writing as process: How writing finds its own meaning. In T. R. Donovan and B. W. McClelland (Eds.), *Eight approaches to teaching composition* (pp. 3–20). Urbana, IL: NCTE.

Tchudi, S. & Tchudi, S. J. (1999). *The English/language arts handbook: Classroom strategies for teachers*. Portsmouth, NH: Boynton/Cook Heinemann.

Journey of a Lifetime

Vickie Moriarity

Many teachers earn their certification and teach in the same state, maybe even the same district, until they retire. My journey is different. I have been teaching for fourteen years, but in four different states: Arizona, Nebraska, Virginia, and Kentucky. While some teachers may not feel this is positive, I feel lucky to have had the opportunity to teach in so many places. Each new geographical change has transformed my writing and my writing instruction.

The Foundations—The Pacific Northwest

Although my teaching career began in Phoenix, Arizona, I grew up in Bremerton, Washington—a small city where the naval shipyards were a source of both pride and commercial activity. I graduated fifth in my class at Bremerton High School and could have chosen any profession, but at the time, I wanted to be a jazz saxophonist. I always envisioned myself as the next Kenny G or David Sanborn. As a result, I enrolled at the Cornish College of the Arts in Seattle. I took courses in jazz theory, rhythm, ear training, and sight reading. I even took English composition, which was, oddly enough, the only C I earned. However, my ambitions of making it in the music world quickly faded as I struggled to pay bills. I dropped out a year later and waited tables full time so I could eat on a regular basis.

Getting It in Writing, pages 175–188

After a failed relationship with my first real boyfriend and a shattered dream of becoming a successful musician, I followed my dad to Phoenix, Arizona. He had recently moved there to make a fresh start of his own. I packed up my few clothes, my books, my saxophone, and said a quick good-bye to my latest beau and the place where I grew up.

Arizona couldn't have been more different. Prickly saguaro cactus, scorching sun, dust storms, and dry riverbeds replaced the towering pine trees, mild temperatures, drizzling rain, and salt water inlets of my child-hood. It was as if I had decided to wander into the desert in search of my true identity.

Once settled in Phoenix, I waited tables again, the fear of not eating firmly rooted in my brain. I enrolled in classes at Phoenix Community College but couldn't find a subject that held my interest. Psychology, paralegal classes, computer programming—nothing seemed to fit like music had once seemed to. When it came down to focusing on a single career, one that actually paid a real salary as opposed to my $2.01 an hour plus tips, I was clueless.

After a Saturday night of deep philosophical discussion with my father following yet another late shift at Coco's Family Restaurant, he said the wisest words I had ever heard. "Vickie, you spend so much time in school. Why don't you become a teacher?" After eight years of confusion, the puzzle pieces fell into place.

I looked into transferring to the Arizona State University the following Monday and found I had more than enough credits to do so. Two years later, I graduated with a bachelor's degree in secondary education with an emphasis in English. I owe this degree to my father. Without his words that night, I would not have figured out what I was meant to do in this life.

Arizona—The Journey Begins—Desert Sands Middle School

Fresh out of college in 1994, I was hired to teach eighth grade language arts at Desert Sands Middle School, a low socioeconomic school in Phoenix, Arizona. I knew from day one that my university education had not prepared me for urban realities. The students came in sporting red, blue, or black shoelaces, oversized monochromatic clothing, and gaudy gold jewelry (indicators of their gang affiliations). They flashed gang signs when teachers dared turn their backs and tested school boundaries with unabashed intention. I diligently posted classroom rules that were routinely ignored. Students rarely brought pencils and paper, threw the pencils they did bring at each other, and had no problems threatening or punching a student in the middle of my lesson if they felt they had been disrespected. These were not the ideal students I anticipated based upon the university's preparation.

As a first year teacher, I dutifully followed the lead of my assigned mentor, the only other language arts teacher on my team. Her lessons were old-school, consisting mainly of weekly spelling tests, grammar exercises from our Heath Composition textbook (by now ten years old), and assigned questions at the end of readings like "The Monkey's Paw" from the literature book. Because my principal wanted us to be "on the same page at the same time" to ensure continuity, there was little time to teach or practice the writing process. The time it would have taken to brainstorm, draft, revise, edit, and present a piece simply didn't fit into my mentor's plans. The second year wasn't much different.

That summer while taking classes for my Master's degree, I reflected on my teaching experience. Had my students become better writers? No. How could I change this? I knew these kids had a lot to share about their lives, but they kept those feelings locked behind tough facades. I asked my principal if I could teach writing separately from the literature. I knew this went against pedagogy, but I needed time to intensely analyze the writing curriculum and figure out how to reach my students. My mentor teacher was excited by the prospect of teaching literature only, and my principal agreed to try it, so I began to research what makes a writing class successful.

My writing instruction improved a little bit my third year. Prior to school starting, a colleague suggested I read Nancie Atwell's *In the Middle: Writing, Reading, and Learning with Adolescents* (1987). As a result, I added the infamous writing folders. Infamous because the writings were so painful to read! The heartache and life experiences that filled students' journal pages were overwhelmingly poignant, but horrifyingly stark. Every other piece contained stories of incarcerated family members or relatives killed in gang-related violence. One piece of writing I recall described how one boy held his dying brother after he had been shot by a rival gang member. I did learn about my students' home lives, however. I did little else with those folders. I was too much in shock, and classroom management difficulties still prevented me from really exploring a writer's workshop climate in my classroom. I couldn't figure out how to be organized enough to effectively incorporate this idea when chaos seemed only moments away each day in my classroom.

My principal discussed classroom management techniques with me at my next evaluation. I remember timidly tapping on his office door for my fall evaluation, extremely nervous since I had already been required to complete a growth plan regarding classroom discipline the previous year when the assistant principal had evaluated me. I had one more evaluation in spring that would ultimately determine my tenure with the district. Mr. Ron Poole, my principal at the time, sat me down and asked how I felt I was doing.

After tearfully expressing my frustrations regarding classroom management, he paused, then said, "Vickie, do you know why I hired you? It wasn't because you were the greatest teacher on earth who had just walked into my office. It was because you had fire, you wanted to do this, and you are teachable." That is when he showed me the book *Positive Classroom Discipline* by Fred Jones (1987). I can truthfully say that Mr. Poole and that book saved my teaching career.

I read *Positive Classroom Discipline* over Christmas break that year. My mistakes glared back at me in many of Jones's examples. Jones wrote about a group of students he followed at a school he was visiting that were perfect in one teacher's room and standing on the top of the coat closet in another teacher's room. Guess which example I identified with? What was the difference? According to Fred Jones, it was classroom arrangement, teacher consistency, and student responsibility training.

When I returned from break, I rearranged my desks a dozen times using the templates in *Positive Classroom Discipline* (Jones, 1987, p. 61). I settled upon a horseshoe arrangement that allowed me a three to five second walk to any student in the room. With renewed hope, I awaited the students' return from Christmas break.

When the students returned, I quickly realized that close proximity prevented many disruptions. The new seating arrangement allowed me to get anywhere in the room in just a few seconds, which seemed to prevent a lot of disruptions before they really started. I learned to teach and walk at the same time so that I could engage all students during a lesson, not just the ones at the front of the room.

I also committed one phrase from Jones's book to memory: "Shut up and wait" (1987, p. 111). This phrase means that when a student is talking back, responding to his or her comments with anger or sarcasm only adds fuel to the fire and gives that student additional ammunition. I learned that the child's goal at that moment is to disrupt the lesson and gain the respect of fellow peers by challenging authority. Confronting that student in front of his or her peers is guaranteed suicide. Since I preferred survival over suicide, it was better to issue the instruction and keep my mouth shut. Sooner or later the student always ran out of comments and went back to work. In the meantime, I kept the respect of the class since I chose not to engage in the same behavior.

I also started placing notes on disruptive students' desks when I walked by that said, "Please pay attention. Your parents' phone number is _ _ _–_ _ _ _." Although students claimed their parents had no power over them, it seemed many preferred to leave their parents out of the teacher–student equation. By keeping the discipline private, many disruptions seemed to stop as quickly as they started, and the nervous tic I had developed during my teaching career diminished considerably.

I also incorporated preferred activity time (PAT), a responsibility training technique (Jones, 1987). The basic premise is that students want more "play" time and teachers want more time on-task. In an effort to reach that goal, I gave each class five minutes of PAT time every Monday that would be used at the end of the week on a fun, yet educational activity such as Jeopardy, an art activity, or some other review game. (Since then, I have accumulated a number of fun, yet educational activities for classes to spend their earned time on each week.)

Students could either add to their existing PAT time by being on time, attending class, and "hustling" during transitions from one activity to the next, or they could lose PAT time by talking when they weren't supposed to, wandering the room, or being off-task. When the whole class was off-task, I simply said, "I need your attention," and clicked the stopwatch. Soon students began saying things like, "Shhh . . . she's timing!" If a single student had the audacity to use the class's hard earned PAT time for a personal mini-vacation from our work, my tougher clientele issued quiet warnings of impending doom if the off-task student didn't get back to work. Needless to say, the student was back on task in record time. I later took ten seconds off each time an unkind word was spoken by the "enforcers" to eliminate some of the intimidation occurring in my class.

The rest of that year was far from perfect, but by developing more consistent classroom management, I could concentrate on teaching writing. I became known as a Fred Jones groupie after that and attended every seminar he offered in my area, watched all his videos, and bought two copies of every book he wrote. Many of the tools I acquired from *Positive Classroom Discipline* are a prominent part of my classroom management repertoire today.

The following year, I was moved to another eighth grade team at the same school. All young and ambitious, no teacher on our team had taught more than four or five years; therefore, it was easy for us to try ideas outside the traditional educational paradigm. The math teacher, Sarah Zembruski and another colleague, Valerie Weide, had created an interdisciplinary unit the year before that made students want to come to school. The social studies, math, and language arts classrooms were divided into the original thirteen colonies. We chalked the carpets delineating state boundaries, had each colony elect a governor, drew state seals and mottos, and researched each colony's natural resources. Students wrote state constitutions and traded resources, such as timber or fish, so each colony could survive. Letters were sent by "Pony Express" and weren't allowed to be "delivered" until the teachers initialed them as error free. We would only tell students where an error was located. They had to figure out what was wrong. Although teachers were still editing all the letters, students began thinking about conventions, applying what they knew, and learning what they didn't.

Students enjoyed writing and sending the letters to the other "colonies," filling out their ledgers when they made a sale or bought goods, and balancing their accounts to ensure they weren't bankrupt. Occasionally, good old King George (a.k.a. teachers donning cardboard Burger King crowns) taxed the colonists, which caused an occasional revolt. Afterward during discussion, students expressed a deep understanding of the colonists' frustrations with England's taxation laws. I discovered the power of interdisciplinary projects that year and the excitement they create for learning. However, while students were now writing for purpose and thinking about conventions, the letters were still formulaic and uninspired. True creativity and voice were still not apparent in my students' writing.

That summer, I took "Writing Across the Curriculum," a professional development course offered by the school district. Teachers wrote personal narratives, memoirs, poems, and short stories. We drafted. We revised. We shared. This was my first experience as a writer outside of university classes. When I realized how good it felt to be recognized for the blood and sweat I poured into my memoir, "Ode to My 1985 Mustang," ideas for classroom writing projects that would help students feel that same pride began to emerge.

In year five, I discovered kids loved to write if they knew they were going to have a live audience. Having toughened up to the realities of urban life, I took the writing folder idea from two years ago and used it as a springboard for original poetry they would perform at our "coffeehouse." After peer conferences and countless revisions (uninitiated by me most of the time), students read original poetry on stage to over 150 parents and classmates, who munched on butter cookies and sipped hot chocolate at our all day "Desert Sands' Coffeehouse Poetry Reading." After each reading, the kids snapped their fingers in approval and said "Cool, Daddio" while parents proudly looked on. Gang members shed tears when recalling the losses of brothers, sisters, friends, and family members due to violence. My students began to see how writing could help them express their thoughts. I learned that students will revise when they truly care about what they are writing and if they know they will be presenting it. I knew this project was a success when a middle-aged woman met me at the parking lot as I pulled in early one morning. Coffee cup in hand, she asked where the new "coffeehouse" was. Apparently, she had heard the coffeehouse buzz in the neighborhood!

Arizona—The Switch to Seventh Grade— Cholla Middle School

I left Desert Sands a couple of years later when the superintendent and I didn't see eye-to-eye regarding the direction of the district and was hired to teach seventh grade language arts at Cholla Middle School in the Washington Elementary School District. This school district was shifting from middle class to poverty because Phoenix was growing. What used to be a rather affluent area was giving in to urban life; once pristine middle class homes now showed their age. Iron bars caged in small cottage windows. Seedy businesses sprouted up, replacing businesses that relocated to newer business complexes. But the area was still considered middle class for the time being. I knew I had come to a better funded school district when I asked the principal for individual desks instead of tables, and she said, "I can get you that, but all the desks won't match." I felt like I had died and gone to heaven!

I continued integrating language arts with other disciplines. Because I was responsible for the literature and writing again, we read more texts that referenced social studies or science content and used the content from other disciplines as springboards for writing. The students paraphrased "Paul Revere's Ride" by Henry Wadsworth Longfellow line by line and presented their paraphrased versions to the class in an effort to enhance reading comprehension and improve writing and speaking skills. Using self-created rubrics, I scored poetry about cells, volcanoes, and historical fiction where students described the action on Civil War battlefields from unusual perspectives (Stonewall Jackson's horse or a rock on the field of Gettysburg). While the pieces lacked purpose and were contrived, students were more creative and voice was emerging in some of their writing. The rubrics really helped students understand my expectations, but I was still a novice teacher of writing with much to learn.

By the end of my ninth year, I felt overwhelmed by the amount of writing I thought I was supposed to grade. I was tired. After attending an English Language Learners conference where a speaker talked about raising expectations, I bought and read the book, *Improving Student Learning: Applying Deming's Quality Principles in Classrooms* (Jenkins, 2003). According to Lee Jenkins, I didn't have to grade everything I assigned. Instead, I could assign several pieces and grade just one. At first I felt like I was cheating, but upon further reflection, I realized that students didn't practice writing enough and this just might be the ticket to increase the amount of quality output. But before trying out this new idea, it was time to move again!

Nebraska—High School Exposure— Platteview High School

I married my husband Tim, a manager for Kellogg's U.S.A., in 2003. In order to do that, I had relocated to Nebraska where he lived. (Long distance romance doesn't work well.) Moving to Omaha brought me new experiences and new challenges in both my personal life and my career. Nebraska was quite different from Arizona. For one thing, Nebraska had snow—and lots of it. Only two or three times in the previous sixteen years had I seen flakes of snow on the outskirts of Phoenix. First, I traded in "Little Red," my 1995 Nissan pickup truck, for a 2003 Ford Taurus that got better traction on icy roads in preparation of my 45-minute drive from Omaha to Springfield, the location of my new teaching position. Then I spent my summer learning how to be a wife and reviewing the content I was supposed to teach at Platteview High School.

When school began, I had to cope with a lot of changes on the job as well. I had only one minority student, a light skinned African-American in my freshman and sophomore classes. This was a complete 180 from what I was used to. To be honest, I couldn't tell one blonde-haired pony-tailed girl from another. I was also teaching four different preps: freshman English, sophomore English, basic English for freshmen, and basic English for sophomores. I have a huge respect for both elementary and high school teachers who think nothing of preparing for a variety of classes simultaneously!

Additionally, I was reintroduced to the world of high school indifference, something I had not dealt with since student teaching. Yes, middle school gang members possessed a certain type of apathy for academics, but I felt their disinterest was easier to crack than teenagers with only sexual exploration and fast cars on their minds. I remember comparing the elements of an essay to a souped up car (the topic sentence is the engine, the word choice is like the paint job, etc.) in an effort to make them understand the six traits of writing. I don't know how much it helped, but I sure learned a lot about cars.

In one class, I had several students remind me they were ADHD; therefore, they couldn't concentrate. We spent a lot of the school year talking about excuse making and how the real working world wouldn't care if they had ADHD or any other problem. I shared with them that I have Multiple

Sclerosis, and while my left hand was numb, I couldn't use it as an excuse for not doing my work. Making excuses was simply not an option. It was up to them to figure how to cope with their disabilities or weaknesses and overcome them if they wanted to succeed after high school.

I floundered as I tried to show my love of Shakespeare but resorted to teaching them Shakespearean insults, the one lesson they might still remember from me. I still conferenced with students on their writing; however, without a close connection with them, it didn't go as well as it had in the past. Because Springfield was a small, close knit community so different from anywhere I had lived before, I didn't feel a bond with these young people yet, something I am sure would have helped me immensely.

On a positive note, I did make students more accountable for their writing by making them practice more often. Using the information I learned the previous summer from Jenkins's book, students wrote three pieces of the same genre before I selected one to grade. When the due date arrived, I rolled a die and graded the writing that coincided with that number. If a four, five, or six came up, I rolled again. If students didn't have the piece assigned, they received a zero for the assignment. As a result, most students completed and carefully revised all their pieces because they didn't know which would be selected. The onus of practicing writing fell to the students, and I spent less time making corrections on papers that would hit the trash can as soon as they were returned.

Virginia—Southern Hospitality—Chatham Middle School

The following year, my husband took a management position with Nestle in Danville, Virginia. Again, I was leaving the familiar. I was going to a very different world—the South. I was lucky enough to get a job at a small middle school fifteen minutes from my home. I worked well with a staff that truly showed me why the South is famous for its southern hospitality. They welcomed me to the school with open arms, and I became very close friends with all of them. A new opportunity to improve as a writing teacher waited.

During an in-service at the school, I was introduced to *The Four Square Writing Method* by Judith and Evan Gould (1999). This book's simple graphic organizer improved my students' understanding of organization, topic ideas, and specific detail more than anything I had used in the past. After the in-service, the four square book was purchased for every language arts teacher in the building.

Another teacher, Theresa Lawrence, and I then developed a school-wide writing program based on that organizer. The organizer was the only change we made, yet our writing scores on Virginia's state tests increased from 60% to 71% that year. More importantly, I conferenced with students during the organization phase faster and more effectively. With one quick glance, I pointed out lapses in reasoning, places to add detail, and redundancy in their writing. As a result, I learned that conferencing with students during the planning stage of writing is much more helpful to them than scribbling comments on their final drafts when it is too late to make changes. The following year, Chatham Middle School's writing scores jumped to an astounding 91%! Unfortunately, my husband was transferred to Kentucky to manage a Nestle plant that made Hot Pockets, so I wasn't able to share in that celebration.

Kentucky—Do I Really Want to Teach?—Bourbon County Continuous Learning Center

Tim and I moved to Kentucky after the school year began, so most teaching positions were already filled. One of the few jobs still open was at an 8–12th grade alternative school in Bourbon County. Two other teachers had resigned from the position, both male, and one had been a prison chaplain prior to taking the job! Neither of my predecessors had lasted longer than six weeks.

The lead teacher, a secretary, and I would be responsible for up to twenty students who were unable to function in traditional classrooms. After several discussions with Tim about this job, I chose to accept it and was hired in October. The contract was for less than a year and I needed to help pay our mortgages—we still hadn't sold our home in Virginia. Because I was hired during the district's fall break, I spent that week researching ways to reach at-risk populations.

When school reconvened, I was introduced to the way things were done at the Bourbon County CLC with a vengeance. Students had no problem telling a teacher to f*** off at this school. Many were there for drug use, fighting, and other criminal behavior. These were the "throw-away" kids, those everyone else had given up on and didn't know how to reach. Several students had, in my estimation, taken over the building, a renovated old house on the school's property. They did as they pleased when they pleased. Two students frequently stopped working whenever they felt like it, usually an hour or so after they got there, and napped on the floor for several hours. If prodded to get up, they exploded, ranted, raved, and attempted intimidation. After one episode where the other instructor had called in sick and only the secretary and I were there, I called the superintendent and told her things had to change or I quit. She held a meeting with me in the parking lot that day.

She agreed that order had to be restored and granted me permission to press charges for out-of-control behavior and teacher abuse at the Bourbon County's Juvenile Court of Justice. I had to be the one to press charges because I had been the target of the behaviors. I pressed my first set of charges against the ringleader. That student removed himself from school the following week, deciding that home schooling was a better alternative for him. Several other students tried to take his place, and I accommodated them with similar charges. I became friends with the man who took my complaints; he had no choice, as I was in his office a lot after my school day ended. Things began to calm down, although not much.

In an effort to reach them, I used an anger management unit I had received from the school's counselor who came in once a week to work with students. This program actually benefited me more than the kids. I practiced deep breathing, counted to ten (sometimes every couple of minutes), and went to my "happy place" a lot. I contacted other alternative schools and learned about carrots (rewards) they had used and had success with. I called one of my friends from Virginia whose brother ran an alternative school. He said he took students on walks for good behavior, so the next week my students and I took walks around the campus or played football until one student got a nasty concussion. The incentive worked for some students, but there were still a lot of outbursts, especially if a student was denied his or her "right" to go outside, and real learning still wasn't happening.

I realized I was in over my head, but not one to give up, I struggled to interest these teenagers in things other than sex, violence, and drugs. I focused on reading things with, or in many cases, to the students that they could relate to. I settled upon *A Child Called It* by David Pelzer (1995), a book that chronicles the author's horrifically abusive childhood. Because of our daily readings, I connected briefly with students, but most had so many problems, both personal and academic, that they had built up a wall against authority. I accomplished little more than honoring the contract that I had signed earlier that October.

I nearly lost my desire to teach that year. There were many times I completely lost control. I wish I could forget the day a student threw a well aimed acorn and hit me in the eye because he felt I had wronged him. I hope I never forget the successful transition of two middle school students back to regular population and a return visit from one of those students after eighth grade graduation. Dressed in suit and tie, he hugged me tightly and thanked me for all I had done. That look of appreciation in his eyes reignited some of the spark I had lost while teaching at the Continuous Learning Center in Bourbon County.

Kentucky—The Appalachian Connection—Bath County Middle School

I survived Bourbon County CLC but had no intention of returning to that environment. I simply didn't want to. So, I applied in several counties close to my home and was hired by Bath County Middle School as a seventh grade language arts teacher. I have never been more grateful. As a seventh grade language arts teacher, I would be responsible for ensuring each student completed a state required writing portfolio comprised of three student-selected pieces fulfilling three different genres. The state's purpose for these portfolios was to show that writing across the curriculum was occurring. In my new classroom, a book that had been left by a previous teacher caught my eye: *After the End* by Barry Lane (1992). After reading it, my spark for teaching was fanned to a full flame. I looked at the way I had previously taught writing in a different light, piecing together all of my previous flirtations with writer's workshop.

I still taught grammar, punctuation, and spelling but tried to use shorter lessons to focus students on common areas needing to be addressed. They then practiced those skills in actual pieces they were writing. I introduced "snapshots" (Lane, 1992, p. 32), where a writer describes every detail as if it has been frozen in time. I showed students how to include an occasional "thoughtshot" (Lane, 1992, p. 44), where a writer reveals what he or she was thinking at a specific moment in time and asked them to add a few of each to current pieces in their working folders. I showed students lots of samples of the types of writing I wanted them to try. I incorporated writer's workshop two to three times a week and held countless conferences while students worked on their pieces individually.

I encouraged students to write about what they knew. I had always told my students in previous years about my run-in with a wallaby at a zoo in Australia. But, after reading Barry Lane's book, I tried something different. I told them the very short version. I said, "When I was six, I went to Australia and was beat up by a wallaby." Students stared at me for about ten seconds, frozen. Then hands flew into the air. As they asked a flurry of questions about my story, I wrote them on the board behind me. After the board was covered, I explained that details make stories come to life. After that, students rushed into my class each morning shouting, "Mrs. Mort! Mrs. Mort! I rewrote my story! Look at how long it is!" Finally, I felt as if the struggles, the research, the bombed and revamped lessons, were beginning to pay off. Mind you, this was thirteen years into teaching! Our portfolio scores improved that year, yet there were still areas of growth I needed to address in my instruction.

I didn't have a good record-keeping system for conferences. I didn't give all students enough time to conference with me. It seemed that I was conferencing with the same students most of the time. Again, it was time to reflect.

A New Way to Reflect

My reflection came in the form of attending a local National Writing Project summer institute at Morehead State University in June of 2007. Funded through a grant from the Department of Education, this intense month long institute provided me opportunities to read the latest professional literature regarding the best practices out there for teaching writing, encouraged me to take on multiple leadership roles in the institute, at my school, and in upcoming National Writing Project events, and provided me the opportunity to put myself in my students shoes by creating both personal and professional publications that I took through the entire writing process.

Today, I can proudly say I am a writer. As a result of this program, I discovered so many new ideas to improve writer's workshop in my class. I learned how to organize writing notebooks that can be useful reference tools for students during the revision process. Not only do these notebooks contain ideas for future pieces, but they also contain mini-lessons done in class that have strong examples from mentor texts (Buckner, 2005). I have learned how to give effective, yet short conferences thanks to our writer-in-residence, Liz Mandrell, who simultaneously made me feel proud of the work I had done but also created a desire in me to improve what already existed as she asked probing questions. I learned how writing is a process and every student is at some point on the continuum. It is up to me to determine where the student is and how best to take them to the next level. I often compare this to a doctor who must determine what symptoms his or her patient has, and what to prescribe to make the person better—only I do that with someone's writing. I can also more readily relate to that feeling of helplessness a student feels when a blank piece of paper taunts them and intimidates them.

Next year I hope to improve my skills at conferencing with students effectively, and I want to keep much better records of those conferences. I read several books that will move me toward that goal this summer. They include Carl Anderson's *How's it going? A Practical Guide to Conferring with Student Writers* (2000), *Teaching the Best Practice Way: Methods that Matter,*

K–12 by Harvey Daniels and Marilyn Bizar (2005), and Jeffery D. Wilhelm's *Engaging Readers & Writers with Inquiry* (2007). As a result, I hope to have more meaningful conferences with students next year and to limit each conference to three to five minutes (Anderson, 2000). I also plan to engage students using more essential questions in an attempt to access higher level learning for my students. Rereading Atwell's books and immersing myself in some new gurus (at least to me) such as Lucy Caulkins, Ralph Fletcher, and JoAnn Portalupi, will also hone writer's workshop, I am sure. I also hope to be more helpful to other teachers who want to teach writing in their own classroom. With all the reading I have done, I hope to be able to point teachers to documentation that shows the value of writer's workshop in the classroom.

Final Thoughts

While I am not planning to relocate to any new states or schools any time soon, I do plan to continue learning new ways to improve my writing instruction. Unquestionably, I will experience bumps along the way, more bombed lessons, and moments of frustration. But this is the thing I love most about teaching; you are never perfect. There is always room for growth. I have found it to be exactly like writing—a journey of a lifetime.

References

Anderson, C. (2000). *How's it going? A practical guide to conferring with student writing.* Portsmouth, NH: Heinemann.

Atwell, N. (1987). *In the middle: Writing, reading, and learning with adolescents.* Portsmouth, NH: Heinemann.

Buckner, A. (2005). *Notebook know-how: Strategies for the writer's notebook.* Portland, ME: Stenhouse Publishers.

Daniels, H. & Bizar, M. (2005). *Teaching the best practice way: Methods that matter, K–12.* Portland, ME: Stenhouse Publishers.

Gould, J. & Gould, E. (1999). *The four square writing method for grades 7–9.* Carthage, IL: Teaching & Learning Company.

Jenkins, L. (2003). *Improving student learning: Applying Deming's quality principles in classrooms.* Milwaukee, WI: ASQ Quality Press.

Jones, F. (1987). *Positive classroom discipline.* New York: McGraw-Hill.

Lane, B. (1992). *After the end.* Portsmouth, NH: Heinemann.

Pelzer, D. (1995). *A child called It.* Deerfield Beach, FL: Health Communications, Inc.

Wilhelm, J. D. (2007). *Engaging readers & writers with inquiry.* New York: Scholastic.

Teacher, Writer, Rebel

A Parallel Journey

Elaine J. O'Quinn

Ancient stories confirm that some of humankind's earliest attempts at writing were based on representations of the gods (Chevalier & Gheerbrant, 1996). In essence, writing was intended from the onset to make visible that which was invisible, to actualize that which had previously only been suggested, and to give divine properties to a human act. From primitive ideograms and sacred carvings to the most complex and nuances of languages, the written word has historically been interpretive, defying the literalism it has come to most often represent in schools. In a concerted and continual effort to teach writing in its most technical, informational, and prescribed forms, schools and the society they represent have continually lost sight of the potential words have to join together the mind, body and spirit to new meaning. Instead of being taught to use words to attain a larger sense of self and the world, most lessons in writing strip students of all personal authority and serve only to propagate institutionally approved knowledge and rules rather than invent new ways of seeing. We have, it seems, almost entirely forsaken the sacred roots of composition.

I do not think this technical approach is an especially "new" understanding of how writing should be defined. In fact, it relies heavily on the

Getting It in Writing, pages 189–203

oldest approximation we know, that which emphasizes rote memory and sanctioned procedure. In my "Teaching of Composition" class, I use what I consider to be a foreboding image from the 16th century of a female form identified as Lady Gramatica to make a point about the continuing influences of the rigid tools of the prescriptive writing classroom. Part of the medieval trivium curriculum that included logic and rhetoric, grammar in the context of its original system is based on structure and rules that clearly define acceptable procedure. In the illustration I share with my students, Lady Gramatica is seen holding a large dead bird in her right hand. The bird has a choke chain around its neck with a small utensil attached that seems intended to incise and discard. Resting on the lady's upper arm is a smaller, live bird with a line of similar instruments etched across its wings. There appears to be a sense of victory over the dead bird. Across the lady's chest is a necklace of "tools" that are the equivalent of scalpels, nails, knives, syringes, and other devices meant to extricate, infuse, pull apart, and pin in place. Above her right arm is the Latin word "Negatio," probably a reference to the metaphysical principle that every determination is a negation of something else; and above her left arm is the word "Affirmatio," confirmation of that which has been established and is no longer in dispute. It is clear that something very important has been determined here. Gramatica's left foot weighs heavily on a short ladder made of ruled and measured lines. A rather large pincer in the open position hangs on the second rung. On the top rung sits another free bird with a tool in its beak. The bird is clearly young, but strong and certain of its position. In her left hand, Gramatica holds a flag with the letters "NRS," perhaps a reference to the Latin phrase Naturalis Recordationis Scientia, the natural science of remembering. She waves it as a possible indicator of the scientific, therefore indisputable, nature of what is seen as right and true.

Whatever the intended meaning of Lady Gramatica's message, those who teach writing must not forget that the craft began as a creative and not a technical act. Magical powers were often attributed to it, and one of its most highly valued properties was that it could be altered yet leave an indelible record (Chevalier & Gheerbrant, 1996). Ironically, it was not until "civilized" societies decided to use writing to uphold particular value structures that it became a tool intended to manage the masses rather than a muse and agent of thoughtful examination. As we all know, it was not by accident that it was illegal in America for slaves to learn to read and write. Likewise, it took decades for writing by women to be appreciated beyond a capacity necessary to keep their fathers' and their husbands' business matters straight. When writing is purposefully reduced over and over again to its most unimaginative and mechanized constructions, its original, creative intent is debased. By suggesting that words stand mostly as vehicles of transport for mere technical knowledge and the reproduction of it, we take away their soul. For writing is not simply about what is; it is also about that which remains hidden and the mystery about that which may never be expressed. The act of writing should do more than simply depict an author's understanding of a subject, an ability to generate records and reports, or a capacity to imitate others. It should also provide a penetrating wisdom that illuminates the world and awakens the reader to it in a sharp new way. It should provide intuitions and insights that unsettle and disrupt a mundane acceptance of the nature of things to recognition of what is still possible. Powerful writing is always about discovery, but by consistently reducing it to its most pedestrian level, it is relegated to a world that appears fixed and absolute. Nothing is transformed, and that which exists simply gets transmitted. Those who honor the craft know that writing is capable of so much more.

If teachers and students alike were to point specifically to a place where the deficit model of education shows up, I think all might agree on the writing curriculum as a constant site. From red pen marks to prescriptive abbreviations in the margins to the sometimes not-so-nice comments on the last page, students have been told of their lack of writing ability over and over again. Many respond by quietly accepting what they believe is their fate; year after year, class after class, they shoulder the comments and grades they are given, simply hoping to do well enough to pass. Others rebel altogether and write only under threat of punishment or total failure. Very few students take up the burden of learning to be better and more creative writers on their own, and most walk away from the experience convinced that writing is only for the chosen or perhaps for some abstract future job. One of my students recently shared this with the rest of my class: "We were told early and often by our teachers that some people can write and some can't. I always assumed I was one of those who couldn't, so I quit trying, except for when I had to." Almost everyone in the class nodded in agreement. Just about everyone agreed they learned little or nothing about self or community or life through school writing. They knew it only as a formulaic exercise in correctness, a means to an end, or a necessary evil. Magic is not a word any of them would have used to describe the promise of their composition experiences, even those who felt their teachers made an honest effort to promote writing as more than just an academic activity.

Sadly, even writing teachers who suffered and endured such insensitivity to their own work while in school are not hesitant to inflict similar injustices on the students they come to teach. Though the memory of struggle and uncertainty as an emerging writer is something no one soon forgets, it does not seem to temper the choice many of us make to teach as we were taught. I should know. I began my writing journey as one of those students and at one point was one of those teachers. While I would not say that my writing as a student was the worst, I certainly recall that it was not the best. My teachers made sure I understood that. Anyone who has ever made a "C" or "B" or even the occasional "D" on an essay did not come away from the process feeling encouraged or empowered to create any more text than absolutely necessary. I can only imagine how those who do worse must feel. Although in private I always harbored dreams of writing creative and meaningful prose, in public I knew my limitations. School dampened any excitement I felt about writing, and the desire to put words to paper gradually began to feel more like a burden than an opportunity. Yet when I began to teach, I never thought twice about how I might be imposing a similar weight on my own students.

In my personal trip down the highway of composition, I learned early never to trust personal insights and ideas and always to keep my writing as brief and ordinary as possible. Benign comments like "could do better" were more endurable than the stop sign of red marks that clearly said "not very smart." Anyone who thinks these kinds of attacks on student writers have no lasting impression either has not persisted in their own writing, has continued to believe that correction is always more important than creation, is not very self-reflective, or cannot see beyond what must have been a good personal experience with writing compared to the stifling experience of so many others. Those of us who struggled with instruction that attends only to the technical writing self can attest to wounds that still bleed fresh at the least touch, wounds that scab over, but never really heal. At best, we have learned to ignore the abrasion when it itches; at worst, every mark we put on a page makes it sear. We endure as writers because we know it was never the memorization of rules, a history of worksheets, the thoughts of a good job, or an attempt to imitate the "masters" that kept us coming back to the blank, stark pages of writing; rather, it was the promise of those hesitant marks to eventually right themselves and speak from somewhere deep within that sustained us as we scratched away, despite the lack of encouragement for, or recognition of, our efforts. I am convinced that even the slightest bit of encouragement as a writer would have kept me from many moments of despair as I worked my way through any number of situations that required writing skill.

It would seem that having had this kind of experience with writing would have prevented me from (a) becoming an English teacher and (b) treating my own students in a manner that in anyway resembled how I had been treated. But the deep dark secret of English teachers is that we tell ourselves that teaching English is not really about writing anyway; it is about literature. So when we teach writing in all the ways we abhorred being taught, it becomes acceptable since that is not really the "English" part of our job at all. Unless there is a major "ah-ha" moment, those who live with the scars resulting from the red slashed across every paper they have ever written will do the very same thing to their own students if given half a chance. The power of the red pen is mighty and everlasting, and for lack of any other model of teaching, even those with an awareness of its sharp edges can find themselves proponents of its sword-like nature. Because the instruction I received in college was very much like what I endured in earlier years, I had no other models of teaching writing. It took me some time to make the leap from unfulfilled student to effective composition teacher, simply because I did not know there was a more dynamic way of teaching. It took even longer to realize that I could teach my students how to be true to their writing selves, think critically about the world around them, unveil new truths, and still learn the conventions necessary for strong communication. My own experience had not taught me this, so it was only through trial and error that I gradually pulled all of the pieces together.

I first learned what it takes to teach writing well after the experience of teaching it very poorly. It was an awareness of how miserably I was failing that forced me to consider what I might do to succeed. As I investigated student writing closely, I could not deny the realities I was encountering daily in the classroom. Not only were students lacking in simple mechanics, they also had no voice, no understanding of how to take their own ideas and turn them into thoughts of inquiry, and no sense of individual strengths of style or habit. They had become accustomed to the teacher giving them topics, leading their thinking, directing their structures, correcting their mistakes, limiting their time spent writing, and dismissing them as authors of their own work. Indeed, for many students, their final product was almost always collaboration between them and me, with most of the effort emitting from my head and pen. They had no authority over their writing because embedded in the way I was teaching was deference to my authority. I made the rules; they followed them.

In my quest for the "truths" about writing and writers that I was led to believe existed, I realized I had saddled my students with assignments that had very little or no meaning for them and structures that confined rather than opened. Space for personal exploration or reflection barely existed. As I consistently saw them struggle, lose interest, and fail to grow, I assumed it was their lack of motivation that was to blame. There was no carryover of instruction, and while I recognized that what I "taught" out of the handbook today was quickly forgotten come tomorrow, it did not occur to me that lack of context and connection, not lack of ability was the culprit. Conferences were directed by my dictates and intuitions, dismantling rather than enabling student agency in a piece, and no matter how many "choices" of topics I devised, it seemed my students never reached eagerly for their notebooks to start composing. Mostly they groaned each time I indicated we were about to write. Completed papers remained worse than riddled with errors; they were dull and uninspiring. I loathed reading them. When it came time to grade, I found I had to pump myself up for the effort I knew was ahead. By the time I finished, I was exhausted, let down, and convinced that my students did not care, would not try, and never listened.

Through week after week of endless frustration, I never once thought that my teaching was the problem. How could it be? I had been taught those worksheets, five paragraph essays, constant attention to the thesis sentence, proper outlines, drill, and rigorous standards would ensure good writers. I was doing everything I had been taught to do. The problem had to rest with the students. I did not consider that I could revolutionize my quest and my classroom simply by shifting the focus from teaching writing to teaching students to write, by looking to help students find their personal center as writers rather than expecting them to objectify those centers as the first prerequisite to good writing. Simply allowing students an opportunity to name their writer selves would have dramatically changed the dynamic of what I was trying to accomplish. However, I had learned that writing was not about self, but about something "over there" somewhere, and I was sure that as the teacher I knew where there was. The only clue I had to the fact that there might be a better way was my own writer's voice, and it was only a faint whisper in the very distant background. Though it nagged at me, it did not have the power of the past and present voices that insisted it was the students who were at fault. Recalling that I often had struggled as much as my students did became an indicator that all was as it should be rather than a warning sign that something was still amiss.

While I know that in life any quest that moves away from the self is destined to fail, I did everything in the opposite when it came to my students' writing. I am fairly certain that knowledge of the world or others cannot be internalized without knowledge of the self, yet I insisted on writing that was rarely made personal and was instead about things the students knew little about through their own experience. Our topics were external and remote; they were canned and flavorless. They moved away from self- knowledge rather than towards it. It took a good deal of agonizing recognition to admit that my approach to teaching writing was moving students away from their centers, not closer to them. I had to recognize that it is only when we know something of ourselves that we can connect our lives to something larger.

That is how we develop and grow in personhood as well as in intellectual capacities. It was clear to me that the results of my approach were rarely very good and almost always painfully bad. Nothing was revealed, nothing really gained. Even if I managed to impose technically correct perimeters around the writing, the words themselves sounded dry and defeated. There was no homeland to travel, only foreign soil to trek. Like wooden soldiers, the words of the writers merely marched up and down the unfamiliar page. The war might be won, but there would be no glory in it.

We like to think that students will be motivated to write by carrots like "this will help you in the future" or "you need this for a good job" or "knowing how to do this is the sign of an educated person." In fact, I know of writing teacher "experts" who believe this, but experience has convinced me that, for the most part, this notion is wrong. Except for those rare students who are as animated about the future as they are the present, these tactics barely register. The only qualifier in this arsenal that I have ever heard a teacher use to encourage writing that made any difference at all in attitude was "we are only going to do this long enough to pass the test, then no more writing for the rest of the year." And then they do just that. When the test is over, so is the writing. The only "future" at stake in this approach is the immediate one, and students sometimes find it minimally acceptable. Appearing well educated for a job that might occur at some future date is just not real enough for most students, no matter how many times we insist that it should be.

Our mistake as teachers comes in assuming students will respond to our pleas to write for predetermined external inducements. For the most part, they simply do not. Students come to us already motivated, but not necessarily by the things we assume move them. One of the teacher's toughest tasks is to find out what needs, dreams, conflicts and desires actually do matter to students and then determine how to turn those interests into tangible writing material that they care about and are willing to express. This does not mean requiring that they disclose their private selves to us; it simply means allowing their writing to have personal meaning for them. How can students possibly care about matters that happen "over there" if they have not been allowed first to connect those matters to the lives they are presently living? They must know that their current and past experiences matter as much as the ones we wish them to connect to further out, if any authentic exploration of the meaning others give to life is going to take place. The pen may write the world, but it must first unfold the experience of it. Linda Christensen's wonderful lesson of having students write their own version of George Ella Lyon's poem "Where I'm From" is one that any teacher can make use of in the classroom to invite students into a careful consideration of their own lives while asking them to connect to the lives of others (2000). It is one that I use often and always with excellent results.

Making these discoveries does not make the task writing teachers face easier, but it does make it more meaningful. I had a clear understanding that becoming a different kind of writing teacher was not going to erase the tensions of teaching, but I knew that it would probably refocus them. Not only did I have to give myself permission to flail and fail in the classroom as I relearned my way, but I also knew I was going to have to accept that my views on writing might be seen by my colleagues as everything from less than rigorous to threatening to just plain wrong. Many teachers immediately balk at the idea of making a place for more writing in their classes, let alone the thought of instituting changes in approach. Too, I had to come to terms with the constant imposition of institutional constructions such as accountability issues, standards of learning, tests, issues of assessment, and the arguments that hold such gatekeepers of tradition in place. Those who have ever chosen to dramatically change the way they do something know that it does not take long to find themselves out of favor with many of the same people with whom they might once have commiserated. As a teacher, touting new classroom activities that everyone is eager to try is one thing, but suggesting an overhaul of teaching and learning strategies is quite another. It is a fine but distinct line between teacher nomads and teacher pariahs. Herding around together in search of new ways of affirming traditional beliefs is one thing; striking out for the unknown in hopes of new discoveries is a rebel move. Few like to wander alone, but teachers who move away from traditional paths often find this is the case. It is a difficult juncture that takes courage, determination, a sense of adventure, and a bit of a rebellious nature. These are never easy characteristics to embrace and display in schools, especially if others see the cause as disruptive and unreliable. After all, most people do not like change, and in schools, especially, change is often perceived of as messy and unpredictable or as faddish ideals doomed to fail, so many opt out of attempting much beyond the proven known.

Unfortunately, it is the newest teachers with the most recent understandings of innovative pedagogy and research that are at highest risk of teaching in ways that may rely more on tradition than discovery. In many instances, they are told to forget everything they learned in college, and many feel they must quickly acquiesce to the pressures of the schools they enter or be an outcast. Knowing how eager and thankful new teachers are to consider different approaches to teaching writing than those they once knew, I find it is disconcerting to see the tensions they must endure in their first positions. For example, English departments in several schools where we place student teachers are prompt and test oriented. The philosophy is to write in a very specific format just during the year the test is given. Beyond that, there is very little writing done. These beginning teachers immediately sense the danger of teaching outside of what seems the expected norm, and in some cases are simply not allowed to try any modes of teaching writing other than what is prescribed by their new departments. New teachers need to be supported as they make their way through the difficult first years, but there is no reason they should be stifled in their attempts to reach the same ends as others in their schools simply because their means may vary. However, this happens time and time again, resulting in very little change in how writing gets taught. Rather than preventing new teachers from trying methods they believe could work, schools would serve everyone better by having regular conversations about current research to determine if there is anything of worth that might benefit all teachers.

Complicating any shift in how we teach, beyond the real and immediate concerns of pedagogy, administration, and what our peers will think, is the response of defeated students who have been bullied and badgered so much by the system and its constraints that they no longer care about or connect to what flows from their pens, as long as they just "get it done." In the end, these are not only the students who hate to write, but also those who have been taught to hate to write and those who have gotten writing in the prescribed ways down to a simple technique. Student resistance is real and stems from a variety of sources. Not only do students balk at what they perceive as "more" work, but they also dislike being asked to work in ways that are unfamiliar to them. It may be that they loathe those worksheets and form essays, but not nearly as much as they dislike learning to do things in a new and different way, especially if that way requires changing habits. As a student writer, I remember thinking that writing was painful and exhausting; however, to learn a different way of doing it after thinking I had finally figured it out would have seemed unimaginable. While I now know that writing is never easy, I also believe schools make it harder than it needs to be, thereby making any reference to it preempted by feelings of dread. Many teachers have been taught to embrace a pedagogy of struggle and strain that makes writing unnecessarily difficult. I am convinced that this kind of institutionalized instruction, one that insists that writing is difficult rather than challenging, creates many more problems than it prevents and hinders the teacher's ability to apply new theories and try new strategies.

In the course of my career I have been guilty of all of the writing teacher "no-no's" I now avoid. I did these things in order to prompt students to write. In both my successes and failures, I learned that writing is a messy process with limited clear-cut solutions, but I stumbled plenty to get to this juncture. When I hear someone say they have found the perfect solution—

for example, 6-traits, process writing, work shopping, I-search, multi-genre, portfolios, blogging, digital composition—I know that all they have really found is one more tool for the vast workbench of what it means to create meaningful text. There are no easy answers when it comes to writing or the teaching of writing, but there is passage and achievement possible within the tension. If we look at all of the tools we have been given as a means to that passage and achievement rather than as an end, we help our students and ourselves in more fruitful ways.

In my earliest endeavors as a writing teacher, I knew nothing about naming the larger structures necessary for good writing. Like many teachers, I just assumed students should be able to write and do so without mechanical error. I am ashamed to admit this, but at some level it was almost satisfying to me to see how many errors I could circle and correct in student papers. For some bizarre reason, those circles stood as proof of my competence as a teacher. My own writing instruction had never included anything more than diagramming sentences, memorizing the prescriptive rules of a handbook, proving I could write a good outline, constructing a strong introduction with a clear thesis sentence, and mastering a formatted essay, so I had a long history of being able to spot errors in any of these arenas. No one had ever talked to me about how to develop (or even identify) a good idea; how to develop those ideas in a way that would address a specific audience; how to exhibit a personal style that presented itself through unique word choice and sentence structure; or, most importantly, how to portray in my writing a voice that was clearly my own. While those who study composition theory know that these are the building blocks to all good writing, my understanding was that those elements simply happened once the proper conventions were in place. Conventions I could do.

Initially, I had no idea that writing is at some level always developmental and that all writers are consistently evolving, whether they are in the second grade, the eleventh, or out of school. Over and over again, I focused on the end product and wondered why the center rarely held. It never occurred to me that aside from a thesis sentence being clear, it should also grab the reader's attention, offer insight, and relate something new (or at least fresh) to the reader. I never stopped to think about how I might teach organization and transition as elements of writing that serve as guides and link together important details and concepts. To my uneducated self, these gateways to writing were mere patterns and elements that should have been clear to writers, if only they paid close attention. Teaching sentence variety meant teaching command over sentence types. It never struck me that issues of style were also involved. Reading papers aloud for a sense of rhythm and flow and expression was unheard of, even though I now know this is one of the best ways to catch all kinds of problems in writing, no matter how experienced or inexperienced the writer. There was no effort on my part to help students find creative ways with words that would pass their message along in a unique and interesting way. These were students; it was not about the message anyway, was it? It was about correctness. Form and formula seemed to be my only guiding lights in teaching writing, and no matter where writers fell on the scale of skill, I expected all of them to perform in a like manner. When they fell short, I attributed it to carelessness and limited effort and not to the fact that their opportunities to grow were limited. I had done all I knew how to do. It was the students who failed themselves. In essence, I assigned writing. I did not teach it.

In retrospect, I now realize that for all the mistakes I made in my teaching, it was my lack of understanding of the concept of voice that was the most harmful to my students. As an English major who admired Walt Whitman above all others, I ask myself how I could have been so blind to the need of writers to develop and refine their own "barbaric yawp." By merely drilling my students on grammar, punctuation and rhetorical format as a way to improve their performance, I was contributing to their inability to find their unique potential as writers. While I never was comfortable in my own writing with the "one could say" or "one might conclude" objectification of subject matter, I forced it upon my students as though it were the golden rule of composition. Where was the individual in what I was teaching, the room to demonstrate personal passion, the chance to elicit excitement? How was I allowing for the spark of originality we know makes a line of writing memorable or the expression that might breathe new life into old words? I know now that these are critical components that must be developed in a writer but not without opportunity and guidance. These are the elements of writing that assure students they can be writers and that make them proud to be so, but it is the work of the teacher to help them realize this potential.

Much of what I have come to understand as a teacher of writing is something I had to learn first as a writer: in order to create authentic texts, the writer must be somehow present. Everything in writing hinges on this concept. Before I understood how critical this tenet is to good writing, I assigned vague prompts to my students, gave them generic lists of topics to choose from, and said "no" to topics I did not think they could "research" well enough. The result was page after page of writing that was as dreary to read as it must have been to construct. Over and over again I subjected myself to papers that I had read at least a hundred times before, papers that either ventriloquated what the "experts" had to say or floundered in trying to recast what others had said. However, once I released students to their own writing selves, I found myself immersed in papers that made me cry, laugh, reflect, and consider. Instead of 75 papers on abortion, drugs, drunk driving, or terrorism, I was reading about what it is like to have a brother in a combat war zone; how it feels to have a sister in prison because of crack-cocaine; how life goes on (and doesn't) when you are the only survivor of a car accident that kills your best friend; and what the search for an adopted child's biological mother is like. My students were writing with meaning because they were writing about things that had meaning for them. Consequently, those subjects took on new meaning for me as well.

Something else I came to know about the teaching of writing is that pedagogies must support the practices of good writers. Process writing cannot be taught with any conviction unless the teacher honestly believes that writers need time to write in environments that provide guidance and feedback and then works to provide that. There is no point in advocating for portfolios if we continue to insist that every piece of writing be dissected and graded without ample opportunity for reflection and revision. Students will not understand the major components of good writing if the focus is always on conventional mechanics. When I determined the actual value of these writing beliefs, my teaching of writing totally changed. I was able to assign more responsibility to the students both for their own work and the work of the others in the classroom. Under my guidance of what constitutes good revision and not simple editing, students learned to help themselves and each other. By teaching them the keys to deep revision, I put what used to be my red pen remarks into a format and language they could use for themselves. I was no longer afraid that an entire class period devoted to prewriting would be looked upon as laziness on my part and a waste of time on the part of my students. Allowing for chunks of writing time on a regular basis changed what happened in the classroom. Accepting that students might be at different stages of writing at any given time and that in the end they would choose which work they wanted me to evaluate gave them ownership of their words that they had never before experienced. Even my own workload became more balanced, and much to my delight, my time was spent in genuine response to papers, rather than in mere correction of them.

To permit others to tap into their abilities as writers can also mean a regeneration of our own writing selves. I might have continued to attribute my own writing difficulties to lack of ability and serious effort had I not finally seen the issues confronting my students as issues that mattered to me as well. It is important to acknowledge not only how my students' writing improved as I became a more astute and knowledgeable teacher of writing, but also to note how my own writing changed. My first observation was that

I no longer struggled with stilted, academic styles that did nothing to advance my arguments. Once I gave myself permission to own my words and style, writing became a joyful activity again. As I learned to see my audience, the lines between talking and writing became fluid rather than rigid. I realized the importance of tapping into the rich, organic nature of conversation while capitalizing on composition's more symbolic and creative qualities. I recognized that being able to imagine the audience I was writing to had a huge impact not only on what I had to say, but also on how I needed to say it. I became more careful in my structures and word choices, knowing that the way words are arranged on a page can either reveal or betray a writer. I learned there was nothing wrong with expressing my passions, as long as I did so in a way that opened up conversations rather than closing them. In many ways, I learned to heal that writing wound of so long ago and freed myself of the teachers who made me believe I could never be quite good enough. In doing so, I freed my own students as well.

Once we view writing as a craft that operates in the world as something more than simple functionary discourse intended mostly to provide answers and solutions, we open the door to a multitude of writing possibilities. Aside from what writing can do for the individual, students need to understand, too, the social value of written language and its ability to enhance democratic participation and community. They need to learn how their personal lives can be enriched by writing, as can the lives of those they somehow come to better know through writing. Both instances are just as meaningful as the one that prepares them to write for future careers or further education, and, I might argue, foundational in their contributions to the society beyond what jobs and educations provide. Writing as a mere source of transmission keeps worlds small. Our intent in teaching students to write and in considering our own writing should always be to expand worlds and make them larger in multiple ways. We cannot do that if we insist on writing that is one-dimensional and leaves no place for new discoveries or reciprocity of thought.

Writing should be a way of opening up channels of communication that previously have not existed, hence the insistence on it as a creative act. It should indicate a revelation as well as a reflection, an offering as well as an invitation. It is based on individual contribution to something larger than itself, and therefore must be allowed to use its own experiences and insights in order to feel a part of that contribution. Because writing is an intelligent act that participates in a socially structured event, it makes meaning only when engaged in the reciprocity of community. When an individual's contribution is lost, the society of which it is a part loses something as well. Eventually, that society will find it cannot sustain itself on the weakened state of its own rhetoric. It ceases the growth afforded by transaction, becomes mired in mindless dictum, and finds itself trapped in the mediocrity of its own making.

The written word has always had the power to create worlds as well as reveal them. Such a power is dangerous because it challenges authority and threatens docility. In fact, so feared is the creational force of writing that in Kabalistic tradition, sections of the Torah are not given in a predictable arrangement for fear that those who read it might try to devise their own world (Chevalier & Gheerbrant, 1996). Writing is revolutionary when used to unveil or promote because it can involve a dramatic and sometimes complete change. Teaching writing beyond the conventional expectation can be risky. It has the potential to profoundly affect not only the writer but also the teacher, the curriculum, and the institutional system itself. For some teachers to practice it at all requires that they close their doors and subvert or agitate their colleagues into action and sometimes even anger. But then, the act of creation can be as unpredictable as it is beautiful, and for many, that unpredictability is threatening and perilous. They prefer not to take the chance.

We live in three worlds: the ethereal that swirls above and around us, the material upon which we dwell, and the invisible that lies mysteriously beneath our feet (Chevalier & Gheerbrant, 1996). Conventional writing instruction tends to insist that all value lies in that which can be properly known and identified. But we are not one-dimensional beings, and we should not respond to the world as though we were. Likewise, expecting students to exist on only one plane of writing is unreasonable. The unknown and the mysterious are as much a force in our lives as is anything common and mundane. We do not conduct our daily lives on one plane without great loss and harm to our deeper natures, and to ask students to separate out their complex selves in order to write from only one plane of perception yields nothing more than artificial observations and pat conclusions. The writing teacher's goal should be to connect the various planes of existence in a way that makes the life we live on the material level more meaningful. Transformation of self and others can only take place when the whole self is allowed to move fluidly among that which is known and unknown. Writing is a relationship that writers have not only with thoughts, ideas, and experiences but also with beliefs, anxieties, fears, questions, and with what is dead as well as alive and what has yet to be. Only when we encourage student writers to explore the meaning of their lives from a variety of perspectives can we feel confident we have given them the means to imagine a world different from one reduced to custom and mere constraint.

References

Chevalier, J. & Gheerbrant, A. (Eds.). (1996). *The Penguin Dictionary of Symbols.* J. Buchanan-Brown (Trans.). New York: Penguin Books.

Christensen, L. (2000). *Reading, writing, and rising up: Teaching about social justice and the power of the written word.* Williston VT: Rethinking Schools.

The McEssay

Choking the Voice out of Student Writers

Kurt Reynolds

It has taken me a decade, but I have perfected my Sunday night ritual: fill a deep ceramic coffee mug with steaming light roast coffee, wedge my iPod headphones into each ear, cradle my gold Cross pen with blue ink (red ink is so 1950s) in my right hand, and select an essay from the stack of College Composition papers on our kitchen table. Then I get lost in the writing.

For the next few hours, I have the best job in the world, and I am not even at work. My pen is almost non-stop. "Tell me more" it scrawls in the right margin of one paper while on another essay it circles an entire paragraph and responds, "Now you're showing! Do more of this!" On another essay it weaves over the first paragraph, "Don't tell us what you are going to write about, show us!" and later in another, "This would be more vivid if you used dialogue." Of course, it often swoops in and notes the wrong use of "there" or spies a missing comma and advises, "End an introductory adverb clause with a comma." But it seeks the potential more than the errors.

In one essay, a student recounts the final bitter words she said to her mother as she left for grade school, only to have her father pluck her out of class later that day and rush her to the hospital, where her mother would die

Getting It in Writing, pages 205–219

205

that night in surgery. Another essay takes me onto the golf course in the hazy heat of late August where the writer's rivalry with his older brother comes down to one final putt. Despite his escalating heart rate and his brother's barrage of insults, the writer drains the putt and defeats his brother.

By now my coffee is cold, and my iPod playlist is repeating, but I'm lost in the work. I am giggling as a student recounts how, as a child, she was fond of discovering new moles and freckles, which her mother dubbed "Angel Kisses." One day she proudly thrust her head in her older sister's face, displaying the newest peck from heaven. "That's not an Angel Kiss, you freak," her older sister declared. "You're growing a third ear!" She believed her sibling, bragging about it at daycare, even believing she could detect conversations from the house next door. Her mother finally had to break the news that it was—alas—just a mole. In another essay, I hurry through downtown Minneapolis, dodging traffic, pedestrians, and vendors, accompanying a student and his father on their trip of a lifetime to see U2 at the Target Center. Their seats are so close the student can see Bono's stubble. After that paper, I spit out a mouthful of icy coffee and scroll through my iPod in search of *The Joshua Tree*.

It was not always like this.

"Okay, who has a topic? Let's hear one," I asked my students.

My sophomores averted their eyes. A boy in the front row made for his untied Doc Martin hoping that would buy him a few seconds. Another boy farther back fidgeted and dragged his pencil across the spine of his notebook, praying I wouldn't call on him. A girl to the left of the fidgeter looked straight ahead but not quite at me, focused on a point just over my right shoulder on the white board.

"Come on now. What do you feel like writing about?"

Let them choose the topic. Allow them to have mastery of the subject matter. Model how much you enjoy writing. Model the writing process. Show them how they can master it to produce excellent essays.

It was the fourth week of my second year teaching sophomore English. I had spent my rookie year just staying a few days ahead of my students, acclimating myself to the role of teacher, struggling with discipline, and trying to get my sophomores ready for the Minnesota Basic Skills Test (BST) in writing. My students had to write an essay, which was then sent to the state for scoring. The scores ranged from one to six, with three being the minimal score for passing. It was implied that we should teach toward a three and that even attaining a four was outstanding. I had learned little about the BST in college, so I devoted the summer to restructuring my curriculum so my sophomores would pass the writing test, and I would not look like a complete failure.

That was exactly how we spent the first part of the following year: writing essays. The only problem? The majority of my college English classes had been devoted to literature. Even the ones devoted to writing focused on teaching *me* how to write. Only one methods class actually focused on teaching me how to teach *my students* how to write, and that was a semester before I even student taught. *Literary Criticism, Shakespeare, Twentieth Century British Literature,* and *Multi-Cultural Poetry* were not going to get 120 sophomores to pass the BST in writing.

Desperate, I turned to the *Minnesota BST Written Composition Handbook.* I found a diagram that demonstrated, using a simple metaphor that my sophomores could easily comprehend, how to create a passing essay: "the hamburger" method. It highlighted the three basic parts of an essay. The beginning of the essay was the top bun, the middle formed the hamburger patty replete with fixings, and the conclusion served as the bottom bun.

After visiting with a friend who taught writing at our district's middle school, I found they used the same diagram for constructing simple paragraphs. This seemed like the perfect segue to take my students to the next step for passing the BST in writing: the five-paragraph essay.

My students already knew that a topic sentence, three supporting sentences, and a concluding sentence made a sound paragraph. How hard would it be to take that format and just expand it, turning their topic sentence into an introductory paragraph that ended with a thesis statement, expanding their supporting sentences into three paragraphs that referenced, with clear topic sentences, their thesis, and finally developing their concluding sentence into a final paragraph that effectively restated their thesis and wrapped up their essay? Obviously, the handbook encouraged the five-part essay formula because nearly every essay scoring above a three was written according to that recipe.

"Come on. Someone give me a topic."

Finally an over achiever broke the silence, "Let's write about our favorite hobby."

"Good topic," I said with my back already to the room. My thumb popped the cap off my Expo marker. Behind me, tablets rustled opened and pencils stood poised.

They know the routine.

"Let's brainstorm some hobbies now," I said with one glance over my shoulder.

"Sports," someone called out only to be met with, "No, we always write about sports."

"Reality TV," someone else yelled.

"Yeah, I have seen every episode of *Survivor*," another student added.

My marker flew across the board to keep pace.

"Playing guitar . . . Working on my truck . . . Video games . . . Weight lifting . . . Work . . . Archery . . . Painting . . ."

"Okay. Okay," I said, flexing my aching hand as I backed away from the board and examined what we had come up with. "Not bad. What should we focus on for our model essay?"

Model the essays for my students so they see the importance of form and focusing on a central idea, just like the handbook advises.

The entire middle row, comprised of junior varsity football players, cried, "Video games!"

The girls let out a collective sigh, but the boys in the front section of the middle row chanted, "Vid-EO" while—on cue—the boys in the back section of the middle row chanted, "games!"

"Vid-EO . . . Games! Vid-EO . . . Games!"

"Okay, okay, okay," I said. "Remember the principal's room is below us, so let's try and keep it to a dull roar." I grabbed the eraser and carved great swaths of white through the brainstorming on the board, leaving just the original "video games" in the middle.

"That's a start. But what type of video games? Are we talking sports games? How about *Madden*? Or quest games, like *Zelda*? Shooter games? *Resident Evil*? How about a classic, like *Pong*?"

One lone student snickered at my joke.

"*Madden*!" a football player called.

"Why?" I urged.

"Each year they make it better. This year there's the franchise mode where you can sign free agents and draft players," a student called out.

"Yeah, there are new playbooks too," another added.

"Okay, so the hobby requires some technical knowledge and skill," I said as I jotted that on the board. "What else?"

"It brings us all together," yet another student began, and I drew an arrow and wrote that on the board. "Nearly every Saturday, we're over at Ryan's. Everybody throws in ten bucks, plus an extra two for pizza, and we draw teams from a hat. You can only use original players, no modified ones. Last year Matt dominated, but this year I own him. Last weekend I raked in $60."

"Yeah, but that's only because my quarterback got hurt in the second quarter," Matt called out from the back, "I was up on you by a touchdown too."

"All right, we've got two things we can develop. But we need a third item," I said.

"It's like a tradition in my family," Jason stated, and I hurried to record the idea. "My dad grew up playing Atari, and my older brothers grew up playing Nintendo. Whenever they're home from college, we hook up the PlayStation to the big screen in the basement and spend our whole day down there while Mom and my sisters go shopping. My uncle even comes over and plays sometimes."

"Great," I said and stood back from the board and surveyed our pre-writing.

Impressive! Just look at all that thinking on the board. Give them a visual pre-writing method. Just like the handbook suggests. Very impressive!

"Now given what we have up here in our brainstorm, someone come up with a thesis."

They know the routine.

Matt finally called out as he surveyed the board, "Madden is one of my favorite hobbies because..." his head bobbed as he followed our cluster-ing, "it is challenging...uh, brings friends together...and it is kinda like a family tradition."

"Okay, we've got a thesis. That's a start. What do we need next?" I asked.

"An outline," the middle row responded.

They know the routine indeed. I could practically see the outlines taking form in their minds.

"Yep. Who wants to time me?"

Have them time me to illustrate how quickly I can devise an outline. Just like the handbook suggests.

"I'll do it," Cheryl said, already looking up at the clock.

"Ready when you are," I said with my marker poised.

"Go."

I knew the routine better than anyone. I quickly jotted down an introductory sentence and a thesis. I organized the three supporting ideas, formulating a topic sentence for each. Then I added at least three examples for each idea. Finally, I restated my thesis in the conclusion and ended with a clincher sentence.

"Done," I said and slammed the marker down.

"Thirty seconds," Cheryl said on cue.

"Now I'll turn you loose to work on your own essay. Remember, brainstorm just like we did up here," I said cocking a thumb at the whiteboard covered in blue marker, "until you come up with three good points. Devise a thesis. Create an outline based on your thesis. Be sure to come up with plenty of examples to support each of your three main ideas. Use details in those supporting paragraphs. The richer you make them, the clearer they will be to the reader. Use transitions to move the reader from one topic to the next. And last, but not least, be sure to have a conclusion that restates your main ideas. I want to see two full pages. Rough draft due tomorrow."

After four weeks of producing perfectly assembled hamburgers . . . I mean essays . . . the students became trained quite effectively. I continued to model the format, typing up essays and copying them to overheads. This format was so easy to master that I continued to crank out the essays right along with my students. All I had to do was give the command "write an essay on your favorite relative" or "write an essay about an important lesson you learned" and we mass-produced them, as if they were McEssays, easily slapped together and readily consumable.

Soon they had the form mastered. I, too, began to feel a mastery of writing as I illustrated the five-paragraph format over and over for my students. Instead of wrestling with ideas and directions, as I had done so often as an undergraduate, all I had to do was select a topic, brainstorm some ideas, determine which three could be best supported, formulate a thesis based on those selections, and begin writing. The essay practically wrote itself.

Why hadn't I encountered this form in college? When a paper was looming on the syllabus, I literally spent weeks holed up in the university library with my sources stacked around me. I randomly explored one idea, only to abandon it when I couldn't fully support it. So I would start after another. After days of writing, I would finally emerge with some ideas gathered and, hopefully, adequately supported. Then I would type them into the proper format and submit the thing to my professor. Think of all those hours wasted!

What a service I was providing my students! They might be bored with cranking the essays out now, but they would thank me when it came time later in the year to write their research papers. When they went off to college and saw what writing was like on that level, they would literally send me "thank you" cards. I couldn't wait to get the mail.

Not long after the mid-term, though, they tired of essays: theirs, mine, and, especially, the student samples from the state. I decided to show them some real essays written by professionals, so I rummaged through the outdated magazines in our school library. I also devised a checklist that called for them to search professional articles for the elements of an excellent essay (after all, I had ordered a set of posters chronicling the five essential parts of an excellent essay and proudly adorned them on my walls). I could not wait to illustrate the importance of precise topic sentences, well-supported paragraphs, and effective conclusions. They would see how real writers write.

The following Monday, I found myself thinking, *It doesn't get any better than this*, as I surveyed my first hour sophomores scattered about my room. *This is what teaching must really look like.* My class finally resembled my vision of an ideal classroom. Mine was not to be the traditional classroom where students sat obediently in neat rows, scrawling furiously to keep pace with my lectures.

One boy leaned against the wall, a *Rolling Stone* obscuring his face, his tablet resting on his chest. Another was lying on his back with his legs arched and feet tapping idly on the carpet, thumbing through a *Sports Illustrated* while a stack of previous issues beneath his head served as a pillow. A cluster of girls was in a corner trading issues of *Teen* and *Cosmo*. Others were in desks or even beneath them. Periodically, students halted reading and scribbled on their assignment sheets.

Completing my circuit through the classroom, I returned to my desk. Before sitting down to get a head start on some correcting, I glanced up and thought once more, *it most certainly doesn't get any better than this.*

Just then Kyle, sitting almost painfully upright in his desk, called out, "Mr. Reynolds, there is something wrong with this article."

I was wrong. It just got better. Kyle was quiet, soft-spoken, and keen. Mine was not going to be a classroom where students had to hoist their arms and wait for me to call on them.

"What do you mean?" I asked, navigating my way toward his desk.

"Well, this article doesn't really meet any of these requirements," he declared, alternating his gaze from the article to the checklist on his desk, before handing me a *Time* article on hazing among Marine paratroopers.

"It must have some," I said, scanning the article, confident I'd locate a clear topic sentence, several supporting sentences, and ample concluding sentences. *There has to be some. This was a real writer published in a respected magazine.*

"And look at that second paragraph," Kyle added half rising out of his desk and pointing. "It only has two sentences."

My eyes scanned the page. *Well, I had to agree. The article didn't clearly address the traditional form. There had to be a topic sentence in here somewhere.* I even brought my index finger up and dragged it across the sentences—a reading practice I had not employed since elementary school—underscoring every sentence, hoping to find those essential requirements, which the *BST Written Composition Handbook* said had to be in every well constructed essay.

"Plus it has seven paragraphs," Kyle stated as if we were in biology and he just pulled a three headed frog from his pocket.

"Whoa. One thing at a time," I said. "Ah, here's a topic sentence. Look at the third paragraph," I said.

Kyle's eyes followed my index finger and poured over the paragraph.

Order has been restored.

"Why didn't she just come out and state her topic right away?"

"Well, you see she is setting the reader up with her first paragraph," I began, smiling at his question. "She is giving us some background information by telling us a little narrative about the paratroopers and how they earn their golden wings. She is trying to hook the reader with that information."

"Oh," Kyle said. "I see." Then he looked me right in the eyes and pondered, "Then why didn't she fully support her second paragraph?"

"Well, here the author is briefly summarizing the hazing from the leaked video that got the military in trouble."

"Okay," Kyle said uneasily and jotted down the topic sentence I had pointed out.

Kyle was right, though. That article wasn't like anything I had my students write. It didn't adhere to a strict form. It didn't bother with a thesis, clear topic sentences, and tidy supporting information. Nor was there a single paragraph containing five sentences. Were these all lies I swallowed from the state? Worse yet, I fed them to my students.

"See what you can find in another magazine," I said and turned back toward my desk.

"Mr. Reynolds," Kyle called.

"Yes?"

"Um, could I, uh, have the magazine back? I really like that article and want to finish it."

I looked down at the issue of *Time*, still clenched in my right hand.

"Oh, yeah. Of course," I said and handed it to Kyle. By the time I was half way back to my desk, I realized my initial theory of teaching writing was collapsing.

All of the essays my students were writing were technically sound. But they failed to inspire interest; moreover, they lacked style and voice. What the state provided was a recipe, and it was a standard recipe for average writing. That writing would get them past the test, but then what? I wanted my students' writing to be interesting like that *Time* article. I wanted students to read each other's essays the way Kyle pored over that article. Instead I was teaching them how to formulate neatly composed drivel, a McEssay.

As I plopped down into my chair and observed Kyle reading the article, the most obvious truth hit me: real writers don't write five-paragraph themes.

Why was I teaching my students to write them? Real artists don't paint by numbers, so would our art instructor teach her students to do so? A five-paragraph essay was just writing by numbers.

Fortuitously, my prep hour was next. Before I filled the recycling box in the staff room with the copies of the state BST handbook and its hamburger method of essay writing, I examined what I should have focused on from the very beginning, the essay that scored the highest, the almost mythical sixes.

They were not McEssays. They had more than five paragraphs. They engaged the reader immediately with dialogue or thoughts. They employed figurative language. They had voice. The style inherent in those essays was as distinctive as fingerprints. They oozed personality. Those essays were written by genuine writers who forgot all about the hamburger method of writing. Instead they wrote with voice and passion.

Today I see that it was the same voice and passion that kept Kyle reading that *Time* article. The same voice and style that I have devoted my career to getting my students to breathe into their writing. The same voice and style that keeps me reading their essays long after my coffee is intolerable and my iPod has shuffled through my playlist several times.

What I didn't realize all those years ago was that the hamburger method of writing was designed to get students to just pass the test. I wanted to do so much more with our class time than just pass a test. I wanted them to develop voice and style, to experiment with form, to analyze and interpret important events from their lives. I wanted them to do what real writers do.

Now I encourage my students to explore the rich, unique experiences of their lives in the personal essay format. I tap into their natural storytelling abilities. I learn more about my students and their lives in two weeks of narrative essays than I ever did teaching the McEssay. Students recount the deaths of parents and grandparents (one even read an essay she wrote in my class at her grandfather's wake), explore rites of passage and epiphanies, and analyze relationships, divorces, and arguments. Their lives have become the context for my class.

Every year my sophomores take the MN BST in writing; every year they are above the state average, never dipping below 93 percent passing. None have yet reached that elusive six rating, but at least they have spent their time crafting skillful personal narratives as opposed to manufacturing McEssays.

The curse of the dreaded McEssay, though, reared its ugly head during my third year teaching. I was reading my way through a batch of personal essays on rites of passage and came across an essay that ground everything I was doing in class to a halt. At the end of the student's first paragraph was a thesis: "Shooting a cow instead of a deer my first time hunting was a major rite of passage for me because it taught me responsibility, safety, and humility." I kid you not.

A thesis statement! I had not even breathed that word in class. Here it was springing up in a personal essay! While I had abandoned this formula, not all teachers in my building had.

As I read through the student's essay, I was amazed at the bits and pieces of an incredible narrative butchered into a McEssay. In Minnesota, especially the northwestern section of the state, deer hunting is a way of life every fall. When a young person shoots his or her first deer, it is a transition from childhood to adulthood.

From the shreds of narrative, I learned that this young man had not seen any sign of deer all week. Deer season was coming to a close, and in the fading light of the November afternoon, from his stand along a tree line, he saw movement a hundred yards away in a pasture. Obviously, it was a large animal. His nerves got the better of him, and he fired. As his thesis so clumsily stated, instead of a deer, he killed a neighbor's Holstein.

While reading the paragraph devoted to how shooting the cow taught him humility, I felt my face flush for the student as I envisioned how he must have eagerly called for everyone in his hunting party to see the large buck he just shot. Unfortunately, the party, likely comprised of the older males in his immediate family, came upon a dead cow instead. I'm sure the poor kid took quite a ribbing from everyone. Not to mention having to pay the farmer for his dead livestock.

I could not deny that this student had a first rate rite of passage that needed to be written. He just chose the worst possible form. Think of the suspense he could have built if he had only structured it as a narrative. What imagery he could have created. Think of the dialogue he could have incorporated. Not to mention his own thoughts and analysis of the event. He took an important experience full of humor, pain, honesty, and learning and wrote it in a form that was none of those, for all of the potential suspense, humor, and tension possible in the essay evaporated when I read the thesis.

The next day I asked the student, who sheepishly averted his eyes from mine, obviously still embarrassed about the ordeal, why he chose this form. He frowned, then shrugged, and finally said, "That's how we wrote last year." The writer was just clinging to a form that worked for him in the past, and it ruined his essay.

Our lives, memories, and stories cannot be reduced to tidy, easily supportable theses. Nor do my students walk around with readily formed theses in their heads. When they enter my room on Monday morning, they do not begin postulating, "There were three contributing factors behind the football team's dominating performance Friday night: a punishing ground game, a defense that forced five turnovers, and a strong punting game that kept the opponent pinned deep in their own territory the entire night." Rather, students walk into my room sharing their stories and versions of what happened at the game. From their stories and experiences, students derive meaning and give shape to their worlds. Why not start there instead?

When the five-paragraph format is either taught too early or as the exclusive format, it inflicts serious damage. When students are shown a template they can follow and have success with, such as passing a standardized test, they cling to it dearly. Paul Heilker (1996) chronicles research done on the negative impact of the five-paragraph format. He cites a study conducted by Russel K. Durst which found that "90 percent of the student texts in his sample were organized this way, students using the thesis/support form to structure literary analysis, autobiographical, informative, and argumentative compositions, and even writing outside of English class" (p. 3).

Instead of being one option for students to use at their discretion, depending on the assignment, the McEssay often becomes the only option they choose, regardless of the assignment.

Earlier I lamented over all the hours I had spent holed up in the university library struggling with my thoughts. However, through that writing, I was able to explore my thoughts fully and examine a topic from multiple angles. It was not until I enrolled in graduate school after my third year of teaching, that I learned the value of all that time toiling with the writing process.

In my graduate program, we began an intensive study of composition theory where I discovered William Zeiger (1985), who emphasizes the importance of exploration in writing through the exploratory, familiar, or personal essay format, yet this exploratory type of writing is rarely emphasized in schools, especially college. Instead the thesis-support format is encouraged because most believe it reinforces the scientific method of thinking and proving a hypothesis.

Zeiger, building on work done by James Kinneavy, states that the scientific process really contains two types of discourse: exploratory and expository. The former "fundamentally asks a question and suggests a tentative answer" and the latter "asserts an answer and supplies proof" (p. 457). When the thesis-support format is emphasized, it really doesn't fully represent the scientific process, only a part. What is being lost is the focus on the exploratory discourse, where one explores ideas in order to reach a hypothesis that can then be tested.

Zeiger's theories gave me a new insight into all my time spent writing my undergraduate work. Now I see how I was, in Zeiger's words, "toughing out" an essay. As Zeiger observes, "Writers who know that the first step in writing is exploration, and who consciously begin the writing process not in the middle but at the beginning, steal a march on the less well informed" (p. 458). By sheer effort and practice, I learned the hard way how to incorporate the exploration process into my writing.

Instead of beginning with the exploratory process and developing a number of possible topics or ideas, I began with the expository process. When a paper was assigned, I formulated a thesis and set about proving it. However, after an hour or two of writing, I often realized that one of my ideas was insufficient. Then it was back to the drawing board. Other times I stumbled upon a better idea. Back to the drawing board again. Sometimes I even realized that my initial thesis was flawed and I had to start all over. All of this was painstaking but essential. Soon I began just writing to see what I really thought about a topic before settling on a thesis. This seems painfully obvious to me now, but every year I see students at the secondary and university levels struggle with this same issue.

Now I keep a quote from E. M. Forster stenciled on my white board: "How do I know what I think until I see what I say?" This reminds me that all the time I spent "toughing out" an essay was essential because I was thinking through my writing. It also reminds me of the importance of the personal narrative, where the reader is able to see the writer's ideas unfold naturally as they grapple with them and, literally, learn what they really think. Too often the McEssay makes it appear like the writer has naturally thought these things all along. It certainly leaves no room for any type of deviation or revelation. It robs the reader of the rich experience of watching the writer's thinking unfold in a natural progression. Zeiger observes this too, "By concentrating almost exclusively on the thesis-support exposition in college composition classes, we are implicitly teaching that the ability to support an assertation is more important than the ability to examine an issue" (p. 458).

Ultimately, Zeiger calls for the exploratory essay to be given the same type of emphasis the thesis-support essay is given. Offer students the chance to write in the exploratory process before emphasizing the expository process. I take this one step further by focusing most of our time on a variety of personal essays.

I do not claim that the personal essay is the only style of writing a student needs. In fact, gasp—shock—gulp, I have actually gone back to teaching the five-paragraph theme. However, I introduce it to students at the end of the course and make them aware that it is just one of many forms they may employ.

I structure my classes this way to offer my students a variety of forms of writing that they can draw upon in the future. In some cases, such as writing for the Advanced Placement test, students will have to employ a very rigid thesis-support format, and they will have that in their arsenals. However, they may have to devise an essay for a college application prompt, such as this one to which Mary Jane Reed (2004) refers in a text devoted to helping students pass college application essays, "You have just completed your 300-page autobiography. Please submit page 217" (p. 9). There is no McEssay that will work there.

We devote the first several weeks to personal essays. I do not allow my students to just tell stories. That is really only part of the personal essay. Students must also tackle a variety of complex strategies: use vivid imagery, incorporate authentic details and dialogue whenever possible, experiment with form and structure, contemplate audience, reflect on and analyze their experiences, and always strive to develop a strong and unique voice. They are, in other words, doing what real writers do.

We spend the final three weeks writing in the thesis-support format. Students struggle with some of the hallmarks of the thesis-support format: devising a thesis, focusing strictly on developing their thesis in the body of their essay, and, of course, refraining from using "I." They struggle most with having to filter out the voices they have been encouraged to develop for the first six weeks. However, I would rather have them already have a distinct voice that needs to be stifled than never have developed one at all.

I, too, must be wary when teaching the five-paragraph essay because it is the only time during my composition classes that I honestly feel like I have control over what my students are producing. This might very well be why so many secondary teachers employ it. When my students are writing their narratives, I have to approach each essay and writer differently. Instead of focusing solely on errors, I am focusing on the potential of the text. How do I coax more of the mind, the personality, and the life behind this story out and onto the page? This is often sloppy and maddening. Often all 30 writers are writing about different things in different ways. It entails sitting down with each of those writers and helping them craft their work. This approach is time consuming and not for the faint of heart.

Bruce Pirie (1997) observes the inherent sloppiness of this approach in *Reshaping High School English*: "We teach structure by sitting down with students who have something they care about saying, helping them sort out how they might try to say it, and looking at examples of how other writers have structured their work" because "it takes time, and the first results of student's own shaping definitely don't look as neat as formulaic essays" (p. 78). To say the least, this is a daunting task, and one I was certainly not up to my first year of teaching, which might be one reason I leaned so heavily on the McEssay.

When I teach the McEssay, I still feel a mastery over what we are writing about because I know the exact formula. I can read a student's rough draft and diagnose immediately what is lacking—"your second topic sentence does not correlate with your thesis" or "you need to offer more support for your third paragraph." This is not necessarily true with a personal essay, where I might offer a student a variety of suggestions, but, ultimately, the decision resides with the writer. The power is out of my hands.

Once my students have written a few five-paragraph essays, I end the class challenging my students to meld their voice and style into their own hybrid McEssay. I encourage them to use their voices in the essay. Some choose to liven up the usual generic introductions by either creating a brief narrative that illustrates for the reader what they are going to focus on or offering personal evidence that illustrates the issue they are going to discuss in their essays. And they can even write a sixth paragraph if they wish.

Ultimately, it is the personal narratives that allow my students to produce their most powerful work. Earlier this year after assigning a personal narrative in which students were to write about a family heirloom, Nicole, a very gifted writer in my College Composition class, raised her hand to share her essay. She described a silver ring with the words "for the love of my life" engraved upon the band. Then she recounted how, as a child, she loved to stare at the ring on her grandmother's finger and hear her recount the story of how Nicole's grandfather gave it to her the day her mother was born. Then she flashed forward in time, recalling how it had been eight months since her grandmother's last story...and six since she had been diagnosed with lung cancer. Finally, Nicole brought us full circle, staring at the words "Beloved Wife and Mother" on her grandmother's tombstone. Her mother handed her an envelope, which still held the aroma of her grandmother's black coffee and cigarettes. Inside the letter was the ring. Plus the note, "Always make me as proud as you do now."

By the time Nicole finished, I had to blink rapidly to quell the tears swelling at the corners of my eyes. I was not the only one doing this. Some had lost the battle and dabbed their eyes with their sleeves or hands. A few sniffled. I found myself searching the ceiling. I was not the one only doing this either. I smiled and swallowed hard. Not a word was uttered. The importance of our essays, our stories, and our lives, hovered in the room.

References

Heilker, P. (1996). *The essay*. Urbana, IL: The National Council of Council of Teachers of English.

Pirie, B. (1997). *Reshaping high school English*. Urbana, IL: The National Council of Teachers of English.

Reed, M. J. (2004). *Teaching powerful personal narratives: Strategies for college applications and high school classrooms*. Gainesville, FL: Maupin House.

Zeiger, W. (1985). The exploratory essay: Enfranchising the spirit of inquiry in college composition. *College English 47*(5), 454–466.

Writing Workshop
One Teacher's Journey

Deborah L. Smith

The Early Journey

The shaping of my writing self began at a very early age. My mother, as a teacher, knew the power of positive feedback and encouraged my creative writing with her time and focused attention. I grew up feeling proud of my writing abilities. I would write story books with illustrations on typing paper folded over and stapled to form a booklet and share these with my mother who would tell me I might grow up to be an author or an artist. My family has never been particularly good at praising, so these comments were embraced and encouraged me to write and draw more. As an early elementary school child, I remember writing a poem about my dog in the form of a Haiku. I was asked to read my poem in front of the class as an example of how to write Haiku. The teacher's praise and the experience of being singled out as "special" for my writing surely built my confidence and contributed to my continued love of poetry as a way to express myself.

As I continued through grade school, I remember having generally good experiences with Language Arts. I always loved spelling bees and

Getting It in Writing, pages 221–242

would often be one of the last students still standing when we played elimination rounds. I had many teachers who read to the class daily, and I was always engrossed in the stories. My second grade teacher, Mrs. Jones, was diagnosed with cancer midway through the school year. She tape-recorded her voice reading aloud to us while she was in the hospital, and the substitute would play her messages to the class and her voice reading *Island of the Blue Dolphins* to us. In the years since then, I have hoped that her children were given her tape-recordings to play to their own children one day. Mrs. Jones' funeral was the first that I remember attending, but I have a stronger memory of her voice reading *Island of the Blue Dolphins* as a class full of second-graders sat mesmerized on the carpet. I remember folding over construction paper and making cards with hearts and flowers to send to the hospital room, where I imagined they sat on a window sill next to a tape recorder.

When I moved on the middle school, I had Mrs. R for English class. We sat reading the grammar book aloud to the class. Each student would read a paragraph and then the next student in the row would continue. I would count off to figure out which paragraph I would be assigned and spend the time practicing reading so that I would not mispronounce any of the words. I also watched closely for anyone leaving their seat lest my paragraph change. Our writing and reading for these two years (7th and 8th grade) were reduced to diagramming sentences and drills to make sure we knew when to use "which" as opposed to "that" or "whom" as opposed to "who." The only writing I remember distinctly from these years was when I would talk in class and the punishment was to write "I will not talk in class" 100 times or 200 times, depending on the offense. Sometimes the writing punishment was more detailed—a paragraph to be copied over and over. Writing until my hand ached and being bored to tears was the only writing I can recall in middle school.

As a teenager in high school, writing came easily to me. I had an excellent senior English teacher who led us step-by-step through the process of writing research papers. We had dozens of note-cards with sources and codes and quotes, and she taught us to piece them together until we had a coherent research paper. In my junior year, a psychology teacher let us each select a famous case to write about. I remember researching Charles Manson and writing a report on his activities and relating his behavior to the psychology concepts we learned in class. The classes where we were given choices for topics and developed longer synthesized writing projects still stand out to me. In addition, I wrote sports reports for the school newspaper and helped to design the yearbook in my senior year. By my junior year of high school, I had decided to become a photographic journalist and to move to New York City. This dream was never fulfilled because it changed over time, but it illustrates that I still had confidence and interest in writing.

In my English courses in college, I found responding to literature to be an especially fulfilling activity. Dr. Matheson at University of Michigan-Flint was my professor for two literature-based courses and for an introductory English course. In the literature courses, she used a modified literature circle where we would discuss the readings in groups of five or six students before holding a whole-class discussion. Dr. Matheson provided study questions that led to deep analysis of the assigned readings, which were complex and varied. After the intense discussions, writing analysis papers to compare characters or to explore themes seemed to just flow naturally from my pencil to the page, and I rarely found writing to be a struggle. In Dr. Matheson's English course, she modeled peer review and editing by asking us to read and respond to classmate's papers. I wrote a paper on drilling for oil in Alaska that was revised and edited based on peer feedback before being submitted for grading. For this assignment, the entire class had to rewrite continually until there were absolutely no mistakes in our APA format or in the body of the paper. Some students turned in that paper over ten times before every mistake was fixed. I was proud that it took me two tries—I tied with one other student for the fewest number of rewrites. I continued to feel successful in my English courses throughout college in part because reading and writing were activities that I enjoyed outside of the classroom.

I have journaled during difficult periods of my life and written poetry as a way to articulate my feelings for as long as I can remember. This poem is one that I wrote soon after learning that my maternal grandmother had died:

Ramblings on Grandma

Bill, put a shirt on with that bathing suit
What would the neighbors think?
Always the model of decorum as she
presided over the picnic table
in the front yard, at the lake
God is great, God is good and we thank him
for this food. By his hands we all are fed
Give us this day our daily bread
Did anyone know that I was praying that there wouldn't be
anything too mysterious in Grandma's Jell-O salad?

Grandma was the easiest person in the world to buy gifts for
as long as you remembered peanut brittle; she was
An exercise bike that never moved

Popcorn balls on Christmas Eve
Mmmm Yummm, Thanks Gramma
Delicate tea cups all in a row
Rock'n' rye floats on Saturday night
The fluffiest chocolate chip cookies in the world
A hot pink bathroom at the top of the stairs
Fells-Naphtha soap after a day at the lake
Sunday dinners
Charades
Kings in the Corners
Jigsaw Puzzles

Lock all the doors
Be careful in life
But bring great joy and love to those around you
She raised 3 wonderful children
Mercy, Mercy, Mercy
It's nice to think that she's happy now
She's with her Lord
And she lives on in our memories
We love you grandma
FOREVER

I still have a poetry notebook filled with teenage angst and tales of unrequited love that are a bit embarrassing in retrospect but that fill me with powerful memories when I reread them. I wrote this one shortly after walking across the campus at Michigan State University when I was a freshman:

Storms

A storm is coming
I can feel it in the air
The electricity surrounds me
This is when I feel most alive
I feel as one with the universe
The power surges through me
The hair prickles on my neck
Clouds blot the sun
Lightning strikes and the crackle fills the sky
Let the rain come and wash me away
To be one with the storm{\ex}

I also turn to the writings of others for solace and inspiration when life seems hectic or significant events occur. As the baby of my extended family, I was not around babies until I had one of my own. My husband and I still joke that I wanted to prop up the section on changing diapers from *What to*

Expect in the First Year next to the changing table so that I could do it just like in the book. I have read books on grief and depression and relationships and discipline based on the events happening in my life and around me. I often feel better just knowing that others have similar issues and concerns about marriage, parenting, or life in general.

Like those who read for pleasure, those who write for pleasure seldom struggle when required to tailor their craft for specific assignments. In my undergraduate years, I did not own a computer so I wrote out my papers long-hand and paid a friend's mom to type them for me. I had no knowledge of the writing process, and thus I never thought about revising or editing my work. Still, I rarely earned less than an A on essays and research papers. I did not reflect on my writing or agonize over word choice; I simply wrote to fulfill the assignments presented to me. I believed that writing was something that I did when I sat down with a pad of paper; in my psyche, the act occurred in a vacuum and was not linked to other events. I did not link the analytical discussions in class and the developing ideas in my head with the ease of sitting down and writing out a paper. I did not reflect on the stages of writing because I believed writing came naturally to me and because the concept had only vaguely been introduced to me.

It was not until very recently that I was able to reflect on this segment of my writing life and realize that all the stages were actually there but in a recursive manner. In university courses, the essays and papers due throughout the semester are normally introduced in the syllabi on the first day of class. This is when my prewriting would often begin. I would begin thinking about research topics or essay formats on the first day they were introduced. In addition, many of the paper topics would relate to readings for each course. This served the double purpose of providing me with a clear reason for reading and focusing my prewriting as I read. There was no clear outline or bubble chart to show my thoughts, but the prewriting stage was actually long and arduous for me even back when I thought that I wrote effortlessly. The next stage of committing my thoughts to paper was supported by weeks and sometimes months of preparation.

The notes that I copiously scrawled on my books, articles, or class handouts could be seen as an extension of my prewriting or a beginning stage of drafting. I would often write questions that would later be explored in essays, or make connections that would lead to inferences presented as supporting details. The underlined passages would regularly turn into direct quotes in the final products of my papers. I even had a set routine for the actual writing of my papers; I would sit and write on my bed in a notebook with my door shut, no music, at a time when the house was generally quiet. When I had a "block," I would take a break and walk around the house, often chatting with roommates, but most often, sitting on the porch and organizing the next section of writing in my thoughts.

For years, I believed that because I wrote out my papers in one draft that was then turned over to be typed that I was skipping all of the stages of writing. It is true that my pages would not be scribbled upon with arrows and crossed out words, but that had all gone into the process beforehand, largely in my head. I often combined drafting, revising, and editing except that I would sit and think about my writing choices and commit to a paragraph in my head before I would write. This process flowed smoothly for me and made writing feel natural.

Generally, this process was sufficient for my life as an undergraduate student. Granted, in a few courses, I had to go back and write an outline after I had finished a paper or turned in a rough draft that was suppose to demonstrate how I had made significant revisions. This process was sometimes more difficult than writing the paper had been in the first place, but besides a few inconveniences, the process served me well. I was not even reflective enough to realize that this lack of reflection into my writing would inhibit me from actually teaching students to write. I never related my own writing with the teaching of writing, even after I had a course on the writing process. In my mind, the writing process was a useful tool for teaching students to write because it broke it down step-by-step, but because I did not see my process as similar, I thought that my own writing was somehow separate.

One Class Can Make a Difference

In my final semester of undergraduate work, I was scheduled to student teach. University of Michigan-Flint does not allow students to enroll for courses as they are student teaching, and I still needed one English methods course to graduate. I had plans to move to Arizona upon graduation and did not want to wait a semester to finish, so I enrolled in a course that I could transfer to fulfill my graduation requirements. This is how I landed in an English methods course at Saginaw Valley State University in Saginaw, Michigan. The professor in this course, Dr. Kay Harley, introduced me to the writing process and to Nancy Atwell's *In the Middle: Writing, Reading, and Learning with Adolescents* (1987). The professor modeled many aspects of writing workshop, including having us keep writing logs where we recorded ideas for writing, transcribed dialogues that we overheard, wrote conversations with ourselves, and tried to turn our observations about the world around us into prompts for writing. Dr. Harley taught about reading workshop and how to implement the writing process in the classroom and required that we create mini-lessons that could be used to teach the conventions of writing, the process of the workshop, and explore the literary craft. Compared to all the other information from my secondary English education undergraduate degree, this stuck, and it seemed imperative to me that I implement a writing workshop program. Perhaps it was because I was student teaching at the same time and had the opportunity to put some of it into immediate use in my placement classroom. Perhaps it was because it was some of the only material presented to me where the professor modeled the method she desired us to emulate. Or perhaps it was because Atwell's book had been the first practical book I had been assigned to read, while so many had been theoretical and difficult to connect with the classroom. Whatever the reason, I immediately recognized writing workshop and Atwell's format as important and applicable and recognized that even though it was not the way I wrote, it would help me to teach writing.

Throughout the course of the semester, this class introduced to me the idea of writing as a process. Atwell's writings are practical and valuable to practitioners because they are based on her own experiences teaching middle school students. The framework that Atwell (1987; 1998) uses to structure her classroom consists of seven basic principles: 1) writers need regular chunks of time; 2) writers need their own topics; 3) writers need responses; 4) writers learn mechanics in context; 5) children need to know adults who write; 6) writers need to read; and 7) writing teachers need to take responsibility for their knowledge and teaching. I participated in a workshop format that included mini-lessons, drafting, peer editing, conferences, and "status-of-the-class" reports. The "status-of-the-class" is a procedural part of the writing workshop where every participant reports on what they will be working on during their in-class writing time. The instructor takes brief notes on a chart so that he or she can keep track of the progress of each individual and so that he or she knows who has the highest priority needs for conferencing. The class met for three hours on Wednesday evenings and about one hour of this time was dedicated to modeling the workshop format.

Yet, for some reason, I was never a true participant. That is, I learned about Writing Workshop and how to implement it and participated in every activity. I kept a "writer's log," conferenced with the professor, revised and edited with peers and found outlets for publishing. I answered all of the reading and writing inventories and kept my writing log and portfolios up-to-date. However, as I forged along as though I had adopted these new methods as my own, in reality I still wrote out my final papers in the same old way. I wrote the required writing log for the course after the fact, going back and filling in ideas from papers that had already been composed. The upshot was that I never genuinely let the process I was learning interfere with my way of writing or my personal writings. My thinking simply was these methods were not meant to be intertwined with academic courses.

As far as teaching was concerned, I thought I had learned a fabulous new method. I figured that I could "fake it." I knew that to conduct a workshop like Atwell's, I would need to follow her principle that children need to know adults who write, but I did not think my own process should be shared with students since it was not linear. I did not yet understand that the process is recursive or that my writing truly did go though the various stages in some form. So the modeling that I did was of writing in a linear fashion, but it was not my true style of writing. I still never gave the writing process much thought in regards to my own writings. It was this lack of reflection that led me to reproduce the linear writing process approach in my classroom.

Putting it in Practice

Upon graduation, I was truly unprepared for teaching. I knew a lot about Shakespeare and Twain, but little about lesson planning and still less about teaching writing, an important component of a Language Arts class, my first teaching assignment. Yes, I had Dr. Harley's class that focused on the workshop format, but I knew nothing of theories of writing, and still less on preparing students to write for multiple purposes. Perhaps that is why I turned to Atwell's writing workshop format—merely because I had no idea how else to proceed, and Atwell provided an easy-to-follow formula for teaching writing.

I adapted Atwell's writing workshop format with very few changes from how she explained it in her first edition of *In the Middle: Writing, Reading, and Learning with Adolescents* (1987). I asked students to keep a writing log with them at all times and followed her procedures for the first day by talking about, our "writing territories," the areas we feel comfortable and confident exploring in writing. I had students make a list of topics that they might write about and we added to the list regularly. All writing was saved in a draft folder, and lists were kept of the finished products in students' portfolios, spelling words, conventions mastered and goals for the workshop. The set procedures for our workshop time included the following:

1. Mini-lesson: Each workshop began with a 10–15 minute mini-lesson about procedures, literary craft, or conventions of writing. These lessons would be determined by my reflections on what the students needed. Sometimes I would focus on common errors

found in writings or would introduce students to new materials available in the classroom. If there was a writing contest, then I would talk about the call for manuscripts, and we would often look at authors' styles for inspiration.

2. Status-of-the class report: As explained earlier, this is a procedural aspect of the workshop. I kept a big chart next to my desk so that I could keep track of each student's progress at a glance.

3. Time for students to write while teacher confers: During this time, students could be on any stage of the writing process. If they were revising, then they could go with a partner to the revision area and read each others' papers and provide feedback. I would move around the room and monitor progress, trying to confer with as many students as possible. I followed Atwell's advice and would not write on students' papers, instead letting them tell me about their writing and probing with questions to prompt improvements and reflection.

4. Whole-class conference: At the end of each workshop, I would call the class back together to share some of their finished pieces and to reflect on the overall process of the workshop. Some days this time was used for organization of folders and updating their list, but most days we would enjoy hearing students "publish" their work by sharing it with the class.

I had very little that I felt successful about in my first year of teaching. The year was 1990, and I was assigned to teach sixth, seventh, and eighth grade Language Arts at Maricopa Middle School in Maricopa, Arizona, a rural town that bordered the Tohono O'Odham nation. My students were a mix of migrant workers, Native Americans, and whites (about equally proportioned), and I was given no curriculum to follow. Instead I was able to order a few class sets of novels and other class sets were left in the classroom. A class set of a textbook that was ten years out-of-date was also left in the classroom. We never broke open the textbooks, instead opting to read *The Light in the Forest* by Conrad Richter, *Number the Stars* by Lois Lowry, *Tuck Everlasting* by Natalie Babbitt, *A Wrinkle in Time* by Madeline L'Engle, *The Outsiders* by S.E. Hinton, *Sing Down the Moon* by Scott O'Dell and others. I was not daring enough to devote all my class time and energy to a workshop format—I felt the need to fit in with a small group of teachers that clung to "junior high" style courses. I did not know how to modify the substantive nature of writing workshop so that my students would produce assignments to meet the state testing requirements, which included writing in multiple formats. Yet every Monday, I ventured into a full session of reading and writing workshop. It was my favorite day of the week, and I loved creating mini-lessons based on students' needs and conferencing with each student on their progress.

Even though I introduced the workshop format carefully following Atwell's description, I still had many students regularly asking "Can I really write anything I want?" I responded by encouraging students to consider their list of "writing territories" that were created on the first day of class and added to regularly. I would ask them what they wanted to write about, and it did not take long for their imaginations to soar and the students to start producing volumes of their favorite forms of writing. I had a student who wrote seven letters in one week because I had a book with addresses for fan clubs and famous people. I had a student who made awesome cartoons with detailed illustrations and an engaging storyline. I had a student who brought in notebooks filled with her poetry to share with me and the class. I even felt that I was successful at modeling the stages with my own writings, though I did not believe that my natural writing involved a process similar to what I asked students to follow. I pretended to prewrite, draft, revise, edit, and publish in distinct stages and did not accept deviations from this format despite never truly following it for myself because I believed that writing workshop would only work if the steps were linear.

It did not take long, however, for my initial elation to wear off as I realized three months later that few students were venturing out of their comfort zone. While I found it great that Julia (not her real name) had decided to write a novel, I felt strong pressure to guarantee that students mastered various forms of writing rather than just the process. Soon after I began teaching, the state implemented the Arizona State Assessment Plan (ASAP), and we were given practice tests and told to prepare students so that they could succeed on the state assessment, which could assess any kind of writing from poetry to persuasive arguments.

Additionally, workshop limited to one day a week felt too segmented and disjointed. It felt more like an interruption of the other projects students were completing, and on Tuesday, the other projects felt like an intrusion on writing workshop time and so it went. Soon I found myself telling students "we'll skip workshop this Monday so that we can finish our other project" and even a single day of workshop was no longer a guarantee.

"Basics" and Back

I would love to report that I deftly overcame these barriers and found ways to interest students in writing multiple genres and found a way to balance the testing pressures and the workshop format. Instead, I drifted away from the workshop approach for a while and found myself assimilating with my fellow teachers' beliefs that control in the classroom was paramount and that too much choice and freedom would undermine a teacher's classroom management. Truth be told, I thought I was offering enough freedom and choice by allowing students to choose their topic when giving them limited options. It wasn't until the middle of my third year, when I attended an in-service workshop led by a high school English teacher in my district that I realized I had moved so far away from the writing workshop format that it really was no longer happening at all in my classroom. I reflected on the fact that while I might refer to the writing process when I told students to revise and edit their work and would sometimes ask students to brainstorm or complete a web before they began drafting, I no longer led my students through the stages or asked them to peer revise or focused on publishing students' writings. I had turned into a teacher who expected students to write for me alone and who tailored her writing assignments not around the interests of the students but around the extant curriculum that was driven by standard exams. Perhaps this was in part because I had not found the link between my own writing and the writing process.

I decided to make a change. I started the process of implementing writing workshop again and broke out the writing folders and opening day pep talk on how we are all writers. I demonstrated how to revise and asked students to read each other's papers and provide feedback. I reread Atwell's *In the Middle: Writing, Reading, and Learning wit Adolescents* (1987) and let students choose their topics, and I tried to recreate the Workshop format that I had implemented in my first year. It, however, just did not work. Possibly it was because by mid-year the classroom expectations had been so firmly established. Maybe it was because that first year had not been all that successful in the first place, and deep down I knew that. Furthermore, it was harder to convince students that this was the way it should be when students were accustomed to a teacher-directed format. The students were confused when I asked them to be creative and decide what to write on their own after I had told them what to write about and led them step-by-step for the first half of the year. We had fallen into a comfortable routine that was not the most effective but that was difficult to bring to a halt.

The New Hybrid

The next four years I taught English as a Second Language (ESL) at the secondary level in Phoenix. It was in this setting that I adapted the workshop approach most successfully. Each of my classes was a 100 minute block devoted to reading, writing, speaking and listening and once again I started off with no prescribed curriculum. In my second year at South Mountain

High School, I became part of the "Literacy Cadre," and it was in this professional development experience that I gained the knowledge and the confidence to make learning the main focus in my classroom.

The "Literacy Cadre" was a program run by Mary Harthun, the staff development specialist at South Mountain High School and Drs. Dee Spencer and David Altheide, professors of Education and Justice Studies at Arizona State University, respectively. The cadre met every Monday night after school for three hours and had regular summer seminars over the course of three years. I was one of the first teachers to volunteer to be a member because of the tremendous amount of respect I had for Mary Harthun, who ran most of the sessions. Mary had run my first-year teacher meetings and had been a tremendous help in my acclimation to the high school.

Much of the focus of the weekly sessions revolved around literacy strategies for instruction. We also reviewed learning theories, kept a weekly log with teaching reflections, and regularly implemented the strategies presented in our classrooms and then reported back to the cadre on what had worked and how we might adapt strategies to make them more effective. Dr. Altheide taught us about action research and we each conducted action research projects in our classrooms. We all traveled to American Educational Research Association's (AERA) conference in San Diego and to the other schools in our district to present our findings. The cadre built my confidence and made me a better teacher. I still have the notebook with handouts, activities, and my reflective logs and refer back to these documents when preparing my college courses.

The cadre greatly influenced my daily classroom practices. After my earlier experiences with writing workshop, I decided not to use the workshop approach in its original form, such as described earlier for my format in Maricopa. I still used all of the elements, but I chose to do so in a more structured format because of my concerns about students being challenged and gaining experience with all formats of writing. Nancy Atwell's newer edition of *In the Middle: Writing, Reading, and Learning with Adolescents* actually laments the fact that her earlier edition reads like "a cookbook," which is exactly how I had read the first edition—as a guide to be followed explicitly. As I became more confident in myself as a teacher, I started to realize that the elements of the workshop can be effectively incorporated into the classroom in a balanced way. There were times when the students took the lead and times when I knew that I needed to lead to provide the challenges that would help my students to grow as writers.

I used strategies learned in cadre to expand students' writing repertoire such as RAFT, which stands for role, audience, format and topic. After students had read and completed class activities to discuss a topic, I would provide choices for each element and they would use writing to expand their knowledge and to synthesize the new information. For example, after a unit on "Coming to the United States," students would select one element from each area and complete the writing:

Role	Audience	Format	Topic
Young child	Mom and Dad	Speech	Why I miss our home
New student	Teacher	Letter	What you should know about me
Border fence	Immigrants	Speech	What I have seen
Immigrant	President	Letter	What should be done to welcome newcomers

The writings that students completed for these assignments were usually quite thought-provoking and demonstrated that the students understood the concepts presented and had related new knowledge with their existing schema.

I also integrated writing and research into students' responses to literature as a way to broaden their writing experiences. I would use Story Impressions to introduce new vocabulary to students. Story Impressions are a strategy where students write creative stories using selected words from the text they are about to read. Before my students read a passage from Shakespeare's *Midsummer Night's Dream*, they would write a brief story that included the following words or phrases: renowned, vexation, bewitched, feigned, gawds, filched, ancient privilege, and dispose. Students would write creatively and then read their stories aloud to the class. After the first time doing this, I had to switch to having students read aloud to a small group because every student in class wanted to share their stories and it would fill the entire class period. After they read their stories, then they would read the passage and compare how they used the words with how Shakespeare defined them. This worked similarly to having students predict because they wanted to learn if they had been close to the actual definition, and it improved their skills at defining words from context. The writing provided a purpose for students' reading.

During these four years of my professional life, I began teaching thematically. Instead of randomly assigning class activities, I would select a general theme to focus student learning. For example, I normally started my semester with a unit titled "Who are you?" In this unit students and I would explore their learning styles, do a "True Colors" personality inventory, and complete reading, writing, speaking and listening activities that focused on building a community in the classroom. We read poems such as "We Wear the Mask" by Paul Laurence Dunbar and wrote autobiographies. I also included a unit on "United States Culture" each year because my students were all immigrants and learning about their new culture was important to them. I would begin the unit by modeling learning activities centered on the current decade that included slang, style, sports, music and pop culture; then students would work in groups to learn about and teach the class about each of the other decades. This project usually took a lot of research in the library and culminated in group presentations on each decade with student-led activities.

In my second year, I began team teaching with Sharon Lea, another ESL teacher. Sharon approached me with the idea of team-teaching and administration quickly approved because Sharon had an excellent reputation. Sharon and I would trade off being the "lead" teacher while the other assisted in the classroom and spent any extra time preparing the next unit of study. Each unit was prepared to engage students in all aspects of literacy. We would design our units by starting with a general theme. We would then consider the state standards and determine which needed to be addressed in our classroom based on student needs and what had already been covered. Next we would select a variety of literature relating to the theme and then determine how to include activities that would engage students in reading, writing, speaking and listening.

Sharon was a fellow cadre member, so we would usually select literacy strategies that were presented in our weekly seminars. Writing was always interwoven through the thematic units and used as a learning tool as well as a skill to hone. For example, if we were studying the format of a poem or the style of a poet, we might ask students to complete a "Copy Text" where students follow the format of the poem and change the words to make it their own. This activity challenges students to develop vocabulary and write creatively by modeling good forms of writing. We also included many forms of journal writing. Students would write in their reading logs after Silent Sustained Reading (SSR) time; they would write in their dialogue journals about general topics and Sharon or I would respond to them in writing; students would complete graphic organizers to organize their thoughts such as webs or "Double-Entry Dairies" where students draw a line down the middle of a lined sheet of paper and pull quotes from the text to place on the left and connect, question, or explain the quote on the right side of the line. Students often completed KWL (Know, Want to Know, Learned) charts as a way to activate their prior knowledge before reading and to give purpose to their readings. The variety of activities that we provided helped to differentiate our teaching so that we reached all of our students.

Sharon and I were both able to go around and conference with students while they wrote, and we individualized the students' writing instruction based on their strengths and needs. I thought it was enough to provide a positive environment, modeling, and encouragement. Yet throughout this experience, I never reconciled the difference between my own style of writing and how I taught the students to write. I still led students step-by-step through the writing process and did not realize that my own recursive style was indeed quite similar. I had grown enough to be reflective on my teaching but not enough to be reflective of myself.

What was still lacking for me personally and for my teaching of writing was metacognition. I never really thought about my own process of writing and never encouraged students to discover their own processes. I imposed Atwell's stages or other processes for writing onto the students and expected them to follow the format for writing. As Kane (2007) states "writing is not magic, nor is it something only the truly gifted can do well, but neither is it something that can be easily produced by simply plugging in the steps of a formula listed over a chalkboard" (p. 214). I read the words in Atwell's and Grave's books about the teacher modeling writing and being a writer with his or her students, and yet I only did this superficially. I kept my real writing process hidden since it never fit the format that I was trying to instill in my students. The writing workshop is a valuable format for teaching writing, but it requires that the teacher be reflective of his or her own writing process and the recursive nature of the writing process. Since it encourages teacher modeling, the teacher needs to truly show students the process that he or she takes and how it differs from the prescribed format so that students can embrace their own process. This hybrid attempt at this stage of my career was more effective than earlier attempts at writing workshop, but it sorely lacked the authenticity that I sensed a real workshop could produce. Sadly, it was not until I left public school teaching and returned to school full-time myself that I became aware of my many short-comings as a teacher. It was in my doctoral graduate work that I developed the critical self-awareness necessary to see that I was reproducing orthodoxies about learning to write that would make it difficult for students to reflect on their writing process just as it had been difficult for me.

New Knowledge

Now I teach at the university level and much of my focus, due to the nature of the courses I teach, is on reading and the complexities of teaching. I write for myself for pleasure and pressure to advance, but it wasn't until recently that I realized that I have once again slid away from the writing workshop approach. I have taught *about* reading and writing workshop in my courses without directly modeling the writing workshop approach. In addition to figuring out how to rectify this situation, I have determined that I need to reflect on my learning to determine how to teach both about writing workshop and about writing to learn and to model both of these for my students. I have started this process in my Adolescent Literature course by including both reading and writing workshop time. I asked students to reflect on their own writing process before I ever introduced the stages, and we all compared our own process with the conventional model. I also provide 20 minutes in each class session to read a novel of their choice and we share what we read and talked about the process of a reading workshop. This is hard to do because there is so little time and always so much to cover, but it shows students that I value reading, and it has been wonderful to see how they love to talk about what they have read. I have had many students comment that they plan to include reading time in their future classrooms because this opportunity has them reading books outside of the assigned readings again. They report that they bring in a new book to read during our weekly session, and once they have started, they are compelled to finish the book. Multiple students have shared that they had not read for pleasure during the school year since starting college because of all the required reading, but they are now reading for enjoyment again.

I have had numerous revelations regarding the teaching of writing and the workshop format that I hope will help me to prepare future teachers to be effective teachers of writing. Many are not new to the teaching of writing, but they have new significance to my teaching plans. I have developed the following five "keys" for teaching writing in response to my earlier deficits as a writing teacher:

1. *The process of writing is recursive rather than linear.* The recursive nature of the writing process is important because it affirms students' own writing processes. If a writer prefers to edit and use spellcheck as she writes her first draft, then that should not be deemed "wrong" because it is part of editing. If a writer would rather start right in on the draft instead of creating an outline or a web, then that should not be deemed "wrong" either. According to Rapp-Ruddell (2005), "virtually all current views of the writing process avoid descriptions of a series of 'writing steps' that all writers proceed through to create written text" (p. 282). Instead, scholars and teachers realize the variety of respectable paths that writers can follow to create their own style.

2. *Teachers must truly bring their own writing into the classroom; "faking it" is not an option.* I believe it is essential in my classrooms to not only show students my true writing form, but to encourage them to reflect on their own processes. Being writing teachers means that we need to dig deeper than we do to write for ourselves. Atwell (1998) coveys her anxiety about sharing her writing with students, but notes that "I can only become their mentor, some- one whose advice carries weight and truth, because I know writing from the inside, and I've shown them I do" (p. 26). Modeling is most valuable when it is authentic. Thus, I have learned not to "fake it" any more. I share my true writing style with students in all its messy glory.

3. *Help students to reflect upon their own stages and understand that each person's process is unique.* Scholars have come to the conclusion that there are endless possibilities for writing processes. Reflect- ing on the stages of the writing process is a valuable tool, but it is not necessary (or even recommended) to follow the stages in any linear fashion, and they do not supersede the natural processes that writers follow. Awareness of the procedures that we each follow for writing can show that the purposes for writing and the targeted audience can influence our process as well (Kane, 2007). The most promising teaching of writing embraces students' own processes and also instructs them in finding the links between their own procedures and the stages of the writing process.

4. *Writing is an effective tool for learning.* Writing to learn is also regu- larly called "writing across the curriculum" and involves "using writing to promote learning by helping students reformulate and extend knowledge of topics" (Armbruster, McCarthey, & Cum- mins, 2005, p. 74). Writing to learn belongs in every classroom in every school. "One of the most important attributes of writ- ing is that not only is it a way to demonstrate what we know—in a report, or a poem, or a set of class notes—but also it is a *way of knowing*, a way of working through confusion and fuzzy ideas, and a way of moving toward clarification and articulation of knowl- edge" (Rapp-Ruddell, 2005, p. 38). A student who knows how to learn through writing will excel in academic settings and beyond.

5. *Writing is more important than process, or learning; it is a reflection of our world and should be valued beyond grades and communicating ideas.* Beyond the academic setting, writing carries a significance that makes one's life more aesthetically pleasing. "[T]he significance acquired by the act of writing will depend on the role played by

writing within the totality of beliefs and practices current in any given society" (Harris, 1995, p. 35). Writing allows for creative thoughts to be expressed and can improve our society with more access for all. When responding to the question "why does writing matter?" Lamott (1994) states, "[w]riting and reading decrease our sense of isolation. They deepen and widen and expand our sense of life; they feed the soul" (p. 237).

The insights that I have gained from reflecting on writing will be foundational as I prepare to rectify my current situation. I don't want to teach in hybrid format—pulling in revision and editing for some papers, brainstorming as a class to get students prewriting on the same topic. I want to find ways to incorporate writing to learn and writing workshop in a purer form and ways to communicate to students the significance of writing.

Plan of Action

My immediate plan was to use the lessons I learned over the years about teaching writing to incorporate writing to learn into my "reading in the content areas" courses, and to model writing workshop for my graduate students in a course on reading and writing programs. This time I did not hold back! I was so excited to dive back into the workshop format and to model the process in the hopes that the current and future teachers in my classrooms would utilize writing in their own classroom practices.

I began by implementing a new writing awareness project in all of my undergraduate courses, using the following adapted assignment from Kane (2007, pp. 219–220):

WRITING PROCESS ASSIGNMENT

This assignment is designed to give you a feel for the writing process stages and to reflect on your own writing process. It will result in a new text about teaching and learning. You are responsible for a short essay that will become part of a class compilation on our webpage. The book must have a theme relevant to a content area literacy course for teachers, so you have two broad options:

1. Write a memoir of some learning experience you have had.
2. Write a description of a teacher you have known.

PLANNING: Before you begin, think about the writing that you do on a regular basis. I know you write a variety of papers for courses, but do you also write for other purposes? Do you keep a "to-do" list? Do you write in a journal or write songs or poetry? Think about your writing and the steps you take as you compose. Maybe you have already begun with the options listed above. Have you been thinking about what you might want to write about?

According to Kane (2007), "researchers, teachers, and writers have discovered that there is no one correct way to write—people have unique styles and preferences that work best for them, and individuals follow different procedures depending on their purposes and targeted audiences" (p. 212).

Writing does not follow a linear path; it is recursive, which means that we move back and forth between stages. For example, I edit for spelling as I write. I have to stop and make sure I have spelled correctly even if it is for a rough draft. Similarly, I might go back and draw a web to flesh out part of a paper when I am writing a final draft.

As you write, be aware of the recursive stages you go through, and keep a record of the piece in progress; save drafts and journal entries. The following paragraphs will help you reflect on the composing process.

PRE-WRITING: How do you think of ideas and identify a topic for your essay? You might read several samples to get your thinking started and your memory jogged. Two samples, Bailey White's "One Eared Intellectual" and an excerpt from Frank McCourt's *Teacher Man* were read to you in class when this assignment was first presented. Notice the crafting of essays or sections of books that relate to describing teachers. Experiment with ways to tell your story.

DRAFTING: Do you write at the computer? Are you following an outline? Do you cluster or work up a mind map? Do you jot down your ideas as they come to you? Do you write out notes on index cards and organize them? How much organization do you do before you ever start writing? Did you go back to the first stage and read more examples of teaching memoirs? Are ideas changed or new ideas coming to you as you write?

PEER REVIEW/CONFERENCING: In class or out of class, meet with two or three people in a writing conference. Each of you should read your piece aloud, pausing two or three times for your peers to take notes, and invite the listeners' responses and suggestions. As you listen to others' texts, respond by completing a "V?P!" chart. Fold a blank piece of paper into four sections and label one section "V". In this section write down or draw what you visualize as you listen. The next section should be labeled "?" and will contain the questions that arise as you listen. The next section, labeled "P" is for predictions and the final section "!" is for connections that the listener makes to the text. In addition to the "V?P!" chart, please offer other feedback to the writer. Be as specific as possible in your response to other's drafts. When you say to your group members, "Oh, that's good; don't change a thing," the writer hasn't learned much. But if a listener explains what made her laugh, what part wasn't clear, or how the ending might be stronger, or when she gives a specific suggestion, such as, "I think a bit of dialogue would make this confrontation between you and the principal come alive," the writer has something new to think about. We will walk through these peer revision steps in class so that we can all learn from each other before you are expected to complete this with your small group.

REVISION: What is the next step that you naturally take when composing? Do you revise next or do you go back to an earlier stage? Revision in the writing process is a step where you "re-vision" what you originally wrote and consider its merit. For some, this step occurs simultaneously with drafting; for others, it never occurs. For this assignment, you have feedback from peers to consider. You might reject some of their ideas; you might surprise yourself with a whole new direction or a different slant or point of view. What you do regarding revision is up to you—just note your process along the way.

EDITING: There are many ways to proofread your work. You might read it out loud so you can hear how the sentences sound or use a spellchecker and grammar check. Be careful with this one! Recent research has found that the number one student writing error is using a wrong word because the spell checker replaces an incorrectly spelled word with a new word that does not fit (Lunsford, 2006). Many people do not pick up on their own sentence level errors, so giving your text to someone else—a parent, sibling, or buddy editor—to go over is a good idea. Offer to reciprocate. Notice if this is a separate stage for you or if you tend to incorporate editing as you go. Do you try to get your ideas down first and then go back to revise and edit or do you follow another pattern?

PUBLISHING: Prepare a final version of your text for classmates and post your essay on the class website. Your final step is to read the postings and enjoy! Feel free to respond to each others' essays with positive comments, questions or your own reflections. Send a note to someone whose essay made you understand a particular point of view, or concept about pedagogy, or teacher behavior. Let someone know if you had a similar experience to the one she wrote about, or if you respectfully disagree on some point. In short, let your fellow writers hear from their fans.

This assignment introduced students in all content areas to the writing process and guided them through the stages. In addition to the essay that students share online, a reflection paper on their own writing process was collected and discussed in class. In contrast to my own experiences, students were asked to reflect on their own writing process—and variations were explored and encouraged as we emphasized the uniqueness of each person's process. This assignment was given early in the semester and then throughout the semester we discussed writing as a tool for learning as it relates to multiple literacy strategies, such as RAFTs, Double-Entry Diaries, Story Impressions, and Dialogue Journals. These were tools that I had always introduced, but I had not emphasized the importance of seeing writing as a tool for learning. I accomplished this by reflecting more on the activities that were introduced and by exploring the learning that students accomplish with their own writing. For example, after I engaged the students in a RAFT activity, I asked students to answer questions such as "How did the RAFT exercise help you to synthesize information from the chapter?" "How might you use RAFT in your subject area?" Or, after completing a reading, I asked students to determine what kind of writing assignment would enhance learning most effectively. This connection I continue to improve and is an area where I continue to grow as a teacher.

In addition, I began using the Atwell text and a true writing workshop format for my course on secondary reading programs. This course was a three hour block two nights a week in summer session that was part of many graduate programs. It traditionally focused on successful secondary reading and writing programs found in the research literature without modeling of some of the most successful elements. To model these elements we participated in literature circles, reading workshop, and then writing workshop for the first two hours of each class session. I reserved the computer lab so that students would be able to choose how they compose. Like my class so long ago, I modeled the workshop, but I also incorporated my years of new learning so that the students reflect on their own processes, and I discussed the reality of aligning a workshop approach with the standards movement and high-stakes testing. Roser and Bomer (2005) note that "depth of understanding doesn't necessarily imply ease of installing a writing workshop; neither does deep knowledge prevent rough spots, quandaries, and even the commission of seeming violations of an increasingly instantiated view of 'the' writing process" (p. 26).

Concluding Thoughts

Writing this essay was a cathartic experience for me; the essay itself served as a model of how writing can be used as a tool for learning. It was through the process of reflecting on my life as a writer, and the insights I made throughout the years that I came to the conclusion that these aspects need to be incorporated more significantly in my courses. My writing helped me to evolve as a teacher of writing. I agreed with Harris (1995) when he states that "the act of writing may have significance in itself, irrespective of what is written down" (p. 33). For me, writing is thinking with clarity and vision. It is a chance to take the jumble of ideas that swirl in my mind and make them real. It does not matter if a written piece is rough draft or finished product; it holds significance. What I write depends on my knowledge, my audience, my freedom to express myself, my mood, and more. It is a reflection of who I am as a person and the context in which I write. I want to convey this passion for the written word and for writing to learn to all my students who participate in the processes as we actively engage in writing and reflection.

References

Armbruster, B., McCarthey, S. & Cummins, S. (2005). Writing to learn in elementary classrooms. In R. Indrisano & J. Paratore (Eds.), *Learning to write, writing to learn: Theory and research in practice* (pp. 71–96). Newark, DE: International Reading Association.

Atwell, N. (1987). *In the middle: Writing, reading, and learning with adolescents.* Portsmouth, NH: Boynton/Cook.

Atwell, N. (1998). *In the middle: New understandings about writing, reading, and learning.* Portsmouth, NH: Boynton/Cook.

Harris, R. (1995). *Signs of writing.* New York: Routledge.

Kane, S. (2007). *Literacy and learning in the content areas.* Scottsdale, AZ: Holcomb Hathaway.

Lamott, A. (1994). *Bird by bird: Some instructions on writing and life.* New York: Anchor Books.

Lunsford (2006). The top twenty composition errors. Retrieved March 23, 2008 from http://bcs.bedfordstmartins.com/lunsford/Lunsford_TopTwenty.aspx

Rapp-Ruddell, M. (2005). *Teaching content reading and writing* (4th ed.). Hoboken, NJ: John Wiley & Sons.

Roser, N.L. & Bomer, K. (2005). Writing in primary classrooms: A teacher's story. In R. Indrisano & J.R. Paratore (Eds.), *Learning to write, writing to learn: Theory and research in practice* (pp. 26–39). Newark, DE: International Reading Association.

No Bad Writing

Deborah M. Stankevich

A writer is someone who writes.
—Pat Schneider

I always fancied myself a writer. Perfectly shaped letters—block and later cursive—led me to believe I wrote well. My letters always gently touched the lines or carefully intersected those horizontal dashes between the solid blue lines that showed the exact middle of the space where the letter should cross and sometimes connect. My elementary teachers, the Felician Sisters at Holy Name of Jesus in Buffalo, said I wrote well. Immaculate letters on a clean sheet of lined paper won the praises of my teachers. Yes, I even spelled well, which was a bonus. Fewer spelling mistakes meant fewer eraser marks. My principal, Sister Mary Richard at Most Holy Redeemer in Cheektowaga, said I wrote well, too. In fact, my "writing" was so beautiful, I was selected to write in "the book" in the principal's office recording important information about the school for posterity. I would go to Sister Mary Richard's office when summoned, step up onto the stool in front of a podium that held this huge leather-bound book, and write whatever Sister gave me to record. Sometimes it was a page; sometimes it was more, depending on what was happening in and around school. I never read what was given to me; I was just supposed to copy the information into "the book." No questions, just

Getting It in Writing, pages 243–254
Copyright © 2011 by Information Age Publishing

copy. I took my time making my letters crisp, precise, and very legible. Sister Mary Richard would look over my work and then send me back to class with a "Well done" and a new pencil. The other kids were so envious. I would come back to class and go directly to my seat. My friend, Patti, would look over and say, "So what happened?"

"Nothing," I would reply. "I just wrote in 'the book.'"

I don't think anyone believed me. I went to Sister Mary Richard's office for something other than talking or not doing my work.

What a great writer I was! I loved the feel of a sharpened #2 Ticonderoga lead pencil in my hand with a Pink Pearl eraser by the side of my paper in case a stray line or smudge should appear, taking away the beauty of the writing. My work was always neat and clean. Heaven help a student who produced an unkempt homework assignment. That visit to Sister Mary Richard's office would not be to write in "the book" but to redo that assignment several times until she was satisfied with the outcome.

It wasn't until my mom gave me a red vinyl 5-year diary for my ninth birthday that I realized I had nothing to say. I opened the box with such enthusiasm, carefully peeling back the tissue paper that protected the cover. "My Diary" was embossed in gold letters in the center of the cover. My eyes widened; my breath caught in my throat. I didn't even realize I was holding my breath until a small "aw..." sound escaped. "For me?" I whispered.

"Happy Birthday, Debcia," my mother said.

I held the diary close to my chest, my mind racing with everything I wanted to put on paper—to remember. "Thank you, Mom," I said excitedly.

Off to my room I raced, plopped down on my chair, and gingerly placed the diary on my desk. Using the tiny gold key, I inserted it into the locket and turned it to the left. A soft click released the curved metal lock and the blank pages presented themselves. Blank pages. Lots of *blank pages*! Oh my God! The pages were blank except for the date clearly printed at the top of each page. I picked up my pen, changed my mind, put it down, and retrieved my sharpened #2 Ticonderoga lead pencil instead. I placed my pink pearl eraser by the side of my diary and got ready to write.

I turned the pages until I reached July 18, 1959. I lifted the point of my classic #2 pencil and while indenting, placed the point on the first line of the page.

"Dear Diary," I began. "Today is my birthday." Perfectly formed cursive letters stared back at me. *Now what?*

My mother opened the door to my bedroom. Peeking in, she said smiling, "Don't write too long. Dinner will be ready soon."

"Okay," I replied smiling back. My eyes gravitated back to those blank pages. Don't write too long! I couldn't even get started. Maybe a little picture would help. I drew a birthday cake with a candle on a plate. This was going to be work!

Every day, I worked very hard trying to find something of importance to say. "Today I went to the park with Patti and Linda." Big deal! "Today I went shopping with Mom to buy school clothes." Was that important? No. "It was raining today, so Jo and I played checkers." So boring, but my writing looked good. Perfectly formed letters forming one or two sentences graced each page of the diary. As it turned out, I went from the sublime to the mundane. I felt I had nothing to say; therefore I had nothing to write.

As a child, I had an extremely vivid imagination, and I liked to tell stories, yet I never saw this as food for writing. They were only stories that I could tell over and over again. Once I recall waking up from a dream of indescribable proportions. I believed it to be the best dream-life story ever. So in the middle of the night, I crept out of my warm bed and wrapped my afghan my mom had crocheted for me around my shoulders and sat at my desk transcribing the greatest story ever told. I couldn't get the words on paper fast enough. I didn't "write" well that night. If fact, I almost couldn't read my words as the story unfolded on the blank pages before me. I didn't care about grammar or spelling, or what the writing looked like. I only cared about the story, the idea, the words, and what they said. That day I was a writer!

Throughout my junior high and high school years, writing was something I did to fulfill assignments for various teachers, and English class was for vocabulary, reading, and grammar. I was pretty good in my English classes. Miss Legierski was the "Comma Momma," or "Grammatician Extraordinaire." This woman could sniff out a punctuation error a mile away and diagram you to death to "help" you understand sentence structure and punctuation. I mean how can you write if someone can't read and understand what you wrote? So throughout seventh and eighth grade, I was filled with grammar and diagramming and vocabulary to help me to become a better writer.

My grades were good and the work easy. Miss Legierski was my role model. I wanted to be just like her—an English teacher. Miss Legierski created an English class assignment that I thought was perfect for me. I was to write a creative piece. Miss Legierski clearly wrote the assignment on the blackboard with a due date by the end of the week. I was excited. All this

English stuff I had been learning was finally going to be put to use. Punctuation, grammar, vocabulary—I had it all and knew this was going to be an A, maybe even an A+.

Every day after school, I worked on writing my story. It was good and I knew it! Hours had gone into this piece. By Thursday, I was ready for my final copy. I picked up my lead pencil from my desk drawer and ever so carefully, in cursive, rewrote my story to be handed in the next day, which was Friday. My letters were perfect. My pink pearl eraser was by my side, ready to obliterate the slightest smudge or stray line. The lead was soft and not very sharp, but the words were placed strategically on the blue lines of the notebook paper, precisely indented, never going over the pink margin guide. As I reread my story, I was filled with satisfaction. This was the best I had written all year. It had a good plot line, characters I enjoyed, and it was fun to read.

The next day, everyone was buzzing about their stories. The usual one or two did not have their work. The rest of my classmates handed in their papers that fateful Friday. It took a week before I got it back. I was excited! This was an A for sure. I just knew it! That Friday, I waited impatiently in class as Miss Legierski began returning papers. Mine wasn't the first or even the second to be returned. More papers were returned, and still I waited. I know! She was going to use my paper as an example of perfection. Every grammar rule utilized correctly. Every comma perfectly placed. Every sentence flawlessly structured. I couldn't stop smiling. I thought my chest would burst as I held my chin high awaiting the coveted pat on the back. I mean—really—I went all through school being told what a good writer I was. And this was no different.

The last paper was held in Miss Legierski's hand as she walked down the aisle between the desks, her full hips swaying back and forth. It was mine, and it was perfect. I knew it! She released the paper and it fell with a mighty plop on my desk and a swish of papers stopped in front of me. My eyes began to well up with tears. I could hear my heart pounding in my chest. My hands shook as I moved the paper closer to me and out of the sight of my classmates. Everyone was murmuring and sharing their grades. I quickly and cautiously, as to not draw attention to myself, slipped the pages within the hard covers of my binder. The large red "C–" and the words "Too light to read!" were scrawled across the front page of my week's work without a single mark on any other page. It wasn't good enough to even read. As class ended and the bell rang, I inconspicuously left the room, all hopes dashed of being a writer. I recall throwing the folded paper out in the lunchroom trash barrel with all the other garbage. Healing those wounds has been an ordeal. I had developed an extremely strong internal critic.

Outside of school, my writer's life was supported by my mom. I had a pen pal in Poland, a distant relative, Irena. We exchanged letters almost every week. Her English was very good and her penmanship easy to read. We wrote in English telling each other about our lives and what we did at school and for fun in our countries. We even exchanged pictures every so often. Air mail postage was expensive, so Mom bought me thin parchment paper, so I could write as many pages as would fit into an envelope. I wrote about my family, my friends, books I was reading. Irena wrote about life in Poland, her family, and friends.

I would sit at the kitchen table with my mother writing my letter to Irena as Mom wrote her letters to friends who lived far away or family who had moved away. She would take me to the post office to buy my air mail stamps. I couldn't wait for the postman to come to see if there was a letter for me.

By the time I entered college, most of my writing was technical and usually for research. My professors wanted to know how much I had learned about a particular subject, not how creative I was. I could use formula-type writing easily. "Find out what the teachers want and then give it to them" was my mantra.

After graduating in 1972 with a degree in elementary education, my husband and I began moving around the Northeast with his job. It wasn't until 1983 when I returned to New York that I applied for a teaching position at East Aurora Middle School. During my interview, the middle school principal asked me what I knew about the Bay Area Writing Project.

"Nothing. But I'll find out," I said.

"Good. If you can create a curriculum to implement this program, you have a job."

I said I could and would have it ready to go in September. Needless to say, I got the job. It was at this point in my teaching career that I became aware of the Bay Area Writing Project, Donald Murray, and Donald Graves. I knew there had to be a better way to teach students how to write. With my middle school principal's encouragement, I took a chance and developed a curriculum that would help students to pass the New York State Preliminary Competency Test (PCT). It was an opportunity of a lifetime. My classes were made up of students that needed preparation in writing to pass the PCT for grade eight. What I learned was that the writing process written about in *Teaching Writing: Essays from the Bay Area Writing Project* (Camp, 1982) was more than a program. It was a new way of thinking about how we write. I learned it was recursive, not linear. A new vocabulary was introduced. Prewriting, writing, revision, editing, and publishing were not always done in that order. There was a difference between revision and editing. From experience, I knew I wrote, revised, and then wrote again. My prewriting or inspiration could happen in the middle of my piece as much as it could happen before I began to put words to paper. I was experiencing what the Writing Project was teaching. What I did know for sure was that in order to become a better writer, one must practice, practice, practice. Using the information I learned from the Bay Area Writing Project, I had my students writing more and enjoying it. It was almost as though I had discovered the key that unlocked the mystery of how to teach writing. Although writing is very structured and has many rules, the actual process of writing and the teaching of writing contradict each other. Students need to explore the process just as I needed to exhibit flexibility to teach writing.

I searched for activities that would encourage creativity. That's where I discovered Bare Books. These white hard covered blank books were used for the final product of my students' stories. Covers were carefully crafted with markers, colored pencils, or paints to depict the essence of the story and create interest. The interior pages were either printed on the computer and glued into the book or carefully printed on each blank page. Computer graphics, artwork, or pictures were gathered to illustrate the book. Knowing that the book was the final product, my students worked diligently to polish a story. The writing process was invaluable to achieve this publication.

Talking to my students about their stories and their work led me to teacher–student conferencing. I realized my students needed time—time to talk, time to write, and more time to talk. Feedback became critical. How do you know if you said what you meant to say unless someone reads it and lets you know?

Yet some of my colleagues were trying to use the writing process in a linear fashion to fit into a school week. For example, Monday students would brainstorm for ideas, or read, or research information that would be used for the week's assignment. Tuesday, students would write their rough draft. Wednesday was revision day. Pretty much students would read over their story with very little input from others and maybe change something so it looked "revised." Thursday, students would edit correcting punctuation, grammar, and spelling. The final paper, written in ink and in cursive was handed in on Friday. Voila! The writing process was completed! This never felt right to me because this is not how I write. I needed more help to understand how this process actually works in the classroom. What I discovered was each district I taught in over the years addressed this issue differently. I had already learned through trial and error that an inflexible writing schedule was not the answer. In addition, it was important to have students write more and given "a rich and diverse array of writing experiences." (NWP & Nagin, p. 13)

I found some books that I thought would create some interest for my students. *Free Stuff for Kids* became a prime resource. We wrote for free stamps, free pictures, free patches and stickers, and free books and food. Before long, my students were finding other places to write for more free "stuff." For the cost of a few stamps, actually quite a few stamps, the payoff came when the letters were answered and free "stuff" starting coming in. My students couldn't wait to get to class to research and write for the next free thing. I discovered having a purpose to write was important. Because this was an experimental writing class, I "borrowed" another teacher's classroom for two periods during the day. In the early 1980s, computers were being introduced into the classroom as tools for learning. This math teacher had four Commodore 64 computers in her class for student use. Wow! Was I impressed! And she let me use them while I was teaching in her classroom. A basic word processing program was installed and provided another tool for my students to use as they composed their letters or wrote their stories.

As I was teaching at East Aurora Middle School and East Aurora High School, the Bay Area Writing Project had taken off and evolved into the National Writing Project. By this time, I had returned to the State University College of New York at Buffalo, my alma mater previously known as Buffalo State College, to complete my Master's program. With computers becoming more accessible in schools, some of my colleagues were questioning the value of the computer lab outside of the classroom setting. Some were enthralled with the idea of giving students a new and exciting learning environment. Others felt the use of computers took away from instructional time and were not beneficial. Students were taken to the computer lab as a reward for work completed rather than for the instruction of writing. This debate became the focus of my Master's project. My ninth grade students would become my experiment to prove that writing on a computer would encourage more editing than writing with pen and paper. One semester of counting key strokes on the computer and cross outs and changes on paper and pencil resulted in an interesting, to say the least, but inconclusive answer to that question. My advisor said my sample was too small to be conclusive. But I did learn how the writing process really works and how it can be implemented into the classroom curriculum.

I was now confident that I had something of worth to write about. My research, my thesis, my project were impeccable. I decided to take a writing class to round out my program, a true writing class with a professor actively involved in the teaching of writing. I entertained thoughts of evenings cloistered with other writers in a workshop setting, sharing and writing for hours. The first night, I entered my class to see neat rows of desks facing the professor's desk with a blackboard filled with notes and an assignment. Hmm . . . not quite what I expected, but it was the first evening. The professor talked about style, sharing some critiques and assigned a critique for the next class. I fulfilled the first assignment as requested and had time to experiment with another piece. I wrote a scene about two people who had not seen each other after a long separation. They had met by chance and were struggling with trying to sound comfortable when it was evident they were still very much in love with each other. I was experimenting with conversation and emotion to show rather than tell the story. I had brought both pieces to class with the hope to share the piece and get some feedback. The professor collected the critiques and indicated that another assignment was posted on the blackboard. We were encouraged to start the work in class. Without any feedback from the last assignment, I began the next critique. While everyone was deep into their writing, I got up enough nerve to approach the professor's desk and tentatively held out my "experimental" piece. She looked at me over her glasses and coolly said, "May I help you?"

"I wrote this and wondered if you could read it and tell me what you think?" my voice just above a whisper.

"Okay," was her only response. I waited with butterflies in my stomach.

After several minutes, she sighed. "Well," she began, "This is really not a genre that I am very familiar with, so I guess it's okay."

Okay? Okay? That's all she could say to me that she thought it is was *Okay*?! I was back in seventh grade staring at a giant C- and the comment "I can't read this!"

"Oh, thank you for your time," I managed to say.

That was the last personal interaction I had with my professor.

What I learned was that if I did not receive some kind of feedback, I was helpless to know if I was on the right track or if my work said what I wanted it to say.

Stories happen to those who tell them.
—Thucydides

After completing my Master's program, I continued to write. My new position at my school district was in administration. I was the public information specialist for the district, which required me to do a massive amount of reading and writing. Of course, the more I wrote, the better my writing became. I continued to write for other university classes, newsletters for the school district, articles for newspapers and magazines, as well as short stories. I was living the process. Prewriting, writing, revising, writing again, editing, prewriting—the process continued. The steps did not matter. They happened in no specific order as I created my pieces. The steps were fluid and I moved through them easily in order to express my thoughts and communicate ideas. They were recursive in nature. It is only by practicing the craft can you completely understand the process and how it works. I had developed a deep understanding and knew I could help my students to become writers. They, too, must write in order to understand the process. They, too, must be able to flow through the steps and revisit them as many times as necessary to finish the piece and to publish. As we know, at some point, we must "let go" of the writing and say "this is finished."

Throughout my teaching career, I have seen different programs and approaches to the teaching of writing. While in Fort Smith, Arkansas, the State supported the program *Step Up to Writing®*. *Step Up to Writing®* featured research-based, validated strategies and activities that help students proficiently write narrative, personal narrative, and expository pieces; actively engage in reading materials for improved comprehension; and demonstrate competent study skills. This program, as stated on its website (2007), was to accomplish the following:

- Align with Writing Next
- Create a common language and approach across grade levels and content areas
- Provide models of student writing for teacher and student reference
- Employ writing as a tool for content learning
- Explicitly connect reading and writing
- Teach all stages of the writing process, with an emphasis on planning
- Provide tips specifically for kindergarten students in Primary Level
- Align with the Six Traits assessment model

But it was missing something. There needed to be choice and strategy for implementing into the classroom. Students needed to be able to choose what they would like to write. I didn't start out thinking that I would write about a particular subject or issue. But I did start out with an idea. Maybe this idea would go somewhere. Or I'll think of a story or personal experience that I may find very interesting. Perhaps that's how the process really works. A writer needs to experience writing. Think about, write about, revisit it, add to it, fix it, share it and continue the process. Maybe that's what it is really about. How clearly I say something will determine if my word pictures are vivid enough to engage the reader or myself, for that matter.

> *The difference between the right word and the almost right word*
> *is the difference between lightning and the lightning bug.*
> —Mark Twain

Developing an effective Writers Workshop within the classroom was critical to teaching writing. It allows the teacher and the students to write and share their work in a healthy and supportive environment. Peer conferencing and teacher conferencing offers time for student writers to discuss their writing and answer those questions that make the writer want to elaborate, correct, change, organize, or rewrite sections to help the reader understand. We all need to reflect on our writing and work to say it better, choose the "right" word to say exactly what we mean. I don't think children just naturally decide to revise their work. My experiences have been that once a child writes the words, he or she is finished. It's only by asking questions and talking about their writing that the revision process begins. This type of teaching takes time and lots of it! In my own classroom, this was facilitated by the way the classroom was set up. The configuration allowed for movement and a great deal of group work to encourage discussion and increase listening skills. By discussing with student writers their writing, students can then see what options they have available to them. It became a matter of asking the right questions.

I met Ralph Fletcher, author of *Writing Workshop* (Fletcher & Poralupi, 2001), at the International Reading Conference in Austin Texas in 2005. He noted the connection between reading and writing. In his book, he broke down the essential components of the writing workshop and provided the teacher with ways "for making it work in the classroom." His practical approach to teaching writing in the workshop format was easy to understand and implement in this simple how-to guide.

Lucy Calkins, in her opening chapter of *The Art of Teaching Writing* (1994), says, "To teach well, we do not need more techniques and strategies as much as we need a vision of what is essential" (p. 3). This is a major paradigm shift for the teaching of writing. Calkins encourages teachers to develop their own vision and create opportunities to teach students the joy of writing. After all the reading, researching, and writing I had done, I was ready to revisit the National Writing Project as a fellow, rather than an observer.

In 2005, I was fortunate to be invited to join the Northwest Arkansas Writing Project (NWAWP) Summer Invitational. The mission of the National Writing Project (NWP) is "to improve writing and learning in our schools by improving the teaching of writing" (NWP & Nagin, p. ix). This professional development paralleled the inservicing that we, at Fort Smith Public Schools, were creating for our staff. This was going to be a summer of writing, exploring, and learning about writing and the writing process. "Improving writing is now seen as important for learning subjects other than English" (NWP & Nagin, p. 73). This invitation could not have come at a better time for me. I had a whole summer to read and write.

So what I learned was that if I value my writing, so will others. It began with me. I was creative; therefore, I was an artist. Only I painted with words. It's similar to when I knit a sweater. Each stitch builds on the previous row to create a block of yarn that is then sewn together into a piece of knitted clothing that can be worn. My stitching, choice of color, and design create a work of art that can be duplicated but never exactly in the same way. There will always be variations in yarn texture, dye lots, and size of needles. So it is with writing. Each time I put my pen to paper, I create a one of a kind piece that can be duplicated but never exactly. My word choices, details, tone, sentence structure all have a major impact on what this piece will look like when I am finished.

That Invitational was critical to me because it validated my own teaching. I was moving in the right direction. I was providing my students with strategies and techniques that would develop their skills and help them become effective and proficient writers.

I like the quote, "Where there is a path, it is someone else's way." (Schneider, p. 55).

Not all who wander are lost.
—J.R.R. Tolkien

I'm still making my own path...

References

Camp, G. (Ed.). (1982). *Teaching writing: Essays from the Bay Area Writing Project.* Portsmouth, NH: Boynton/Cook Publishers Inc.

Calkins, L. M. (1994). *The art of teaching writing.* Portsmouth, NH: Heinemann.

Free Stuff Editors. (1982). *Free stuff for kids.* Minnetonka, MN: Meadowbook Press.

Fletcher, R. & Portalupi, J. (2001). *Writing workshop: The essential guide.* Portsmouth, NH: Heinemann.

National Writing Project & Nagin, C. (2003). *Because writing matters: Improving student writing in our schools.* San Francisco, CA: John Wiley & Son Inc.

Schneider, P. (2003). *Writing alone and with others.* New York: Oxford University Press.

Sopris West Educational Service. (2007) *Step up to writing*. Frederick, CO: Cambium Learning Group.

For Further Reading

Atwell, N. (1987). *In the middle: Writing, reading, and learning with adolescents*. Portsmouth, NH: Boynton/Cook Publishers, Inc.

Graves, D.H. (1983). *Writing: Teachers and children at work*. Portsmouth, NH: Heinemann.

Gruwell, E. (2001). *The freedom writers diary: How a teacher and 150 teens used writing to change themselves and the world around them*. New York: Broadway Books.

King, S. (2000). *On writing: A memoir of the craft*. New York: Scribner.

Murray, D.M. (1982). *Learning by teaching: Selected articles on writing and teaching*. Portsmouth, NH: Boynton/Cook Publishers Inc.

Murray, D.M. (1985). *A writer teaches writing*. Portsmouth, NH: Heinemann.

Reeves, J. (1999). *A writer's book of days: A spirited companion & lively muse for the writing life*. Novato, CA: New World Library.

Those Who Made the Journey

April Brannon

April Brannon is a former middle and high school English teacher. She currently teaches English and English Education courses at California State University, Fullerton and summer school at Bernalillo High School in New Mexico.

M. Patricia Cavanaugh, Ph.D.

Dr. Patricia Cavanaugh is a professor in the English Department at Saginaw Valley State University in University Center, Michigan. She is primarily responsible for English Education. She is the recipient of the 2008 Franc A. Landee Award for Teaching Excellence and the Braun Fellowship. She is always so pleased when she sees that her current students understand and perform well and when her former students contact her to discuss how they are using a strategy or activity that she taught them.

Cheryl Cormier

Cheryl Cormier has been an educator for over 25 years. She received her B.A. in Elementary Education/Communication Disorders from Boston College and her M.S. in Speech-Language Pathology from Worcester State College. Over the years, she has integrated her work in education with her love for literacy. She was a 2001 fellow at the Summer Institute at the Boston Writers Project. Her love for literacy has played a major factor throughout

Getting It in Writing, pages 255–260
Copyright © 2011 by Information Age Publishing
All rights of reproduction in any form reserved.

her life, ranging from motivating special needs children and establishing several journal writing groups to dealing with the death of her daughter. She is now a sixth grade writing teacher in a small town west of Boston. This is her first publication.

Helen Eaton

Helen Eaton lives in Fayetteville, Arkansas. She co-founded and co-directed the Northwest Arkansas Writing Project Open Summer Institute for seven years. There she enjoyed seeing educators spend two weeks of their summers discovering the writer within, developing a writing community, and gaining a fuller understanding of the writing process. She taught Writing Across the Curriculum for the University of Arkansas Masters of Arts in Teaching program for two years. As a Writing Teacher Consultant for the National Writing Project, she has also led many writing inservices in schools across Arkansas. When she isn't teaching, she enjoys reading, gardening, cooking, and painting. She feels like she's living the all-American dream with a husband, a daughter, a son, a dog, a cat, and a house with a porch.

Jessica Fragale

Jessica Fragale is a National Board Certified Elementary School Teacher. After obtaining her Masters in Education from Pepperdine University, she began work at Santa Monica Boulevard Community Charter School in Los Angeles, CA. There she teaches a third, fourth, and fifth grade multiage class. Jessica enjoys working with her school's population of English Language Learners as well as her work in the creation of a community garden.

Gary French

Gary French takes great pleasure in riding his 1978 BMW motorcycle from his home in sunshiny Punta Gorda, Florida, to Woodland Middle School in Northport, Florida, where he inspires learning with his extremely talented eighth-grade students. He has worked as a teacher, executive vice president, stock-photo copy right agent, actor, bookstore manager, biodynamic farmer, and counselor.

In addition, he has intermittently spent periods of time contemplating life while sailing, playing guitar, painting houses, bartending, pizza making, shingling roofs, laying tile, repairing fences, driving buses, busing tables, mowing lawns, and splitting wood. He expresses his heartfelt thanks to Debbie for putting this book together and to Jennifer for everything else.

Anne Smith Gleason

Anne received her Bachelor of Science degree in Biology in 1976 and returned to school when she was 40 years old to attain her Teaching Certification. She taught preschool (part-time) for ten years and has been teaching third grade for eleven years.

Anne credits her father and her own love of learning as inspiring her to be a teacher. She is married, has four children, 29 nieces and nephews, and four grandchildren. Children have always been a part of her life. While Anne takes her job very seriously, she says, "If I can't have fun teaching third graders, then I'm doing something wrong."

Sharla Keen-Mills

Sharla Keen-Mills, M.Ed. is National Board of Professional Teaching Standards certified in Early Adolescent English and Language Arts and a Teacher Consultant of the Northwest Arkansas Writing Project. She has co-directed her writing project's Summer Invitational Institute and serves on its steering committee. Ms. Keen-Mills served as the Literacy Consultant for *An Arkansas History for Young People* by Shay Hopper, T. Baker, and J. Browning (University of Arkansas Press, 2006). She has also contributed articles to *The Flavor of Our Words*, edited by Helen Eaton, S. Totten, and L. Terrell (NWAWP, 2006) and *Spark the Brain, Ignite the Pen*, edited by Samuel Totten, H. Eaton, and S. Dirst (Information Age Publishing, 2006). She published "Dirt and Honey: Place According to Welty and Yaeger in *The Secret Life of Bees*" in the National Writing Project Professional Writer's Retreat Invitational Anthology, Santa Fe in June 2007.

Ms. Keen-Mills has taught social studies and language arts for 20 years and is currently teaching creative writing and pre-AP English at a junior high school in northwest Arkansas, where she lives with her husband on a lake in the Ozark Mountains. They enjoy fishing, gardening, and the NHRA Drag Races.

Kim Kendrick

Kim has taught in Nebraska, Hawaii, Iowa, and Arkansas. Her work with junior high students with learning disabilities and high IQs in Arkansas earned her a national and state award for her lessons in economics education, which led to being a nominated finalist for Arkansas Teacher of the Year and being invited to a National Teacher Forum in Washington, D.C. in 2000.

Carol Malaquias

Carol Malaquias holds a Master of Education from Lesley College and has been teaching fifth grade on Cape Cod, Massachusetts for nineteen years. Her students do nature writing in a central arbor in the schoolyard and on the dunes, beaches, and swamp trails of the Lower Cape. Carol likes to write memoirs, and her travel adventures continue to inspire her writing. She and her physician husband have two grown daughters, a new son-in-law, and a Cavalier King Charles grandpuppy.

Faith-Ann McGarrell

Faith-Ann McGarrell currently serves as Assistant Professor of Teaching, Learning, and Curriculum at Andrews University in Berrien Springs, Michigan. She taught English and Language Arts, grades seven through twelve, in Ocala, Florida and Chicago, Illinois for six years before entering the college and university classroom, where she taught Basic Writing and Freshman Composition in Michigan. Her interests include academic service-learning in writing composition, creative writing, young adult literacy, and arts in education. Her dissertation, *Teacher Success, Assessment, and Evaluation Practices in Service-learning Composition Courses,* and subsequent articles emerged out of an interest in discovering the power of connecting the community to the classroom. She currently teaches courses in foundations of education, language arts and arts methods, and curriculum and instruction.

Vicky Moriarity

Vickie Moriarity earned a Bachelor of Arts degree in Education from Arizona State University in 1994 and a Master's degree in Secondary Education from Northern Arizona University in 2000. A teacher for sixteen years, Vickie considers herself lucky to have taught middle and high school students in Arizona, Nebraska, Virginia, and Kentucky. She lives in Mt. Sterling, Kentucky with her husband Tim, a realtor, and their four cats. Vickie currently teaches seventh grade language arts at Bath County Middle School in Owingsville, Kentucky.

Elaine J. O'Quinn

Elaine J. O'Quinn is an Associate Professor of English at Appalachian State University in Boone, North Carolina. She teaches courses in the Teaching of Composition, Young Adult Literature, World Literature for Children, and Issues in English Studies. She is also a faculty member in Women's Studies and Appalachian Studies. Dr. O'Quinn's research interests include identity development and its place in the English classroom, moral imagination as it applies to the teaching of literature and writing, and the study of girlhood and the texts girls choose to read. She has presented widely and has written numerous book chapters. Her work has appeared in a variety of journals, including the *ALAN Review, Education and Culture, Feminist Collections, Girlhood Studies: An Interdisciplinary Journal,* and the *Journal of Adolescent and Adult Literacy.* Dr. O'Quinn lives in Boone, North Carolina, with her wonderful husband and her two darling cats.

Kurt Reynolds

Kurt Reynolds is in his eleventh year teaching composition and literature classes at Lincoln High School in Thief River Falls, Minnesota. It just so happens to be the greatest job in the world.

He earned his MA in English from Bemidji State University in 2006. During the summers he is a teaching consultant for the Red River Valley Writing Project at the University of North Dakota. He also takes part in a Teaching American History grant through the Minnesota Historical Society and Hamline University.

Kurt and his wife, Kristie, and their children, Casey, Korey, and Kenzie live in Red Lake Falls, Minnesota. He can be reached at kreynolds@trf.k12.mn.us or on the web at www.teacherscribe.blogspot.com.

Deborah L. Smith, Ph.D.

Deborah L. Smith taught English as a Second Language and English for eight years before returning to school full time to earn her doctorate in Curriculum and Instruction. She is now a teacher educator, field placement coordinator, and chair of the Writing Committee at Saginaw Valley State University. She is dedicated to improving classroom climate and literacy learning for disadvantaged urban children through the preparation of urban teachers; her current research focus is on the development of an Urban Literacy Cadre for Detroit area schools.

Deborah M. Stankevich

Deborah Stankevich received her B.S. and M.S. from State University College of New York at Buffalo. She is a Teacher Consultant for the National Writing Project, attending the 2005 Northwest Arkansas Writing Project (NWAWP) Summer Institute at the University of Arkansas in Fayetteville and sitting on the steering Committee for NWAWP. For over 30 years, Deborah has taught in New York, Massachusetts, Connecticut, Pennsylvania, Florida, and Arkansas on multiple grade levels and college. She has written for *Good Life* magazine. Her short stories were published in *The Flavor of Their Words*. Her blog *Living the Dream* (blog.geneseecountryinn.com) recounts her life as an innkeeper and owner of the Genesee Country Inn. Deborah lives with her husband, Richard, her dogs, Bentley and Cooper, her cat, Sam and a tank of community fish. She is currently working on her novel when she is not taking care of her guests at the Genesee Country Inn Bed and Breakfast in Mumford, New York.